£8·95

KU-185-914

The Political Economy of
European Trade

The Political Economy of European Trade:
An Introduction to the Trade Policies of the EEC

R.C. Hine
Lecturer in Economics
University of Nottingham

Wheatsheaf Books

DISTRIBUTED BY HARVESTER PRESS

First published in Great Britain in 1985 by
WHEATSHEAF BOOKS LTD
A DIVISION OF THE HARVESTER PRESS PUBLISHING GROUP
Publisher: John Spiers
Director of Publications: Edward Elgar
16 Ship Street, Brighton, Sussex

© R.C.Hine, 1985

British Library Cataloguing in Publication Data

Hine, R.C.
    The political economy of European trade: an introduction to
    the trade policies of the EEC.
    1. European Economic Community countries—Commercial
    policy
    I. Title
    382′.094   HF3499.5

    ISBN 0-7108-0119-X Pbk

7108012+6

Typeset in Times 10pt by M.C. Typeset, Chatham, Kent
Printed in Great Britain by
Whitstable Litho Ltd., Whitstable, Kent
All rights reserved

+59577·

THE HARVESTER PRESS PUBLISHING GROUP
The Harvester Press Publishing Group comprises Harvester Press
Limited (chiefly publishing literature, fiction, philosophy, psychol-
ogy, and science and trade books), Harvester Press Microform
Publications Limited (publishing in microform unpublished arc-
hives, scarce printed sources, and indexes to these collections) and
Wheatsheaf Books Limited (a wholly independent company
chiefly publishing in economics, international politics, sociology
and related social sciences), whose books are distributed by The
Harvester Press Limited and its agencies throughout the world.

To Anne,
Richard,
Naomi and
Sophie

Contents

List of Tables

List of Figures

Preface

This book has developed from a series of lectures that I have given at the University of Nottingham. In preparing the lectures I felt that academic writing on the economics of the EEC's trade policies tended to fall into two groups: single chapters in general texts on the Community's economic policies which could do little more than map out some of the principal features of EEC trade measures; and monographs and journal articles on particular aspects of policy, such as the Lomé Convention, which were too detailed for the non-specialist reader who was unfamiliar with the general subject area. This book seeks to follow a middle course by providing—in one volume—students of European integration with a reasonably comprehensive introduction to the nature of current EEC trade policies, the economic principles which underlie them, and the problems and choices which confront policy-makers.

I would like to record my gratitude to my colleague, Geoff Reed, for his intellectual stimulus over the last decade, and in particular for reading the draft of this book and making many helpful comments. Thanks are also due to Peter Holmes of the University of Sussex for his constructive criticisms of the draft, to Professor Jack Parkinson for his support and encouragement, and to my typist, Mrs Christine Johnson. As usual, the responsibility for any errors and omissions is mine alone.

R.C.H.

Abbreviations

ACP	African, Caribbean and Pacific (countries which participate in the Lomé Convention)
billion	1000 million
CAP	Common Agricultural Policy
CCP	Common Commercial Policy
CCT	Common Customs Tariff
CEN	Comité européen de normalisation (European Committee for Standardisation)
CENELEC	Comité européen de normalisation électrotechnique (European Committee for Electrotechnical Standardisation)
CET	Common External Tariff
cif	cost, insurance and freight (valuation of traded goods)
COMECON	Council for Mutual Economic Assistance (grouping of East European countries)
EC	European Communities (EEC, EURATOM and European Coal and Steel Community)
ECU	European currency unit (a basket of EEC currencies)
EEC (6)	European Economic Community with initial membership of Belgium, France, Germany, Italy, Luxembourg and the Netherlands
EEC (9)	EEC (6) plus Denmark, Ireland and the UK (from 1973)
EEC (10)	EEC (9) plus Greece (from 1981)
EDF	European Development Fund
EFTA	European Free Trade Association
fob	free on board (valuation of traded goods)
GATT	General Agreement on Tariffs and Trade
GDP	Gross domestic product
GR, 1981, etc.	Fifteenth General Report on the Activities of the European Communities, 1981
GSP	Generalised System of Preferences
ICA	International Commodity Agreement
IMF	International Monetary Fund

MFA	Multi-Fibre Arrangement
MFN	Most-Favoured-Nation (tariff treatment)
NATO	North Atlantic Treaty Organisation
NICs	Newly Industrialising Countries
NIEO	New International Economic Order
NTB	Non-Tariff Barrier to trade
OCT	Overseas Countries and Territories
OECD	Organisation for Economic Cooperation and Development
OEEC	Organisation for European Economic Co-operation
u.a.	unit of account
UNCTAD	United Nations Conference on Trade and Development

1 Introduction

Although attempts have been made to unite the nation states of western Europe over many centuries, significant progress in this direction has been achieved only since 1945. After the second world war, a chief problem became how to allow Germany to regain normal control over her national affairs without in consequence exposing Europe to the risk of further military conflict. A solution proposed in the Schuman Plan was to place the European coal and steel industries—on which military strength depended—under international control. The plan became reality in 1952 when the European Coal and Steel Community (ECSC) was set up to link the coal and steel industries of Germany, France, Italy, the Netherlands, Belgium and Luxembourg in a common market. Britain was invited to take part but declined on the grounds that the High Authority which was responsible for supervising the ECSC was 'undemocratic and responsible to nobody'.[1]

The initial success of the ECSC encouraged more ambitious attempts to establish a European Political Community, with control over a fully integrated army. However, these moves foundered in 1954, mainly because of opposition from France. More modest proposals then began to be discussed concerning closer economic cooperation which might in the longer term lead to political integration. The Benelux countries (Belgium, Netherlands and Luxembourg) put forward a memorandum calling for the establishment of a European common market and for specific measures concerning energy and transport. These ideas were endorsed at a meeting of ECSC Foreign Ministers at Messina in Italy in June 1955. Events then moved ahead rapidly, and the European Economic Community, embodying a general customs union of the six ECSC countries, came into being in January 1958. Britain had the opportunity to take part in the EEC from the outset but withdrew from the discussions because of a disagreement with the ECSC countries over the form which the EEC should take, as well as an underestimation of the commitment of the six to press ahead with economic integration.

The legal basis of the new European Economic Community was the Treaty of Rome, which sets out the aims and obligations of the member countries. The Treaty calls on the member states (i) to work closely together to free the movement of goods, services, labour and capital within the Community; (ii) to formulate and apply common (EEC) policies for trade, agriculture, transport and competition; and (iii) to coordinate their macro-economic policies. The foundation of these cooperative activities was to be a customs union within which goods could move freely across national boundaries. The conditions of trade with non-member countries were to be regulated by a Common Commercial Policy (CCP) and the centre piece of the CCP was to be a common external tariff—the Common Customs Tariff (CCT) in EEC parlance. The CCT would ensure that goods entering the Community would be treated alike, regardless of the particular member country through which they were imported. The introduction of the CCT also meant that national tariffs, and the freedom to adjust them, had to be abandoned.

The Treaty of Rome was brought into effect in January 1958. Although there have been many setbacks and the ambitious aims of the original founders of the Community have certainly not been fully realised, a complex pattern of cooperation between the member states has developed and common measures affecting many aspects of economic life have been agreed. This book will focus on just one dimension of EEC policies: that of trade. Specialising in this way becomes increasingly necessary as the area of Community activities expands. It also permits one to look at the interrelationship through trade of areas of policy which in a more general text might be treated separately, and to pay more attention to the international context in which Community policies operate. At the same time, it is important to bear in mind that trade measures do not exist in isolation. They reflect—indeed are usually an integral part of—domestic policies in many fields. A proper understanding of EEC trade policies therefore requires familiarity with a wide range of Community policies. A detailed treatment of the latter lies largely beyond the scope of this book. Thus qualified, the study of the Community's trade policies gives a valuable insight into the nature of the Community, its economic impact, and its relations with the rest of the world.

The Common Commercial Policy remains the most developed expression of the EEC's external relations with non-member countries. It is a complicated tapestry woven over 25 years and reflecting a variety of influences, most notably:

- the legacy of previous national policies, including the colonial trade links, and the diverse national attitudes towards trade;
- the Community's international obligations under the GATT;
- external events like the rise in oil prices, and the emergence of powerful rivals such as Japan;
- internal events like the growth of unemployment;
- the Community's decision-making process which has enhanced the influence of protectionist pressures because of the need to reach a package-deal acceptable to all.

Because of the complex way in which these various factors interact, there is no ideal sequence in which to treat them in a book of this kind. Since the primary aim here is to provide an economic interpretation of the EEC's current trade policies, no attempt has been made to provide a comprehensive chronological review of the development of EEC policies. However, salient features concerning earlier policies are described in the main text, and in this introduction a brief overview of the development of EEC trade policies is given.

The general organisation of the book is as follows. First, the economic effects of discriminatory trade arrangements like the EEC are explored with the aid of customs union theory (Chapter 2). Then attention is directed to the international context within which EEC policies have evolved. (Chapter 3 examines the trade rules embodied in the General Agreement on Tariffs and Trade and their implications for the EEC customs union, and Chapter 4 considers EEC trade patterns and the 'shared interest' in a common trade policy.) Next, the general measures that govern EEC trade are described. In Chapter 5 the measures for freeing trade between the member countries are first discussed, then in Chapter 6 the instruments of policy used in relation to non-member countries are examined. It should, however, be borne in mind that the measures represent two sides of the same coin since, for example, the stimulus to intra-EEC trade from customs union formation will depend in part on how restrictive policies towards non-member countries are. EEC trade policies have become highly differentiated in regard to both products and partner countries. So the trade arrangements for certain products where there are special EEC measures, like the Common Agricultural Policy, are examined in Chapter 7. EEC policies towards particular groups of countries are now surveyed in relation to their content and economic impact. This forms the major part of the book since differentiation in the trade treatment of its partner countries has been the cornerstone of EEC trade policies. The order in which policies are reviewed follows broadly the position of countries in the EEC's hierarchy of trade preferences, starting with the most preferred. (Chapter 8, the EFTA; Chapter 9, the Mediterranean countries; Chapters 10, 11 and 12, the developing countries; Chapter 13, the US and Japan; and Chapter 14, the Eastern European countries and the OPEC group.) Finally, in Chapter 15, some conclusions on the current state of the EEC's trade policies and the choices facing Europe's trade policy-makers are suggested.

1.1 Overview of the development of the EEC's trade policies since 1958

In reviewing the major landmarks in the development of the Community's trade policies since the Treaty of Rome was brought into effect in 1958, it is helpful to distinguish three phases: (a) a transition phase (1958–68), (b) an emergent phase (1968–74), and (c) a recession phase (from 1974).

THE TRANSITION PHASE 1958–68
The Treaty of Rome stipulated that the customs union and the common EEC policies should be introduced by stages over a twelve-year transition period to give sufficient time for enterprises to adjust to the new economic environment. In the event, the Community was able to speed up the transition process, thanks partly to the buoyant economic conditions of the 1960s which enabled jobs lost in the import-competing industries to be quickly replaced by jobs in the export industries. By 1968, the Common Customs Tariff was in force, whilst tariffs and quotas on internal trade had been dismantled. Progress was much slower in relation to non-tariff barriers (see Chapter 5) but some success was achieved, for example in replacing the national forms of indirect taxation, with their varied arrangements for rebates on exports, with a single EEC system of Value Added Tax (VAT). National rates of VAT, of course, continue to vary widely and this means that tax adjustments still have to be made when goods cross internal boundaries between EEC countries.

As the EEC made progress towards common policies in areas such as trade and agriculture, the nature of Community control over the policies became an increasingly contentious issue. The Treaty of Rome had laid down that there should be a movement by stages towards majority decision-making, which would indeed be essential if the EEC were to develop into an economic, and eventually political union, as the founding fathers had hoped. The French government under President de Gaulle, however, argued for more national safeguards. After a major crisis in the Community in 1965, the member countries 'agreed to disagree'; in practice this meant that the French view prevailed, so that on matters judged to be of vital national importance individual countries can veto proposals which they find unacceptable. Although this helps to protect national interests from being over-ridden, it does mean that policy-making in the Community is very slow and decisions on major issues are usually made only under conditions of crisis. It also contributes towards the difficulties of negotiating with non-member countries, since once a balance of interests within the EEC has been struck, and a Community negotiating position has been adopted, it is very difficult to adjust that position. Third countries are then left with a take it or leave it decision. On the other hand, the process of haggling and horse-trading within the Community makes it fairly easy for non-member countries to keep themselves informed about the state of play within the EEC.

When the Community was founded in 1958, many of the developing countries were still colonies of the EEC member states—France in particular was anxious to preserve its preferential trade position with its overseas territories. But this was consistent with a common EEC trade policy only if the preferences were extended to all of the EEC countries. To this end, special arrangements for the member countries' African colonies were incorporated in Part IV of the Treaty, and when the colonies became independent in the 1960s these arrangements were continued in the Yaoundé Conventions, and later the Lomé Conventions. Some Mediterranean countries similarly were able to substitute EEC trade preferences for their previous colonial trade advantages. In this way, tariff discrimination in favour of a select group of developing countries became an important feature of EEC trade policy.

In relation to non-member developed countries, the formation of the EEC had most impact on the Community's neighbours in western and southern Europe. As the EEC customs union took shape during the 1960s, non-EEC countries were increasingly discriminated against in the Community market: their goods faced tariffs where goods from other EEC countries were admitted freely. A number of European countries responded to this situation by forming themselves into a free trade area, with the primary objective of negotiating more favourable trade arrangements with the Community. As the initial attempts to do this failed, Britain and some of the other countries made individual attempts at negotiating either full or partial (associate) membership of the Community. During the 1960s these national approaches made no headway, mainly because of opposition from the French. In southern Europe, Greece and Turkey were more successful in their overtures to the EEC, though their association agreements made provision for a very long transition period before full membership could be considered.

Meantime, there was concern in many developed countries over the implications of the formation of the EEC for the future trade relations of the western world. The US took the lead in pressing for a major series of multinational trade negotiations under the General Agreement on Tariffs and Trade (GATT), known as the Kennedy Round. These took place in 1964–67, and resulted in a major reduction in the level of tariffs in the EEC and elsewhere. Thus the GATT—the forum within which the principal trading countries have sought to establish orderliness in international trade relations since the second world war—was successfully used to soften the discriminatory and potentially divisive consequences of EEC formation.

THE EMERGENT PHASE 1968–74

During the transition period, the Community was feeling its way; it was anxious not to upset its main trade (and defence) partners like the US, and was pre-occupied with elaborating and implementing its internal arrangements. From about 1968, however, EEC trade policies began to assume a more definite shape, for two main reasons. First, the CCT was in place, and responsibility for many key areas of trade administration—including the negotiation of trade agreements with other countries—had shifted from the individual member states to the Community. The EEC, as a major trade bloc, became the focus of requests from many countries which wished to improve the conditions of access for their exports to European markets, and the Community felt obliged to respond.

Secondly, the Kennedy Round—which had helped the EEC customs union to gain international acceptability—had been successfully concluded, and the Community derived from this a greater confidence in its ability to act as a single, very powerful, unit in world trade affairs. Moreover, with the trade talks over, the Community felt able to interpret its GATT obligations in a looser fashion, without fear of torpedoing the complex series of negotiations. Thus, the Community began to respond to pressure from the Mediterranean countries for special trade links by granting preferences under the guise of establishing free trade areas or customs unions, even though the actual arrangements might not conform strictly to international trade rules under the GATT.

The major influence on the shape of the Common Commercial Policy during this phase was the 1973 enlargement of the Community to include the UK, Denmark and Ireland. This enlargement affected the general trade policy stance of the EEC in conflicting ways. On the one hand, the UK, with its long-established global trade links, could be expected to oppose a too inward-looking CCP. On the other hand, the chronic low growth and (pre-North Sea oil) balance of payments problems of the UK promised powerful support for a protectionist response to the trade difficulties of declining industries.

Enlargement also necessitated major adjustments to certain EEC trade policies, especially towards the EFTA and the UK Commonwealth countries. The UK and Denmark had been founder members of the EFTA, and were resolutely opposed to re-erecting trade barriers against their former partners. Equally, the other EEC countries would not agree to the UK and Denmark alone having special trade links with the EFTA. A solution was found by extending free trade with the remaining EFTA countries to the EEC as a whole, thereby creating by the late 1970s an industrial free trade area covering most of western Europe.

The problems posed by the UK's trade preferences in favour of the Commonwealth countries were tackled in a similar way, through the Lomé Convention. This extended the EEC's trade and aid arrangements under the Yaoundé Convention to the developing African, Caribbean and Pacific countries in the Commonwealth. The Commonwealth countries in Asia were, however, excluded—ostensibly on the grounds that their economic structures were different from those of the African members of the Yaoundé Convention. Some limited compensation for the excluded countries was granted under the EEC's version of a UN-backed scheme of tariff preferences for manufactured exports from developing countries (the Generalised System of Preferences, or GSP) which the EEC was first to apply in 1971.

During the second phase, as the EEC itself began to play a more active role, the EEC found it increasingly difficult to reconcile the non-discriminatory approach advocated by the GATT with an

acceptable resolution of various trade policy problems accumulated during the transition period and added to by the 1973
enlargement. In particular, the EEC resorted to trade measures
which although they were claimed to conform to the letter of the
GATT, nevertheless had the effect of creating a web of regional
trade preferences, seriously threatening the whole GATT edifice.
Similary, the new Common Agricultural Policy showed that in
responding to the difficulties of declining industries the EEC was
prepared to deploy non-tariff instruments in a highly protectionist
manner. EEC protectionism in certain areas continued to be
reinforced by national measures such as Italian import quotas on
Japanese goods.

THE RECESSION PHASE FROM 1974

Since 1974, the major factors influencing the evolution of EEC
trade policies have been the western economic recession and
growing competition from Japan and the newly industrialising
countries (NICs). In 1973, and again in 1979, large increases in oil
prices led to massive balance of payments deficits in energy-
importing countries and contributed to an upsurge in inflation.
EEC countries attempted individually to combat these problems
through restrictive domestic economic policies which in turn
resulted in output stagnating or declining, and in unemployment
rising to massive levels. Any growth in imports which competed
with domestic production was viewed as leading directly to job
losses, and protectionist pressures—both at the EEC and at the
national levels—intensified. Within the Community, the progress
made towards a unified internal market was thrown into reverse.
The growth in the volume of world trade slowed down, and in 1981
trade actually declined. Even with economic recovery from 1982,
protectionist sentiments remained dominant.

The influence of the recession can be seen in most aspects of
EEC trade policies during the last decade. For developing
countries it is shown in the increasing restrictions on their textile
exports to the EEC under the Multi-Fibre Arrangement; the
unwillingness of the EEC to make substantial new concessions
under the renewed Lomé Convention; and the EEC's retention of
tight safeguards under the GSP and especially against the NICs.
Similarly, in the EEC's trade relations with other developed
countries, the recession contributed to the slow progress and
rather meagre results of the Tokyo Round (though the negotiations may have helped to keep the lid on protectionist pressures); a
series of trade disputes involving agriculture, steel and East–West

trade; and trade conflicts with Japan leading to so-called voluntary export restraints affecting a range of EEC imports.

The economic slowdown has also hampered negotiations on the Second Enlargement. Although Greece became a member of the Community in 1981, the entry of two further prospective members—Spain and Portugal—has seemed like a moving target, always about two years away.

The recession has made national governments reluctant to hand over their remaining trade controls, for example, in relation to safeguard measures, to EEC operation. Most importantly, the EEC remains a collection of national markets rather than a single integrated market. This is partly because some governments fear that if they were to liberalise intra-EEC trade fully then they could not control the backdoor entry of low-cost third country goods via another member country. Greater freedom of intra-EEC trade seemed to hinge upon a more restrictive treatment of external trade: a 'Fortress Europe' approach.

The EEC has been roundly criticised by supporters of the GATT open trading system for its increased non-tariff protectionism in certain sectors like textiles, for its discriminatory regional trading arrangements, and for its tendency to use competitive countries like Japan and the NICs as scapegoats for its own internal failures (e.g. inflexible labour markets). It should also be pointed out though that European policy-makers have been faced with major changes in the international environment caused by the energy price shocks, and have had to respond to enormous social problems generated by structural changes in industry and massive unemployment. Indeed, domestically, the European governments have been attacked for not taking tougher action against imports. Viewed in this light, the world trade system has perhaps done well to remain as open as it is. None the less, a beggar-my-neighbour policy of protectionism is an unenlightened and dangerous response to deep-seated problems of structural change in the European economy. As the OECD Secretary-General has pointed out, the current western economic recovery will not of itself dampen protectionism, which was fostered by structural unemployment in Europe, a strong dollar which made US industries uncompetitive abroad and debt problems in developing countries.[2] In turn protectionism could stifle world economic recovery.

2   The Political Economy of Customs Unions

Since its formation, the EEC has evolved a complex network of preferential trade agreements with non-member countries. The degree of preference and the commodity coverage of these agreements vary widely so that the EEC has created a 'pyramid of privilege'.[1] At the apex of the pyramid are the Community's most favoured partners, such as the African countries, and at the base are those countries like the United States and Japan whose goods do not receive preferential access to the EEC market. In between comes an assortment of bilateral and regional arrangements offering various trade and aid advantages, and sometimes requiring in return concessions in favour of EEC exports.

This hierarchical and shifting system of trade arrangements has been shaped by a combination of factors: the historical legacies of the member states' former trade policies, geographical proximity, political pressures and economic self-interest. In later chapters we shall examine how these factors have influenced the EEC's trade policies towards specific groups of countries.

The purpose of this chapter is to provide a more general perspective on the nature of the EEC's internal and external trade arrangements, and in particular to consider the economic implications of discriminatory trade arrangements. This will be approached through a review of certain aspects of the theory of international trade in general and of customs unions in particular, in order to address three principal issues: (i) what economic advantages do countries derive from their participation in international trade, and under what circumstances may these advantages be outweighed by other factors (section 2.1)? (ii) what economic consequences may be expected from the formation of regional trading arrangements, like the EEC's customs union (section 2.2)? (iii) what economic motivation might there be for membership of a preferential trading group (section 2.3)? Finally section 2.4 relates the trade-creation/trade-diversion concepts of customs union theory to the political economy of preferential trade agreements.

2.1 The economics of trade and protection

International trade involves the exchange of goods between countries. An exchange takes place in a market economy because it is to the advantage of both parties.[2] The reason why it is mutually advantageous is basically very simple: the two parties at the margin must value the goods which they possess differently—i.e. each party disposes of something which it rates less highly than that which is received in return. The crucial question then becomes, why do the trading partners value their goods differently? The general answer lies in the complex interaction of conditions of demand and supply. Across a range of goods there are differences between countries in the interrelationship of costs of production and consumer tastes and preferences. From this diversity springs the basis for mutually advantageous trade.

ECONOMIC THEORY AND THE GAINS FROM TRADE

The theory of international trade traditionally focused its explanation of the gains from trade on differences in the costs of production between countries and the advantages of specialisation. It can easily be shown on the standard assumptions that specialisation and trade permit a country to obtain more goods and/or more leisure-time than a system of national self-sufficiency (autarky). (See *Standard assumptions of trade theory,* below.) For example, suppose that for each of two goods, say cricket bats and baseballs, the costs of production are constant in both Americana and Europa, but at different levels. For simplicity, assume that manufacture requires only one scarce resource, labour. This enables us to express the costs of production in terms of man hours per item, as follows:

	cricket bats	*baseballs*
	(costs of production in man hours per item)	
Europa	5	10
Americana	10	5

Suppose further that in international trade one cricket bat can be exchanged for one baseball. Then Europa could gain by specialising in the production and export of cricket bats. To obtain one baseball rather than spending 10 hours producing it at home, Europa would be better-off by making a cricket bat for export (at a

STANDARD ASSUMPTIONS OF TRADE THEORY/CUSTOMS UNION THEORY

The standard assumptions in the pure theory of international trade include:

- perfect competition in goods and resources markets;
- resources are assumed to be completely mobile within countries but not between them;
- there are no transport costs;
- tariffs are the only form of trade restriction employed;
- there are no externalities: that is, there is no divergence between private and social costs, nor between private and social value at the margin of the various quantities consumed;
- trade is balanced so that imports and exports are equal;
- there is full employment of all resources.

The orthodox theory of customs unions shares these assumptions. It usually employs three countries, which is the simplest possible situation, and is comparative static (i.e. equilibrium situations before and after an exogenous (policy) change are studied). Much of customs union theory is partial equilibrium in approach and thus focuses on changes in the market for one good on the assumption that all other prices remain the same. This is clearly a very unrealistic assumption, since the formation of a customs union is likely to involve many price changes, and caution should therefore be exercised in using the results of partial equilibrium analysis to interpret the changes that might occur in a customs union involving many goods.

In this chapter, customs union formation is assumed to affect the welfare of three groups—taxpayers, consumers and producers— their welfare is measured by the amounts of tariff revenues, consumers' surplus and producers' surplus, respectively.

cost of five man hours) and exchanging it for a baseball from Americana. Trade gives Europa more sports goods and/or more leisure. A similar gain is open to Americana through specialisation in the production and export of baseballs. In this way, each country is specialising in producing the goods which it can manufacture at lower cost than its partner. This is the principle of *absolute advantage,* and it is probable that most of world trade is conducted on this basis.

Less obviously, both countries in our example could still benefit from trade even if, in absolute terms, one were more efficient than the other in the manufacture of both goods. What matters for trade is that there are differences in the *relative* efficiencies with which goods are produced: each country can then gain through specialising in the production and export of the good in which its relative efficiency is greater. This is the principle of *comparative advantage:*

	cricket bats	baseballs	cricket bats	baseballs
	(costs of production in man hours per item)		(opportunity costs of production)	
			in baseballs	in cricket bats
Europa	8	10	$0.8(^8/10)$	$1.25(^{10}/8)$
Americana	6	5	$1.2(^6/5)$	$0.83(^5/6)$
	absolute efficiency		relative efficiency	

This shows Americana as having an absolute advantage in both sports goods, but a comparative advantage in baseballs since the opportunity cost of producing baseballs is lower in Americana than in Europa. Europa has a comparative advantage in manufacturing cricket bats. Suppose, as before, that in trade one cricket bat exchanges for one baseball. Then, by specialising in the production and export of cricket bats, Europa can obtain baseballs through trade at a unit cost of only 8 hours (the labour required to make a cricket bat for export) instead of expending 10 hours to produce a baseball at home. Similarly, Americana can benefit by specialising in the production and export of baseballs: cricket bats can be obtained at a unit cost of 5 hours (the labour required to make a baseball for export) instead of expending 6 hours to produce each cricket bat at home. By specialising according to their comparative advantages both countries gain from trade, even though Americana imports cricket bats which in absolute terms it could produce more efficiently at home.

THE SOURCES OF COMPARATIVE ADVANTAGE
In our numerical example we assumed that costs of production differed between countries without offering any explanation as to why such differences might occur. A large part of the literature on international trade theory is concerned with this issue and its implications, and two principal lines of argument have emerged, both based on the assumption that there are no significant taste differences between countries. One view is that cost differences arise because the resources available to countries vary (for example, one country might have abundant labour, and another an abundance of capital). Each country will then have a cost advantage in the production of those goods which require a heavy input of its abundant resource—a country with abundant labour will be able to produce labour-intensive goods at low cost. The other main view considers that cost differences arise because of differences in the technological know-how available to countries. The spread of know-how may be held back by patent protection or for other reasons, so that the innovating companies have a cost advantage which they can exploit more fully through trade.

The resource endowment and technology arguments offer a powerful understanding of the basis for trade between countries at different levels of development. But over 40 per cent of world trade takes place between the (comparably) developed market economy countries. This includes a substantial two-way exchange of manufactures between European countries which, broadly speaking, have similar resource endowments and a shared access to modern technology, especially through multinational companies.

The explanation for this trade seems to require a more active consideration of consumer demand. Following the work of Lancaster,[3] a product like a car can be considered to possess a number of essential characteristics—fuel economy, seating capacity, and so on. Consumers will vary in the combinations of these characteristics which they prefer: some will want small, fuel-efficient cars for town use, others large, high-speed vehicles for long-distance travel. This variety of tastes will pose a problem if there are important economies of scale in production. Without international trade, each country would have to balance off the benefits to consumers of having a wide variety of products from which to choose against higher production costs. With trade, however, each country can specialise in those varieties which are in strongest demand at home and can manufacture them in long production runs. Minority tastes can be catered for by imports

from similarly specialised foreign manufacturers. This explan.
is consistent with the observation that much of the trade betwee
developed countries is *intra-industry* in nature; that is, it involves
the two-way exchange of differentiated goods within the same
product category.[4]

FREE TRADE AND PROTECTION

Using the principle of comparative advantage, it is possible to
show that given certain assumptions about the nature of the world
economy (full employment, for example) world production of
goods and services will be maximised under a system of *free trade*.
Such a system came near to realisation in the mid-nineteenth
century and was actively canvassed by Britain, then the main
industrial power. However, free trade arrangements tend to break
down because individual countries can gain from restricting their
imports. A country whose trade is large enough to influence world
prices can benefit from reducing its imports, which will tend to
depress their price; with the volume and price of imports falling,
fewer exports are needed to pay the import bill; with fewer
exports, the prices of the export goods will tend to rise, reducing
further the quantity of exports needed. This is the *terms of trade*
argument for protection. Clearly, however, it is a game that more
than one can play. With retaliation from trading partners, it is no
longer certain that the country which starts the protectionist ball
rolling will in the end be better-off.

Free trade also tends to disintegrate because of pressure from
sectional interests. While free trade may bring some benefit to all,
protection can provide substantial assistance to a few. For
example, if any industry's survival is threatened by lower cost
imports, protection could shield those who own industry-specific
resources (e.g. specialised machinery or labour) from large losses.
The use of tariffs to deal with a problem of this kind is open to the
objection that it is not the first-best policy because it has
undesirable side-effects such as raising the price which consumers
must pay. An alternative approach might then be to avoid any
restriction of imports and instead to pay government compensation to those who suffer losses from import competition. This may
not be easy, however: the losses may be difficult to trace and to
evaluate, and the necessary administrative machinery may be
costly or lacking. Now, if society takes the general view that
producer-groups threatened by import competition should be
shielded against significant income losses, then some kind of
protection at the border—on a temporary basis—may be the only

tion.[5]

*on would need to be closely supervised within an
*ramework of rules if the liberal system of trade is
*lermined, as the experience of the interwar years
*ws. During this period, international trade became
*cted by tariffs, quotas (fixed limits on the quantity of
imports), *d many other devices. The chief reason for this lay in
the Depression and high unemployment throughout the developed
world. Countries tried to solve their own unemployment problems
by restricting imports, thereby hoping to preserve jobs in home
industries, and by encouraging exports. As more countries
followed suit, the restrictions on trade compounded the national
problems. A similar danger lurks at the present time. Slow
economic growth and rising unemployment have generated a
powerful protectionist tide, though it has yet to reach the
proportions of the inter-war period.

After the war, a determined effort was made to encourage trade
and specialisation by negotiating reciprocal reductions in tariffs
and the abolition of quotas. Job losses in industries whose
protection was reduced could then be offset against higher
employment in export industries which had better access to foreign
markets. The process of freeing trade from restrictions was very
successful and, along with a stable exchange rate system, was a
major factor in the post-war growth and prosperity of the western
world. In western Europe there were pressures to take the
liberalisation process a stage further on a regional basis. These
pressures led to the creation of the EEC customs union in 1958 and
the European Free Trade Association in 1960. Although the
formation of the EEC in particular was heavily influenced by
political considerations, it was also believed that regional economic integration would lift the economic performance of the
countries taking part. Indeed, the hope of those who wanted to see
a 'United States of Europe' was that Europeans would be
encouraged by the material benefits of economic integration to
seek political unity.

2.2 Trade creation and trade diversion in a customs union

The EEC's ambitious attempt at regional economic integration
involves action in a number of fields including the free movement
of labour, rules on competition and the Common Agricultural

Policy. But the central feature is the trade arrangement which takes the form of a customs union. A customs union comprises two or more countries which agree (i) to abolish all tariffs and quantitative restrictions on trade between themselves; and (ii) to establish a common external tariff on imports from non-member countries. These two components give the customs union a dual character since internal free trade is combined with protection against external competition.

In the EEC, the common external tariff is known as the Common Customs Tariff (CCT), and under the CCT the customs duty on a particular good will be the same regardless of which member country is chosen as the point of entry for goods into the customs union. Once the duty has been paid, a good enters into free circulation in the customs union; that is, it can cross frontiers between the member countries without any further customs duties being paid. In principle, on these internal frontier crossings, there is no reason for distinguishing between goods produced within the union and those from outside which have entered free circulation, at least as far as customs duties are concerned.

The nature of the customs union does however raise a problem over the disposition of the tariff revenues that are collected through applying the common external tariff. This problem arises because the country which collects the tariff revenues is not necessarily the country in which the imported good is consumed. Germany is a case in point since many of its imports from outside Europe arrive via other EEC countries, especially the Netherlands. Thus some of the tariff revenues which Germany used to collect before it became a member of the EEC are now collected, for example, by the Dutch customs authorities. This redistribution of tariff revenues affects the balance of payments positions of the member countries. In the case of the EEC, it has been agreed that all tariff revenues (less an allowance for the costs of collection) become the property of the whole Community. They are paid into the European Budget which funds joint EEC measures, such as the CAP.

Until relatively recently, it was thought that since the formation of a customs union involved the removal of some tariffs it represented a movement towards free trade. If free trade was accepted as a desirable objective, the formation of a customs union appeared to be a step in the right direction. Jacob Viner, in 1950, was the first to demonstrate the error in this line of thought.[6] His argument hinged on a distinction between what he called 'trade creation' and 'trade diversion'. Viner recognised that the removal of tariffs on trade between two countries would be likely to increase their mutual trade, but whether or not this was desirable depended on why the trade had increased.

Consider the formation of a customs union between two countries—a home country and a partner country. Some extra trade between these countries could occur because consumers in the home country switched some of their purchases from higher-cost home production to lower-cost partner production as a result of the abolition of tariffs on intra-union trade. Viner labelled this source of increased trade *trade creation*. Assuming that full employment is maintained, trade creation is beneficial in that production is shifted to a lower-cost source. Within a customs union, trade might also increase because of *trade diversion*. This involves a switch in home consumption from low-cost production outside the union to higher-cost partner production, caused by the selective removal of tariffs on imports from the partner country alone. Trade diversion is harmful in that production is shifted to a higher-cost source. Viner concluded that whether or not a customs union was desirable on economic grounds depended on the balance between trade creation and trade diversion. Only if the balance was in favour of trade creation could a customs union be described as advantageous.

Viner's arguments can be illustrated with a simple numerical example involving three countries: A is the home country, B is the partner country and C the rest of the world. Table 2.1 shows the production costs of shuttlecocks in the three countries and the tariffs applied by country A, before and after A forms a customs union with country B.

Table 2.1   A numerical example of trade creation

	A	B	C	A	B	C
	(pence per item before the union is formed)			*(pence per item after the union is formed)*		
Production costs	35	26	20	35	26	20
100% tariff in A	—	26	20	—	—	20
Price in A	35	52	40	35	26	40

Disregarding transport and handling charges, etc. the price of shuttlecocks to badminton players will depend on the production cost plus any tariff. If country A has a 100 per cent tariff, imports will be priced out of its market: the tariff is prohibitive. A's consumers will buy only the home-produced good at 35p each. The formation of a customs union between A and B would, however, lead to *trade creation*. Imports from B, with no tariff charged, would reach A's players at a price of 26p each and would completely displace the home-produced good. Assuming that resources are efficiently redeployed, there will be a saving for country A of 9p per shuttlecock.

If the initial rate of tariff in our example had been lower, say 50 per cent, a quite different situation would have emerged. A 50 per cent tariff is not sufficient to maintain a shuttlecock industry in A; the players' demand in A is met entirely by imports from C at a tariff-inclusive price of 30p (see Table 2.2). The formation of a customs union between A and B in this case would lead to *trade diversion*. Imports from B would now be available to A's players at a price of 26p, and they would switch all their purchases to this source.

Table 2.2 *A numerical example of trade diversion*

	A	B	C	A	B	C
	(pence per item before the union is formed)			*(pence per item after the union is formed)*		
Production costs	35	26	20	35	26	20
50% tariff in A	—	13	10	—	—	10
Price in A	35	39	30	35	26	30

This change would however be damaging to A's terms of trade since it would pay country B a price of 26p, compared with the previous price of only 20p paid to country C.

Viner's model was a deliberately simple one, designed to demonstrate the essential point that customs union formation need not be beneficial. In particular, it is assumed that costs of production stay the same regardless of the level of output. Country B, in our example, could increase production to meet A's demands without running into higher costs because of shortages of key resources. Moverover, Viner's model focused on the cost of production and left aside the important effect which falling prices might have on consumption.

This *consumption effect* is an aspect of customs union formation that has been explored by later writers. It is seen as a source of gain since the distorting effect of the tariff on consumer choice is reduced as prices move closer to world levels. As our numerical example illustrates, both trade creation and trade diversion lead to falling prices for consumers and hence to a consumption effect.[7] In the case of trade creation, the gain from the consumption effect adds to the gain from switching to a lower-cost source of supply. With trade diversion, the consumption gain works in the opposite direction to the production effect; in certain circumstances, trade diversion could be beneficial.[8]

Figure 2.1 shows the production, consumption and trade effects of customs union formation for a small country which had previously protected its home producers by a tariff (t) applied to all imports. For the particular product in this example, the effect of t is to increase the price to consumers, from the world level of Op_1 (the price at which world supplies (S_w) are available) to a tariff-inclusive price of Op_3. It is assumed that home production, shown by the supply curve (S_h), and consumption, shown by the demand curve (D_h) respond to the price level so that production at Oq_2 will be higher than without protection, and consumption at Oq_3 will be lower.

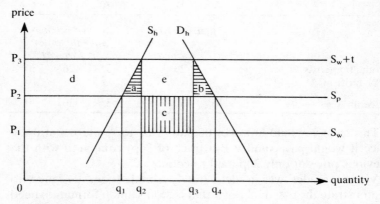

Figure 2.1   The trade effects of customs union formation

Now suppose that the home country forms a customs union with a partner country, whose supply price for the good in question (given by S_p) is above the world price. Because these partner supplies are exempted from the tariff under the rules of the customs union, they will be available to consumers at a price (Op_2) lower than the world price plus tariff (Op_3). The partner supplies will pull the market-clearing price in the home country down to Op_2, and this will cause production to fall to Oq_1, and consumption to increase to Oq_4. Imports from the world suppliers will cease because they are too expensive to home consumers. Imports of q_1q_4 will be supplied entirely by the partner country.

This particular example shows a mixture of trade-creation and trade-diversion effects; in other instances, the two effects can occur separately.[9] The trade which has been diverted amounts to q_2q_3 since this was the level of imports from the world source before the customs union was formed. The remainder of the increase in imports from the partner country is attributable to trade creation, which has two components: a *production effect* (i.e. the displacement of higher-cost home production by lower-cost partner production: Viner's trade creation) and a *consumption effect*. The impacts on the volume of trade are q_1q_2 and q_3q_4, respectively.

The adverse effects of trade diversion on the home country can be measured by multiplying the volume of trade diverted (q_2q_3) by the increase in the price of imports at the frontier (p_1p_2). In Figure 2.1 this is equivalent to the shaded area, c. The height of the supply curves above the quantity axis measures the marginal cost of domestic production (S_h) and the marginal cost of imports (S_p, S_w). The saving of costs by importing q_1q_2 from the partner country rather than producing it at home can thus be represented by the shaded area a: this is the production effect. The formation of the customs union led to an increase in consumption of q_3q_4. The price which consumers would be willing to pay for the marginal unit of the good in question is measured by the height of the demand curve (D_h) above the quantity axis, and the price that consumers actually paid in the customs union is Op_2. The difference between these prices over the quantity q_3q_4 represents the beneficial effect of the customs union for home consumers: area b. Summarising, we have:

(a + b) as the production and consumption effects of *trade creation*

(c) as the *trade diversion* effect.[10]

In general, we have identified the source of gain from customs union membership as trade creation, and the source of loss as trade diversion. For a customs union to be beneficial to the member countries, and to do least damage to the rest of the world in terms of lost exports, it should be primarily trade-creating and should involve the minimum of trade diversion. This situation is more likely to occur where: (i) the home and partner countries currently produce a similar range of goods but at different costs; that is, their economies are actually competitive but potentially complementary. This gives a large scope for trade creation to shift production from higher to lower cost sources; (ii) the union is large relative to the outside world—the more of the world is included, the less scope there is for trade diversion.[11] Similarly, the less trade the union members have initially with non-members, the better; and (iii) the initial tariffs on goods traded between the partner country are high, but the initial tariffs on goods traded mainly with the outside world are low.[12]

These generalisations help to establish the circumstances in which the formation of a customs union might be beneficial, and we shall make use of them later (see section 2.4). It should be emphasised, however, that since most customs unions will involve a mixture of trade-creation and trade-diversion effects a more definite judgement on their economic desirability can only be made by careful measurement of the actual or potential trade and welfare effects. This itself poses many difficulties (see section 4.2).

2.3 Economic arguments for customs union formation

Even if the formation of a particular customs union were overwhelmingly trade-creating, it does not follow that customs union membership is the best trade policy for the countries concerned—they may be able to find a better policy which is non-discriminatory. Indeed, Cooper and Massell[13] argue that there will always be a superior non-discriminatory policy, and conclude that the orthodox analysis of customs unions offers no economic rationale for union membership. They observe that all the benefits of union membership are associated with trade creation, which comes about through a lowering of prices. But they argue that a similar fall in the price level, and hence the trade-creation effect, can be engineered by an appropriate reduction in the tariff on *all* imports.

In Figure 2.1, this would require a reduction in the tariff from $p_1 p_3$ to $p_1 p_2$. With world supplies now available at a tariff-inclusive price of Op_2, the trade-creation effects would be the same as with customs union formation. But there would be one crucial difference with the new arrangement: there would be no trade diversion. With the same rate of tariff applied to world and partner supplies, consumers in the home country will prefer the cheaper world imports. Cooper and Massell argue that there will always be an appropriate non-preferential trade policy which will be superior to customs union membership: it will secure all the trade creation gains *and protect home producers to the same extent* but will avoid the trade diversion losses.

Cooper and Massell's argument focuses on the home country as an importer. It might be objected that any trade diversion loss to the home country is balanced by an equivalent gain to the partner country, which can export at the high union price. But the high price is needed to cover the high costs of producing the good in the partner country, it does not create a surplus which would be big enough to offset the terms of trade loss which the home country has suffered. There is no escaping the conclusion that, within the orthodox analytical framework, trade diversion is harmful to the union as a whole.[14]

Their argument is convincing within its range of assumptions. It follows that either there is no economic argument for customs union membership and/or some of the assumptions of the orthodox analysis are unrealistic. The latter view is held by the Wonnacotts. They are concerned over 'the curious case of the missing foreign [i.e. rest of the world] tariffs'.[15] Now orthodox analysis is logically consistent on this point: it is assumed that the rest of the world is so large that its supplies to the customs union members can be regarded as perfectly elastic; that is, whatever supplies the union needs can be obtained at a constant world price. Such a large country would have no purpose in applying a tariff against such inconsequential exporters as the home and partner countries.

The Wonnacotts, however, consider that the assumption that the rest of the world is large is an analytical convenience which should not be further removed from reality by assuming that tariffs are not used: tariffs are almost universally applied. The Wonnacotts suggest too that a third country (the rest of the world) may be large only in relation to certain goods. The third country might then retain tariffs on these goods as bargaining counters to negotiate better trading conditions for its exports. If the possibility of a third country tariff is accepted, this opens the way for an economic argument in favour of customs union formation.

Consider the example illustrated in Figure 2.2. The home country (right-hand side) initially applies a large enough tariff to keep out all imports, resulting in a market-clearing price of Op_3. The partner country is a low-cost producer with, for simplicity, no domestic consumption of the focus good. It cannot fully exploit its comparative advantage because of the prohibitive tariff in the home country and the tariff t_w ($= p_1p_2$) in the rest of the world (ROW). To sell in the ROW market, the partner country's exports

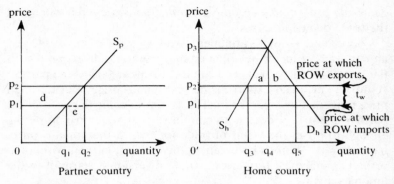

Figure 2.2   Customs union formation when the rest of the world applies a tariff.

must be priced at not more than Op_1, so that after the imposition of the ROW's tariff they can be sold at Op_2, the ROW's market price. At the export price of Op_1, the partner country's exports to the ROW amount to Oq_1.

Assume now that the partner and home countries form a customs union and that supply and demand in the union happen to balance at a price of Op_2. This entails imports of q_3q_5 to the home country which are met by the exports of Oq_2 from the partner country. For the home country the result is straightforward trade creation of q_3q_5, with the production and consumption effects shown by a and b, respectively. The partner country is also better-off since both export volume and export price have increased. The consequent gains in export revenues are shown in Figure 2.2 as areas (d + e), but area e represents the cost of the extra output q_1q_2. The gain to the partner country from customs union formation is represented by area d, which we may call the export effect.

The home country could have achieved its trade-creation effect, as Cooper and Massell suggest, by unilaterally abolishing its tariff since this would also result in the home country price level falling to Op_2. But the same possibility of unilateral action is not open to the partner country. Its export effect can only be obtained if other countries reduce their tariffs. How then can the partner country persuade the home country to form a customs union? Since the customs union would cover the whole range of goods, it is likely that for some goods the partner country will be the potential low-cost exporter, and for others the home country will be in this position. Hence both countries will derive beneficial export effects from customs union formation which they could not obtain by unilateral action.

The Wonnacotts' argument is particularly convincing in that it seems to fit in well with trade negotiation practice. Countries do not usually reduce import tariffs unilaterally, even though this would, on balance, appear to be beneficial.[16] Instead they use their tariffs on imports as bargaining counters to obtain better access for their exports to other protected markets.

Are there any other economic arguments which could be used to justify membership of a customs union? In section 1.1, *The recession phase from 1974,* we touched on the terms-of-trade effects of national tariffs, and this principle can also be applied to a customs union. In particular, it is possible that the members of a customs union, through the use of an appropriate rate of tariff, could collectively obtain better terms of trade with the rest of the world than they could achieve if each acted alone.[17] Notice that we are here thinking of the (realistic) situation where the rest of the world is not so large that it would regard its trade with the customs union as inconsequential. It is worth pointing out, however, that members of a customs union are constrained by legal and practical considerations in their selection of tariff rates. Under GATT trade rules,[18] the common external tariff must not on the whole be higher or more restrictive than the former national rates. Further, in fixing their tariffs, the union members have to take account of possible retaliation by other countries. Nevertheless, terms-of-trade advantages do provide a second possible economic rationale for customs union membership.[19]

A third possibility has to do with *externalities* (i.e. divergences between private and social costs and benefits, as when an industrialist does not in his private cost/benefit calculations take account of the pollution caused by his factory which imposes costs on society through damage to buildings, etc.). Harry Johnson devised an ingenious argument based on externalities which could be used to support the formation of a trade-diverting customs union.[20]

Suppose that a country valued the possession of a large manufacturing industry for its own sake; for example, as a symbol of development. In other words, quite apart from the benefit of the goods produced, the country actually derived a *social* benefit from the presence of manufacturing industry. Now if the country is an importer of manufactures, tariffs can be used to establish a larger industrial sector than free trade would permit. But for an exporter of manufactures the situation is different: tariffs would be ineffective and the rules of international trade prohibit export subsidies on manufactures. Johnson's suggestion is that the exporter should seek to join a trade-diverting customs union. Under the right circumstances, the private and social benefits which the exporting country could derive from its increased exports would more than outweigh the terms-of-trade loss of its partner country. Johnson's argument is interesting but probably not of much practical consequence for European countries.

A fourth argument for customs union membership focuses on *economies of scale*—the concept that a larger volume of production may permit a reduction in unit costs, for example, through a spreading of overhead charges. Assume that all markets are protected by tariffs. A particular market may then be too small for economies of scale in national production to be fully exploited, and customs union membership may enable average costs to be reduced by opening up export markets. But the position of other countries in the union must also be considered. If they previously imported low-cost goods from another source, customs union membership may make them worse-off: indeed, these losses may exceed the producing country's gain. The possibility of exploiting economies of scale does not guarantee that customs union formation is beneficial.[21]

From a free-trade perspective, the economies of scale argument hinges on the assumption that the rest of the world applies a tariff on imports—in effect it is a variant of the Wonnacotts' argument. Without this tariff, all worthwhile economies of scale would already be exploited through exports to the rest of the world. However, from a protectionist viewpoint, the economies of scale argument for customs union formation may meet the Cooper and Massell challenge if the cost-reduction effect in one country exceeds the trade diversion loss in the other.

The importance of the economies of scale argument lies in the size of the gains that may occur. In Figure 2.1 the trade-creation gain was represented by the areas a and b. What order of magnitude can be put on these in relation to, say, consumers' expenditure on the product in question? Area b is given by $(p_2 p_3) \times (q_3 q_4) \div 2$. The maximum size of $p_2 p_3$ is determined by the tariff rate—say 10 per cent; $q_3 q_4$ depends on the slope of the demand curve, say 0.2, and the tariff rate. Putting these together we have:

$$(0.1) \times (0.2 \times 0.1) \div 2$$

or 0.001 (i.e. 0.1 per cent) of the value of total annual consumption. Area a in Figure 2.1 can be assessed similarly. Clearly, these are minute proportions. As Waelbroeck remarked, on this basis 'the welfare significance of the EEC appears to be less than that of the Concorde aeroplane'![22]

If we allow for the existence of economies of scale, however, very much bigger welfare gains become possible. These gains apply not just at the margin on the increased trade flow, but over the whole volume of production. In the case of Australia, for example, Dixon has shown that with reasonable assumptions about scale economies, the structure of tariffs and the willingness of consumers and producers to alter their product-mix in response to price changes, the removal of even quite modest tariffs can lead to very significant welfare gains.[23]

This brings us to a key issue. Surely, it may be objected, countries like France, Germany and the UK have home markets which are large enough to allow their firms to achieve whatever economies of scale may exist. Indeed, judged by the amount of labour that they employ, plants in western Europe are similar in size to their counterparts in the USA, the largest national market.[24] However, labour productivity levels in Europe are only 35–50 per cent of US levels, so the average capacity of US plants is much greater. In addition, with access to a huge domestic market, US firms have plants which are much more specialised than those in Europe: they produce fewer product lines, with much longer production runs. This permits them to employ high-capacity, labour-saving plant and equipment, to mechanise more operations, to reduce set-up times for machinery, and to achieve economies in indirect labour in stores and in production and quality control. The cost advantages from longer runs appear to be very substantial.[25]

It can be argued that in Europe before the EEC was formed there was a tendency for each firm, within its protected national market, to make a full range of products, but at relatively high cost. The arrival of tariff-free trade within the EEC customs union then forced firms to concentrate their limited resources on their more successful product lines, and to manufacture these on a more substantial scale to meet export demand. Trade between the EEC countries intensified and became increasingly intra-industry in nature. More specialised production and longer production runs enabled costs to be reduced. This stylised account suggests that the formation of the EEC may have resulted in much larger welfare gains than are indicated by orthodox customs union theory, since economies of scale bring benefits over the whole volume of production.

A further gain from customs union formation may be the

increased competition that can occur when barriers to trade are reduced. In the past, national markets in Europe tended to be dominated by a small number of relatively large, home-based firms which had settled for 'peaceful coexistence' behind tariff walls. The removal of tariffs within the EEC brought increased competition from foreign-based firms. This may have reduced the losses from monopolistic behaviour (e.g. output restriction) by national firms and from inefficiency within firms (e.g. managerial slack). As with economies of scale, the gains from increased competition are potentially large since they are not confined to marginal increases in output.

There are some doubts, however, about the effects of regional trade liberalisation on competition. Meyer has argued that exporters generally conform to existing price relationships in their foreign markets.[26] Even so, imports will increase the pressures on home-based firms to improve their performance, and could affect their ability to raise prices. Corden has pointed out that although the removal of tariff protection increases the competition in the import-competing industries, the pressures on exporters may be eased, since they no longer have to surmount the tariff barrier in foreign markets.[27]

Gains from economies of scale and increased competition are part of what are termed the *dynamic effects* of customs union formation, as distinct from the once-for-all static effects examined in orthodox customs union theory. Kreinin has defined these dynamic effects as 'changes in the growth rate resulting from expansion in the size of the market and the attendant addition of productive resources'.[28] Advocates of regional economic integration lay emphasis on the dynamic effects, since even a small change in the growth rate is likely to be far more significant over a period of time than a once-for-all effect like trade creation.[29] The elaboration of a suitable analytical framework within which the dynamic effects of customs unions can be quantified poses great problems, and so the importance of the dynamic effects remains a matter more of belief than of established fact.

2.4 The political economy of preferential trade

In this section it is argued that preferential trade arrangements are likely to lead to a conflict of interests between various groups, such as consumers or producers, within the preference-granting country. The resolution of these conflicts through the political process may enable the better organised producer groups to exert a systematic influence on the trade policies of a country or a customs union like the EEC, both in the choice of preferential partner and in the detailed content of trade agreements.

Much of the theory of customs unions is concerned with defining the conditions under which the formation of a union will be beneficial to the participants. For the most part, the gains from forming a customs union have been associated with trade creation, and this has led to a number of generalisations being advanced as to which countries might represent the most suitable union partners. For example, Grubel and Lloyd suggest that the gains from customs union formation may be greatest 'the more competitive or similar are the lists of the member countries' tradable differentiated goods produced *before* the union and the more production of these differentiated goods is subject to economies of scale.'[30] The advocacy of trade-creating customs unions is based on the view that they increase the *potential* welfare of the member countries because those who gain could compensate those who lose. In a trade-diverting customs union, under standard assumptions, this would not be possible.

If it is presumed that compensation will not take place—which seems likely to be the case in practice—then the desirability of customs union formation will depend heavily on the views which a society holds about the welfare of its constituent groups, and changes in their welfare. Corden, for example, has suggested that some countries may be characterised as having a 'conservative social welfare function', one component of which would be that 'any significant absolute reductions in real incomes of any significant section of the community should be avoided.'[31] In a trade-creating customs union losses of this kind are likely for owners of specialised resources in import-competing industries. Without a system of compensation, joining such a customs union would be unacceptable to a country possessing a conservative social welfare function, unless membership could be phased in so gradually that no significant losses would occur.

From a practical standpoint, the drawback with most customs union analysis is that it has, in effect, abstracted from distributional issues in its judgements about the conditions under which customs union membership would be desirable. But conflicts between different interest groups are likely to be key issues in relation to forming a customs union or practising other discriminatory trading arrangements. In order to understand the policy choices which countries make where such conflicts arise, it is necessary to take more explicit account of the political decision-making process in parliamentary democracies.

In recent years, attempts have been made to develop economic models of political behaviour which can be used to investigate national tariff structures. The models assume that there is a political 'market' in trade protection measures. The supply of these measures is controlled by the government, which uses this control to maximise its chance of re-election. The demand for protection comes from different groups of people whose welfare is affected by industry-specific protection. In such a model, 'a tariff can be viewed as a price which equilibrates political markets.'[32]

In the *adding machine* model, the pattern of protection reflects the voting strengths of particular groups. This might seem to rule out any protection at all, since consumers of any product will be more numerous than producers. However, for consumers, the effect of a tariff on a particular product will usually be too small to influence voting behaviour. The government may then gain votes by giving protection to an industry, especially if it is large and labour-intensive, and located in marginal constituencies.

An alternative view sees political decisions as being much influenced by the activities of *pressure groups* who lobby politicians and cultivate close links with government departments responsible for implementing trade policies. These groups seek to maximise the potential benefits from protection for their industry, net of the costs of organising and lobbying. They may face counter-pressure from groups representing consumers, importers and retailers. The *incentive* to lobby is also important. Caves has suggested that this incentive will be greater when an industry has fared badly compared with the economy at large.[33] Misfortune of this kind will increase the likelihood of a sympathetic response from the public which will be heeded by the government, it will also increase the perceived value of public assistance to individual firms, and will reduce the probability of free-riders (i.e. those who would share the benefits of group action but do not contribute towards the costs).

The effectiveness of models of political choice in explaining the pattern of protection between industries can be evaluated empirically by using economic variables (e.g. the degree of import penetration) as proxies for some of the political factors. Caves pioneered this approach in 1976 in a study which compared the ability of three models—the adding machine, interest group and National Policy models—to explain the structure of Canadian tariffs on manufactured goods. He concluded that his statistical tests broadly supported the interest group model as having the greatest explanatory power. In relation to the EEC countries, a number of studies have recently been undertaken as part of an inquiry into the penetration of markets of industrial countries by exports of manufactures from developing countries. Glismann and Weiss,[34] for example, concluded that in Germany the extent of government subsidies afforded to an industry will be greater the higher is the import penetration (i.e. ratio of imports to exports), the lower the number of firms, the more evenly the industry is distributed throughout the country, and the lower is the level of (EEC) effective tariff protection. The latter finding suggests that, to some extent, domestic subsidies are a substitute for EEC tariff protection. Studies of this kind have helped to give a fresh insight into the way in which protective measures are evolved: they represent the beginnings of a new political economy of trade policy in which both economics and political science have important roles to play. However, as Cable has pointed out,[35] there is a danger that some aspects of the decision-making process which are less readily quantifiable (how well an interest group is organised, for example) may be neglected.

Decision-making on trade policy in the EEC is complicated by the multinational character of the Community and the procedures employed in the decision-making process. All important decisions are made by the Council of Ministers, in which each country has one representative (see *Decision-making bodies in the EEC*, below). Where important national interests are involved decisions have to be unanimous, thus giving each country a veto. The aim of national pressure groups in the first place is to influence their own government on a particular issue by working through the national parliaments and through government departments. In addition, there is increasing collaboration at the European level between pressure groups in the various EEC countries (e.g. COPA, the farmers' group; and EUROFER, the steel producers' organisation).[36] Working in Brussels, where the headquarters of the EEC is based, they aim to keep EEC administrators in the European Commission fully informed of their members' views on policy issues. The Commission itself has some influence over trade policy in that it is responsible for drafting policy proposals, for the day-to-day operation of trade policies and for ensuring that the rules set out in the Treaty of Rome are observed. A third institution, the European Parliament, which brings together elected representatives from each of the member countries, has little power over the development of trade policy, although it does

DECISION-MAKING BODIES IN THE EEC

Under Article 4 of the Treaty of Rome, the operation of the EEC is entrusted to four principal bodies: a Commission, a Council, a Court of Justice and an Assembly (now known as the European Parliament).

The Commission has essentially a threefold role (Article 155):

(a) to ensure that what is set out in the Treaty is being fully observed, i.e. to act as a watchdog; (b) to suggest new or modified policies for the Community; and (c) to implement, on a day-to-day basis, certain aspects of EEC policy, especially concerning agriculture and trade (e.g. the Commission has the daily task of fixing the size of the variable levies charged on EEC food imports).

The Commission is headed by a President (from 1985, Jacques Delors) and thirteen Commissioners, nominated by the national governments for (renewable) terms of four years. Each Commissioner is responsible for a specific area of EEC policy and can call upon the services of a large professional and administrative staff based mainly in Brussels. The Commission staff work in twenty departments (Directorates-General), two of which are concerned with EEC trade: DG I, which deals with External Relations, and DG VIII, which is responsible for EEC development assistance. DG I is subdivided into eight Directorates, five of which focus on trade relations with particular foreign countries: (1) North America/Australia/New Zealand/Japan; (2) developing countries in Latin America and Asia; (3) Europe; (4) state-trading countries, and (5) countries which are negotiating for membership of the EEC (Spain and Portugal). The remaining three deal with trade relations in the GATT and OECD, plus agricultural trade, industrial trade (including textiles and steel), and general questions and instruments of trade policy like export credits and anti-dumping measures.

The main decision-making power rests with the Council:

'the Commission proposes but the Council disposes.' Each member country has one representative on the Council, appointed by its national government.The choice of representative varies from meeting to meeting, depending on the issues under discussion—e.g. if decisions have to be made about farm support prices, each government will normally send its Minister of Agriculture; major issues of policy command the attendance of Foreign Ministers. The Council meets about sixty times a year, with about fifteen sessions devoted to trade matters and twelve to the CAP. A large part of the preparation for these meetings is carried out in COREPER (the Committee of Permanent Representatives). COREPER is able to clear out of the way much of the uncontroversial technical material and can identify for the Council issues on which political decisions are required involving a balancing of national advantages and disadvantages ('package deals'). The Council also has the backing of a Secretariat, about a thousand strong, based in Brussels.

Breaches of Community law are dealt with in the Court of Justice. The judges are drawn from the member countries and can try cases involving individuals, firms or national governments. Where there is a conflict between Community law and national law, Community law has precedence. The judges have the power to impose heavy fines. Against governments, however, the only real sanctions are that if a government habitually puts national interests above Community law, then it cannot expect other governments to comply where its interests are affected, and the Community may disintegrate.

The fourth body, the European Parliament has little real power in relation to trade policies. Since 1979, members of the European Parliament have been directly elected. They have a right to be consulted on trade policy issues only when the EEC has a special relationship with a non-member country, involving an EEC aid programme, or the possibility of future EEC membership.

have the right to consultation with the Council on some policy initiatives (see *Decision-making bodies in the EEC*).

The real power for decision-making on trade policies rests with the Council of Ministers, and hence with the national governments. In making decisions about trade arrangements with non-member countries, the Council is influenced by a wide range of considerations such as historical ties with member countries or the need on strategic grounds to retain political allies in militarily sensitive zones. Economic factors also have a role to play and will certainly be important in determining the detailed content of any trade policy. Customs union theory gives some insight into how these economic factors might operate where the EEC's trade policies involve geographical discrimination (e.g. the extension of the customs union to new members, or the granting to non-members of preferential terms of access to the EEC market).

For this purpose it is helpful to distinguish two types of trade creation: that which is int*er*-industry in nature, and therefore involves the closure of part or all of a home industry, and the expansion of the corresponding, lower-cost industry in the partner country; and that which is of an int*ra*-industry kind, involving a two-way expansion of trade as the industry in both the home and partner countries concentrates on a narrower, but more complementary, product range. Thus EEC trade policies which discriminate between countries will have three broad effects: inter-industry (one-way) trade creation, intra-industry (two-way) trade creation, and trade diversion. These effects will have differing consequences for the various interest groups in the Community.

Which European industries might be vulnerable to inter-industry trade creation as a result of the preferential reduction of protection depends on the trading partner in question. For example, preferential access for developing countries' goods might lead to a contraction in EEC production of labour-intensive manufactures (e.g. textiles) and of some foodstuffs (e.g. sugar); similarly, preferential agreements with developed countries like the USA could pose a threat not only to high-cost food producers in the EEC but also to some technologically advanced industries. Owners of resources—both physical and human—in industries forced to contract would experience losses as the present value of their services declines. It is important to observe that it is not just those whose resources are forced out of an industry who would lose, but all those who own resources in that industry because of a general decline in profitability. Thus a powerful producer lobby could be expected against any agreement which might generate substantial inter-industry trade creation, like that mounted by farmers in the Mediterranean zone of the Community in relation to the terms of EEC entry for Spain. To the extent that the vulnerable industry is concentrated in particular regions, local lobbies will bring together both those directly affected and those whose interests are damaged by the decline in the region's economic base. If any industry is especially important to a certain member country, then that country may use its power of veto in the Council of Ministers to modify the Community's policy. Consumers, of course, would stand to gain from inter-industry trade creation in the form of cheaper goods, but their gains are much more thinly spread than are the losses to producer interests, making it more difficult to organise opposition.

In the case of intra-industry trade creation, adjustment costs may be lower than for the inter-industry variety because new opportunities will arise within the industry as export markets are opened up in the partner country. There is less likely to be organised producer opposition to the loss of protection in the home market since some firms will benefit from increased exports, possibly enabling them to exploit economies of scale more fully, and firms themselves may bring in imports to improve their product range and thereby strengthen their competitive position in the home market. Not only will producers be less united than in the case of inter-industry trade creation, but public support for protection will be less because of both the lower adjustment costs and also the observation that the more enterprising and export-oriented firms may favour a preferential trade agreement. Again, consumer groups could be expected to support a trade-creating agreement.

It has been implicit so far in the discussion that the goods in question are final goods destined for purchase by households. A good deal of trade however involves raw materials and intermediate products. In general, raw materials do not raise major conflicts of interest because potential Community production is small. Intermediate products (components, parts, bulk chemicals, semi-processed materials, etc.) pose greater problems because they tend to be more homogeneous than final goods, and as such are more vulnerable to inter-industry trade creation. The consumers in this case are manufacturing firms, who could be expected to mount an effective lobby against special treatment for intermediate goods (e.g. exclusion from a preferential trade agreement). The outcome of this clash of interest between intermediate goods producers and end users depends on many factors including how important the cost of the intermediate goods is in relation to total costs in the final goods industries; the protection given to final goods (e.g. under the CAP, processing industries are given protection to compensate for the higher cost of foodstuffs in the EEC); how diverse and numerous the end users are compared with the intermediate goods producers (e.g. the engineering industries in comparison to the steel industry); the extent to which end users produce tradable goods; and the degree of vertical integration between intermediate and final goods industries.

Trade diversion would be detrimental to the interests of the EEC as an importer, though a package deal might be arranged in which the EEC's partner also makes trade concessions which will be trade diverting in favour of EEC exports. Our earlier analysis of trade diversion suggested that such an arrangement would be, on balance, damaging to both partners. However, this need not necessarily be the case if, by reducing their imports from the rest of the world, the EEC and its partner could improve their terms of trade. In turn, however, this would depend on the response of countries which suffer a deterioration of their terms of trade. Even if they are not powerful enough to retaliate, their worsened export prospects could reduce their ability to import from the Community.

Clearly, each detailed aspect of the EEC's trade policies generates a different constellation of political and economic pressures. Nevertheless, the discussion of inter- and intra-industry trade creation and trade diversion suggests that there may be some systematic influences on the way in which EEC trade policies evolve, both in relation to the choice of preferential trade partners and in the detailed content of the Community's trade agreements. In particular:

(i)   In its choice of preferential trade partners, the EEC will encounter strong internal opposition to agreements which would lead to inter-industry trade creation but will find support for negotiating trade agreements whose primary effects are intra-industry trade-creating. This implies that where agreements are sought—perhaps mainly for politico-strategic reasons—with countries of similar economic structures, they will be not only easier to achieve than with countries of dissimilar structure but will also, as Grubel and Lloyd suggested, yield important economic benefits. On this basis, the original EEC countries appear to be particularly suitable partners: intra-industry trade flows between them are large and have increased since the Community was formed. Similar considerations apply to the trade links with EFTA countries.

(ii)   Where, for political reasons, trade preferences are granted to countries with dissimilar economic structures, there will be pressure within the Community to

   (a)   restrict the product coverage to exclude sensitive areas where inter-industry trade creation might be expected;

   (b)   restrict tariff concessions to not more than the existing volume of trade; in this way the EEC makes some sacrifice of tariff revenue without adversely affecting its producer interests;

   (c)   phase in concessions in sensitive areas over a long period so as to give resource owners the opportunity to withdraw gradually, thereby minimising their losses;

   (d)   offer tariff adjustments which are primarily trade diverting;
   and

   (e)   develop complementary areas of policy like technical and financial aid as an alternative to concessions which might lead to inter-industry trade creation.

It must be emphasised that these observations are not intended as a prescription for what should happen, but as an interpretation of the pressures which may actually shape EEC trade policies. In later chapters, we shall have the opportunity to consider the extent to which particular EEC policies follow the pattern suggested above.

3   The EEC and the GATT rules for International Trade

When, in the 1950s, the EEC countries began to draw up plans for their future economic cooperation, they recognised that they did not have a completely free hand to choose whatever trade arrangements suited them best. For one thing, each country was already involved in a network of trade agreements and obligations which could not be abandoned overnight. More importantly, they all subscribed to a set of rules—embodied in the General Agreement on Tariffs and Trade (GATT) – which governed the bulk of international trade relations. If the EEC were to be acceptable to the other major trading countries—and in view of the Community's heavy reliance on world trade this was vital— then its trade measures had to respect these rules.

The purpose of this chapter is to describe the GATT rules (section 3.1), and then to consider how the EEC's customs union, an essentially discriminatory arrangement, was reconciled with the GATT approach towards trade relations with its emphasis on non-discrimination (section 3.2).

3.1 The General Agreement on Tariffs and Trade: Origins and Principles

Towards the end of the second world war, the United States, Canada and Britain held discussions on future international economic arrangements. There was a determination to steer the global economy away from the economic depression, unemployment and protectionism of the 1930s and to create a new world economic order based on new international institutions. Thus were conceived the International Monetary Fund, to handle short-term capital flows, the International Bank for Reconstruction and Development, to deal with long-term capital flows, and an International Trade Organisation (ITO) to regulate world trade. The ITO was intended to have a comprehensive role covering, for example, not only trade liberalisation, but also the establishment of commodity agreements and the coordination of counter-cyclical policies.

In 1947, while discussions were taking place on the ITO, tariff negotiations were held in Geneva and resulted in the signing of the General Agreement on Tariffs and Trade. The GATT was intended to form part of the ITO, but as the discussions on the ITO eventually foundered, the GATT came to have a life of its own. The main purposes of the GATT are to provide a framework of rules for the orderly conduct of world trade and to supply a vehicle for the negotiated reduction of barriers to trade. The Agreement itself consists of two main parts: (i) a list (schedule) of national tariffs fixed through international negotiations, and (ii) a set of rules for the conduct of international trade. These rules, whose original form was heavily influenced by the views of the United States, continue to provide the framework under which trade between the market economy countries is supposed to be conducted today; they are outlined in the following paragraphs.[1]

THE RULE OF NON-DISCRIMINATION

This is the most important feature of the GATT system, and gives the Agreement a multilateral rather than a bilateral character. It requires that any 'advantage, favour, privilege or immunity' affecting customs duties or other trade charges which is granted to trade with another 'contracting party' (GATT member) must be accorded immediately and unconditionally to like products traded with any other contracting party. This means, in particular, that for each product category under negotiation a country must establish a single rate of tariff which applies to imports from all other member countries. Each GATT member then receives most-favoured-nation (MFN) treatment.

The merits of a non-discrimination rule are that it encourages countries to take part in negotiations to liberalise world trade since they know that any concessions obtained will not be undermined by greater concessions given to other countries at a later date. It encourages the spread of tariff reductions, since any tariff concessions agreed between two GATT members must be extended to all other GATT members. It puts a powerful brake on tariff increases since they have to be applied on imports from all GATT members, who are in a stronger position to resist than individual member countries would be. Finally, it can be argued that, in practice, it 'gives the best prospects for the supply of the imported good being from the country which is the most efficient, that is, the lowest cost producer of the good.'[2] This argument, however, has to be tempered by the (second-best) rule that, so long as one or more distortions (tariffs, subsidies, etc.) to trade exist 'it is not possible to say that non-discrimination will *necessarily* result in a more efficient production pattern than would tariff reductions that discriminated between countries.'[3]

It should be added that the GATT non-discrimination rule is not as simple as it initially appears.[4] First, it clearly continues to involve discrimination between home producers and foreign producers since home production is not subject to import tariffs. Secondly, tariff rates are still free to vary between products, so that a country can structure its tariffs to give more liberal access to the goods of a favoured partner than are provided for goods from other sources; in other words, because of differences in tariff rates by product, and in the composition of trade, the average rate of tariff actually applied may vary widely between imports from different countries. Thirdly, the GATT rules provide for certain exemptions, notably for customs unions and free trade areas (see section 3.2): thus discrimination is accepted as long as it is complete!

THE RECIPROCITY RULE
Even in the best of times, unilateral tariff cuts are not likely to command strong political support in western countries for two reasons. First, the views of consumers who might benefit from tariff cuts are generally not well articulated whereas producer groups whose interests might be damaged are able to mount powerful political lobbies. Secondly, tariff cuts on imports can be used as bargaining counters with which to obtain reciprocal concessions from other countries—notably better access to export markets. Employed in this way, reciprocity becomes a lever with which protection can be dismantled, but it has the drawback that it favours those who have been most protectionist in the past (as the United States had been in the 1930s), and those with the largest markets. Small countries with low tariffs are thus in a weak bargaining position. In order to improve their position, it was agreed early on in the GATT that binding (fixing) a low tariff against an increase for a period of years was to be regarded as equivalent to cutting a high tariff.

NEGOTIATIONS AND CONSULTATION
The GATT was an attempt to put order into an international trade system which had degenerated into beggar-thy-neighbour disarray

during the 1930s. In future, changes in trade policies were not to be made without consultation and a system was set up for trying to resolve the inevitable disputes that occur in a complex trade environment. Once negotiated, tariff rates were to be fixed for a period of at least three years. After that, if tariffs were to be increased then the country concerned must accept that its trading partners would be free to make equivalent changes affecting the conditions under which it exported. From 1955 on, tariffs were fixed without time limits.

The GATT has organised a number of major bargaining sessions in which tariff reductions have been negotiated. The rules of non-discrimination and reciprocity make for very complex negotiations. The aim is to produce a package deal which is acceptable to all member countries, through largely bilateral negotiations. In the early rounds of negotiations, a product-by-product approach was employed, in which each country negotiated tariff reductions with its principal suppliers and then extended the concessions to all contracting parties. This approach proved cumbersome and vulnerable both to protectionist lobbies and free-riders (smaller countries who benefited from tariff cuts under the MFN rule but failed to make cuts themselves), and in the last two rounds of GATT negotiations an alternative across-the-board or linear approach has been used instead. Under the linear approach, a target rate of tariff cuts is first agreed by the GATT contracting parties. Each country is then permitted to put forward a list of exceptions, since it would be very inefficient if wide-ranging tariff cuts were prevented by reservations in one or a few countries about tariff cuts on a handful of perhaps minor items. Negotiations then take place to narrow the list of exceptions and to agree on smaller tariff cuts for these products. If the list of exceptions is long, it may prove necessary to reduce the targeted rate of linear cut, and there is a danger that the negotiations will return to the product-by-product approach.

PROTECTION BY TARIFF

When the GATT was being established, the US argued for the principle that tariffs should normally be the only form of protection, though quotas could be used to help cope with major balance of payments problems. Tariffs had the advantage of working within the market mechanism and it was argued that they provided a clear indication of the extent of protection that was being provided. They also gave an incentive to exporters to lower their costs in order to overcome the tariff disadvantage, and were amenable to across-the-board reduction. By contrast, quotas and other devices tended to be applied by governments in an arbitrary way outside the market mechanism: they are more consonant with a command economy than a market economy. The GATT, consequently, sanctioned protection by tariffs only.

In fact, however, quota restrictions were very widely used in western Europe after the second world war. They were gradually eliminated as economic recovery proceeded, balance of payments conditions improved, and currency convertibility was achieved. Most of the quota eradication was carried out not in the GATT, but in the Organisation for European Economic Co-operation (OEEC)[5] which had been set up initially to administer Marshall Aid.

Negotiations in the GATT gradually brought down the level of tariff protection, but as tariffs declined, the importance of non-tariff barriers to trade (NTBs) became more apparent: Baldwin likened the process to the draining of a swamp—as the water level fell, so more and more obstructions began to emerge.[6] With the recession, an increasing proportion of world trade has been affected by NTBs, especially so-called voluntary export restraints. Thus the GATT's success in reducing tariff barriers has been offset—probably to a very substantial extent—by the growth of NTBs, which by their very nature are much more difficult to control. Tackling non-tariff barriers to trade became the major goal of the Tokyo Round, the latest, most ambitious and comprehensive set of trade negotiations ever held in the GATT.

3.2 The EEC customs union and the GATT

As described in section 3.1, each contracting party to the GATT agreed to apply a uniform most-favoured-nation tariff on imports from every other contracting party. There was, however, an exception to this rule which was of great importance to the EEC. Article XXIV of the GATT permitted the member countries of a customs union (or free trade area), on certain conditions, to give preferential treatment to imports from other member countries whilst still maintaining non-discriminatory treatment as between non-members.

The GATT rules made clear that the aim of a customs union or free trade area should be to facilitate trade between the member countries rather than to raise barriers to the trade of other GATT members. This could be interpreted as a demand that customs unions should be trade-creating rather than trade-diverting. A number of conditions are set out in Article XXIV to try to ensure that the formation of customs unions and free trade areas does not harm the trade interests of other contracting parties, and is not used simply as a device to circumvent the non-discrimination rule. The conditions concern (i) the speed with which the customs union or free trade area is established—it must be completed 'within a reasonable length of time'; (ii) its trade coverage—it must cover substantially all trade between the member countries; and (iii) in the case of a customs union, the height and uniformity of the common external tariff.

The first two conditions are designed to prevent countries getting around the non-discrimination rule by making selective tariff cuts on trade with certain countries, and labelling these as the first stage in the creation of some future but long-distant customs union. This was clearly not the case with the EEC customs union since it was fully established within a decade and covers all trade. From the viewpoint of customs union theory it should be added that a partial customs union might be preferable to one which covered all goods: trade diversion could be avoided by retaining some tariffs on trade between members. In practice, however, a partial customs union would probably have the opposite effect because protectionist pressure groups would oppose tariff cuts leading to trade creation and welcome instead the removal of tariffs which led to trade diversion.

Article XXIV specified that the common external tariff of a customs union was not to be 'on the whole higher or more restrictive than the general incidence of duties and regulations of commerce' that had been applied by the member countries before they formed the customs union. The EEC claimed that its use of the arithmetical average of the previous national duties met this condition, especially when the limitations on duties on raw materials were taken into account. There was no difficulty either in meeting the requirement that each member country must apply 'substantially the same' duties on their trade with non-member countries.

Superficially, the GATT rules appear to safeguard the export interests of non-member countries. The participants in a customs union are specifically prohibited from using the introduction of the common external tariff as a pretext for raising the general level of their tariffs on trade with the rest of the world. Of course, *some* exporters to the customs union might face higher customs duties on their products in *some* member countries, as part of the averaging process, leading to trade suppression. But this should be matched by reductions in duties in other member countries, leading to external trade creation. More seriously, the GATT rules in no way protect non-member countries from losing exports to the customs union through trade diversion. Even if the rules required the customs union to adopt the lowest of the previous national duties for each product as the common external tariff, trade diversion could still occur, though its extent would be lessened. The damage to the export interests of non-member countries occurs through the discrimination in tariffs between imports from members and non-members. Since discrimination is an inherent feature of a customs union, no general set of rules about fixing the level of the common external tariff can entirely prevent trade diversion from occurring, though they might help to minimise it.

There were lengthy discussions in 1957 over the compatibility of the proposed EEC customs union with the rules of the GATT. After this, it was agreed 'to set aside for the time being legal and formal considerations when discussing the problems which arise and to apply the established procedures of the General Agreement for consultation in the examination of specific problems.'[7] Under Article XXIV(6) of the GATT Agreement, if a country joining a customs union raises its tariff on imports from non-members in order to comply with the common external tariff other GATT countries can claim compensation for damage to their export trade. Such compensation has to take account of trade with those countries which reduced their tariffs down to the common level. Renegotiations on this score were opened in September 1960 and were brought to a successful conclusion in May 1961. The way was then open for the EEC to implement its CCT.

It is most unlikely that in framing Article XXIV the authors of the GATT had in mind anything like the development of huge regional trade groupings like the EEC; instead, their concern was not to prevent the economic merger of a small country with a neighbouring state. Thus many GATT members had serious misgivings about the creation of the EEC customs union. However, no effective challenge to the EEC was mounted because the most powerful GATT member, the US, took the view that the political advantages of a more united western Europe outweighed the potential damage to the trade interests of non-member countries.

The use of Article XXIV to legitimise the formation of the EEC set a precedent which the EEC has exploited repeatedly in the elaboration of its trade relations with third countries. By this means the EEC has been able to spin a worldwide web of preferential trade agreements, whilst claiming to adhere to the rules of GATT. However, as will be shown in later chapters, the conformity of these agreements with the GATT is debatable. The free trade areas linking the EEC with the EFTA countries, for example, exclude agricultural products. Similarly, the customs' unions which are supposed to be established between the EEC and certain Mediterranean countries (e.g. Malta and Cyprus) are unlikely to be completed 'within a reasonable length of time'. What matters more is not the individual conformity of particular agreements with the GATT rules, but the effect which the proliferation of discriminatory trade arrangements has on the whole GATT system.

Although the clash between GATT principles and EEC practice is perhaps most evident in the EEC's preferential trade agreements, the EEC is also guilty—along with most GATT members—of undermining other aspects of the GATT approach, for example, in its increasing use of non-tariff measures (see, in particular, Chapter 7). These actions have contributed to the current malaise of the GATT system. It should be added that although EEC practices seem often to be at odds with the spirit of the GATT, the Community—or at least the more liberally-inclined member countries—is very reluctant to breach openly the letter of GATT (see the discussion of the safeguards issue in section 10.1, below). The EEC is only too aware of its vital interest in the continuation of an open trading system. The implications of EEC policies for the GATT system will be reviewed in Chapter 15.

4 EEC Trade Patterns and the Shared Interest

In Chapter 3 it was argued that the shape of EEC trade policies is constrained to some extent by the rules which govern world trade. EEC policies will also reflect the pattern of the Community's external trade, since their underlying economic aim is to obtain the most advantageous conditions for trade. This means, for example, providing exporters with the best possible conditions of access to foreign markets, ensuring that needed imports are available on secure and advantageous terms, and protecting strategic or otherwise favoured industries which are vulnerable to import condition. The structure and direction of EEC trade are briefly reviewed in section 4.1. Section 4.2 examines the extent to which the present trade patterns of the Community have been altered as a result of the formation of the EEC customs union, and draws attention to the serious difficulties faced by any attempt at quantification. Patterns of trade are also one consideration in relation to the ease with which a common EEC trade policy can be established. The degree to which the EEC countries, through the structure and direction of their trade and also their attitudes towards protectionism, have a 'shared interest' in common EEC trade policies is discussed in section 4.3.

4.1 The pattern of EEC trade

Excluding trade between the member countries, the EEC accounted for about 18 per cent of world trade in 1982, and is the world's largest single trade unit, surpassing both the US (15 per cent) and Japan (8 per cent). The Community's share of world trade has been rather stable, fluctuating between 18 and 21 per cent over the last decade as the rise in oil prices has boosted OPEC export earnings and as the NICs have rapidly expanded their trade shares. In value terms, EEC exports in 1983 were valued at 300 billion ECUs and imports at 320 billion ECUs. The EEC's leading trading members are Germany (29 per cent of EEC external trade), the UK (20 per cent), France (17 per cent) and Italy (15 per cent), though the smaller countries have a higher share of trade in relation to their GNP.

The broad commodity pattern of EEC trade (see Table 4.1) is long-established and reflects, at least in a general way, the relative resource endowment of the Community—capital- and knowledge-rich, but short on land and other natural resources. Thus the EEC exports chiefly manufactures, especially machinery and motor vehicles, in exchange for raw materials, tropical foodstuffs and energy. The impact of the oil price increases over the last decade or so is reflected in the evolution of the commodity structure of imports (by value): the share of fuels has doubled since 1970 to about 30 per cent, whilst the relative importance of food and beverages has declined. The structure of exports has, however, been more stable. Onto this traditional trade pattern which is rooted in the Community's colonial past has been grafted a new and increasingly dominant element: the intra-industry exchange of manufactures with other industrial countries.

Table 4.2 describes the EEC's trade with its main commercial partners. The magnitude of the trade flows has been influenced by many factors including the population size of the partner country, its level of economic development and pattern of resource endowment, geographical proximity, differences in political systems, and government restrictions on trade. Reflecting its economic size, the US is the EEC's biggest trading partner, followed by Saudi Arabia, Switzerland, Sweden and Japan.

Fostered by their geographical closeness to the EEC, their strong political and cultural links with the Community, and a preferential trade arrangement, the EFTA countries are a major export market for the EEC and a key source of imports. In contrast to the strong intra-industry element in EEC trade with EFTA, the Community's trade with the developing countries is largely inter-industry in nature. The basic pattern of trade is an exchange of EEC manufactures for developing countries' foodstuffs and raw materials. A number of changes have, however, taken place in recent years, including the rapid growth of manufactured exports from a few developing countries—the NICs—and an increasing (subsidised) export of food from the EEC to some parts of the Third World, not to mention the massive increase in the value of exports from the OPEC countries to the Community. Trade with the centrally-planned economies is small considering the size of these economies and their geographical

Table 4.1   The commodity structure of EEC trade in relation to trade partners, 1982

Commodity	Industrial countries		Traditional oil exporters		Other developing countries		Eastern trading area		Total trade	
	X	M	X	M	X	M	X	M	X	M
Primary products:										
Food	51	57	5	1	6	17	3	2	66	79
Raw materials	9	15	0	0	0	3	1	2	10	22
Ores and other minerals	4	7	0	0	0	3	0	0	5	13
Fuels	49	50	2	67	2	10	0	16	56	143
Non-ferrous metals	10	10	1	0	1	3	0	1	11	14
Total	123	139	8	68	9	36	4	21	148	271
Manufactures										
Iron and steel	20	17	3	0	3	1	3	1	28	19
Chemicals	54	50	5	0	8	2	3	1	72	55
Other semi-manufactures	24	29	2	0	3	2	1	1	31	32
Engineering products	151	151	30	1	29	5	7	1	225	159
Textiles and clothing	27	26	1	0	2	7	1	2	32	35
Other consumer goods	28	25	4	0	3	3	0	1	36	29
Total	304	298	45	1	48	20	15	7	424	329
Total all commodities	435	445	54	69	59	56	19	28	583	609

Source: GATT, *International Trade 1982/3* (Geneva, 1983), Table A20.
Notes: X = EEC exports, M = EEC imports, in billion dollars. 'Total trade' includes trade of countries not listed, and 'total all commodities' includes items not classified by kind. 0 signifies a trade flow of less than $500,000.

Table 4.2   The direction of EEC trade, 1983 (billion ECU)

Partner country/group	EEC Exports	Imports
Intra-EEC	337	336
EFTA	69	67
Mediterranean countries	52	47
African, Caribbean and Pacific countries[a]	19	21
Other developing countries[b]	97	101
(of which newly industrialising countries)[c]	(15)	(24)
USA	50	53
Japan	7	21
USSR and East Europe	20	28
OPEC	52	61
World	645	665

Source: Eurostat, *Monthly External Trade Bulletin*, no. 6, 1984.
Notes: certain countries belong to more than one of the groups identified.
[a] Signatories of the Lomé Convention: includes also Overseas Countries and Territories plus Overseas Departments.
[b] Includes China and other Asian centrally-planned economies.
[c] Brazil, Mexico, Hong Kong, Malaysia, Singapore, South Korea and Taiwan.

closeness to the Community. For political reasons, neither group of countries wishes to become heavily dependent on imports from the other; EEC exports of manufactured goods are exchanged mainly for oil and gas imports.

The EEC's overall balance of trade has been fluctuating but generally in heavy deficit in recent years, reflecting a variety of influences including (i) the increase in oil prices in 1973–74 and again in 1979, which led to a massive trade deficit with the OPEC countries; (ii) a growing trade deficit with the US from 1972 to 1980, when the dollar strengthened; (iii) a trade deficit with Japan which escalated sharply at the end of the 1970s; (iv) a stable trade surplus with other European countries; and (v) a varying but large surplus with the Mediterranean countries. It should be noted that the countries which have the most preferential trade arrangements with the EEC—the countries of the EFTA, the Mediterranean, and Africa—are those with which the EEC is in trade surplus. The EEC's trade performance is, of course, only part of the broader balance of payments position in which earnings from invisibles (e.g. tourism, insurance and transport services) as well as capital flows play a major role (see Table 4.3).

During the 1960s, the share of intra-EEC trade in the Community's total trade increased rapidly because trade within the Community grew during that period about twice as fast as

Table 4.3   The balance of payments of the EEC countries, 1981
(billion ECU)

Merchandise exports	+550		Investment flows		
Merchandise imports	−557		long-term assets	−53	
Visible trade balance		−7	liabilities	+45	
Invisibles—credit	+251		net		−8
Invisibles—debit	−238		short-term assets	−121	
Invisibles balance		+13	liabilities	+128	
Private transfers (net)		−6	net		+7
Official transfers (net)		−12			
Current account balance		−12	Capital account balance		−1
			Errors and omissions		−1
			Change in reserves		+14

Sources: Eurostat, Balance of Payments, no. 2, 1984, and Eurostat, Eurostatistics, no. 7/8, 1984.

trade with the rest of the world. Close to a half of the EEC member countries' trade now takes place within the Community. The growth in the share of intra-EEC trade was consistent with the trade-creating and trade-diverting effects of customs union formation identified in Chapter 2. But it could also have been due to other factors, for example to the commodity pattern of intra-EEC trade with its emphasis on the fast-growing trade in manufactures. A more sophisticated approach is required to ascertain the EEC effect on trade and to judge the relative importance of trade-creation and diversion. Studies which attempt to do this are reviewed in section 4.2.

4.2 Measuring the trade effects of the EEC

Although there have been many attempts to quantify the effects of the formation of the EEC on trade flows, disagreement remains not only over the magnitude of these effects but also over how best to measure them. There are two broad approaches to measurement. The first, sometimes referred to as the *analytic method*, tries to explain trade flows in terms of all the major economic influences which shape them, such as national incomes in the importing countries, production capacity in the exporting countries and barriers to trade, including tariffs. With such a model it would, in principle, be possible to examine what the consequences of a selective removal of tariffs within a customs union have been or might be.

The attractions of the analytic approach are that the effects of customs union formation on trade are explained in terms of the known economic influences, and that estimates of the trade effects of customs unions may be made in advance (*ex ante*), if we are prepared to make the usual heroic assumptions about the future level of national incomes, etc. The main problem with this approach is that our knowledge of the factors which influence international trade flows, and their quantitative significance, is still sketchy. Because of the difficulties of predicting the values of many of the relevant variables, *ex ante* models are usually kept very simple, concentrating on the importing country and factors such as the level of income and relative prices of imports and domestic products. Even so, the problems are considerable, for example in relating changes in tariff rates to changes in prices in the importing countries.

The inherent difficulties with the analytical approach have led most researchers concerned with the trade effects of the formation of the EEC to use a cruder approach known as *residual imputation*. The essence of this approach is that one tries to explain developments in EEC trade by reference to certain key economic variables apart from tariff changes. Any unexplained developments are then attributed to the effects of customs union formation. Most residual imputation studies of the EEC have been based on an extrapolation forward of the EEC's trade experience in the 1950s, focusing particularly on the relationship between imports and income or consumption. The validity of such an extrapolation may be questioned in view of the special circumstances of the 1950s, such as the introduction of currency convertibility and the widespread abolition of quota restrictions. Moreover, it is likely that the results obtained are highly sensitive to the choice of those years that are included in the base period.

An alternative residual imputation technique is to examine the development of EEC exports in another market which is broadly similar to that of the Community, but one in which the EEC's exports do not get special tariff treatment. The experience in this market can be used to construct an *antimonde*, that is, a picture of how the EEC countries' trade would have developed in the absence of their customs union. There are two particular problems with the use of this technique: (i) it is hard to find a market comparable to that of the EEC—the US seems an obvious choice but its market is larger and more integrated than that of the original EEC; and (ii) the EEC is such an important trading entity that its formation has influenced the subsequent development of a all other markets.

In comparing measurement techniques a crucial consideration is their ability to distinguish separately the trade-creation and trade-diversion effects. Both lead to an increase in trade between the member countries, but, as was argued in Chapter 2, their relative sizes will have a strong bearing on the economic desirability of a particular customs union. The inability to separate trade creation and diversion is particularly a problem with simple import shares techniques. They may reveal that, for example, the formation of a customs union is associated with an increase in the share of a country's imports coming from its partner countries, but additional information about the effects of the customs union on the total level of imports would be needed if a breakdown between trade creation and diversion is to be made.

Since the EEC was established, a large number of empirical studies into its effects on trade have been made employing various measurement techniques, though predominantly of the residual imputation type.[1] Not surprisingly, the results obtained vary widely, though this is partly accounted for by the dates at which the studies were undertaken, because the EEC effect appears to have increased strongly over at least the first decade of its existence. Crucially, virtually all studies conclude that trade creation has exceeded trade diversion by a considerable margin, typically between five and ten fold. Furthermore, the total effect on trade appears to have been very large—for example, one study[2] suggested that, by 1969, intra-EEC trade had increased by about a third.

On a more disaggregated basis, there is some empirical support for the argument in section 6.1 that the member countries that had high national tariffs tended to experience mainly trade creation, and the low tariff countries mainly trade diversion (see Table 4.4). There is also some evidence that the impact of the EEC on non-member countries has been uneven. For example, a study by Balassa[3] found that US and Japanese exports to the Community had actually benefited from the formation of the EEC customs union, whilst neighbouring European countries had suffered trade diversion.

It is disconcerting to find that where studies try to disaggregate the EEC effect by sector, there are frequently conflicting results. To the extent that there is consensus, it appears that trade diversion occurred for foodstuffs, chemicals and possibly textiles, whereas the machinery sector experienced trade creation.[4]

Increased trade between the EEC countries should have

Table 4.4   Trade creation, trade diversion and the height of national tariffs in the original EEC member countries

Height of national tariffs pre-EEC		EFTA[a] 1967	R & T[b] 1968	V & S[c] 1969
		Trade-creation as % of trade creation + trade-diversion		
high	France	96	44	93
↓	Italy	76	95	90
	Belgium	73	35	83
↓	Netherlands	58	33	80
low	Germany	51	0	94

Sources:
[a] EFTA Secretariat, The Trade Effects of EFTA and the EEC, 1959–1967 (Geneva: EFTA, 1972).
[b] S. A. Resnick and E. M. Truman, 'An empirical examination of bilateral trade in Western Europe', Journal of International Economics, vol. 3, 1973, pp. 305–35.
[c] P.J. Verdoorn and A. N. R. Schwartz, 'Two alternative estimates of the effects of EEC and EFTA on the pattern of trade', European Economic Review, vol. 3, 1972, pp. 291–335.

permitted increased specialisation, along intra-industry and/or inter-industry lines. Balassa[5] investigated the nature of trade specialisation in the original EEC by analysing the product composition of trade between each pair of EEC countries over the periods 1958–63 and 1963–70. If inter-industry specialisation had been the dominant influence, then the lists of export products for each pair of countries should have become steadily more different. In fact, for 19 of the 20 bilateral trade flows examined, the export products became more similar: trade was increasingly taking the form of an exchange of similar goods. Grubel and Lloyd[6] confirmed the growing importance of intra-industry trade in the Community. They estimated that 71 per cent of the increase in trade between the EEC countries from 1959 to 1967 was intra-industry. In the early 1960s, according to Meyer,[7] intra-industry specialisation particularly affected the machinery and transport equipment sectors, and later in the decade spread to chemicals and consumer durables.

In short, there is empirical evidence that the formation of the EEC led to a substantial increase in trade between the member countries, and that most of the additional trade between the member countries was intra-industry in nature. The general finding that trade creation greatly exceeded trade diversion suggests that the effect of the customs union on the economic welfare of the member countries was on balance beneficial; some neighbouring European countries may however have been harmed by trade diversion. Beyond the trade effects of the EEC, what remains uncertain is, unfortunately, the most crucial issue of all: how was the rate of economic growth of the member countries affected? From the perspective of the 1980s, it appears that the rapid economic growth enjoyed by the EEC countries in the 1960s owed much more to the buoyant economic conditions of the time than to the formation of the Community.

4.3 The shared interest in a CCP

The ease with which an EEC common commercial policy can be created and maintained depends ultimately on the political commitment of the member countries to the Community. It also reflects the extent to which the member countries have shared interests in the structure, direction and management of their foreign trade. The closer and more homogeneous these interests are, the easier will it be to establish a Community approach and to use the Community's bargaining power to obtain more favourable conditions of trade than would have been available to the member countries acting independently.

THE MANAGEMENT OF TRADE: NATIONAL ATTITUDES TOWARDS PROTECTION

According to the Treaty of Rome, the CCP was to have a liberal stance towards trade with non-member countries, which would be facilitated by the strengthening of EEC industry within the larger market provided by the customs union. Article 110 of the Treaty declares that 'by establishing a customs union between themselves the Member States intend to contribute, in conformity with the common interest, to the harmonious development of world trade, the progressive abolition of restrictions on international exchange and the lowering of customs barriers.' These aspirations are in conformity with the spirit of the GATT and were no doubt intended to allay the fears amongst non-member countries that the EEC might become an inward-looking organisation. In practice, the CCP represents an uncomfortable compromise between the more liberal and the more protectionist elements.

In general, Germany, the Netherlands and Denmark are inclined to take a more liberal stance on Community trade issues than France, Italy and the UK, who have more frequently tended to adopt a protectionist approach.[8] These differences in national attitudes towards trade restriction appear to have persisted over time; for example, before the CCT was established, Germany and the Netherlands had lower average tariff rates than France and Italy. Similarly, prior to 1973, the UK had an average tariff rate above the CCT level. Attitudes towards protection have no doubt been reinforced by differences in economic performance over recent years. During the 1970s, the UK, France and Italy had the slowest growth in labour productivity in industry and the fastest increase in hourly wage costs (in national currencies) in the Community.[9] It should be added that national views on trade restriction are strongly influenced by the issues in question—for example, the Netherlands and Denmark, whilst having a generally liberal approach in relation to external trade, nevertheless strongly support protectionism under the CAP where their important national trade interests are involved.

COMMODITY INTERESTS

In terms of the product structure of their foreign (non-EEC) trade, the positions of the four large EEC countries (Germany, France, UK and Italy) are broadly similar: they export predominantly industrial goods (including chemicals, these account for 80 per cent or more of exports) in exchange for fuels (less so for the UK), food (less so for France) and raw materials (see Table 4.5). The smaller EEC countries have a higher dependence on agricultural exports. In general, the product structure of the EEC countries' trade appears to give them a shared interest in world trade, with the possible exception of the UK because of its indigenous oil resources.

THE DIRECTION OF TRADE: FOREIGN TRADE PARTNERS

The principal foreign trade partners of the member countries are similar:

for exports: USA, Switzerland, Sweden, Saudi Arabia
for imports: USA, Saudi Arabia, Switzerland, Japan

However, when considered in more detail, the geographical patterns of trade of the EEC members diverge, reflecting their locations within Europe and their historical trade links, especially with former colonies. Thus Denmark and Germany have strong commercial links with the EFTA countries; France, Italy and Greece with the Mediterranean region; France with the Francophone countries in North and sub-Saharan Africa; Greece with the Arab oil-exporting countries; and the UK with the Commonwealth countries.

Table 4.5 EEC trade with non-member countries by product groups, 1983 (billion ECU)

		EEC member countries								
Exports	EEC(10)	G	F	It	UK	N	BL	Dk	Ire	Gr
Machinery	113.4	48.5	21.1	15.3	17.4	4.4	3.2	2.7	0.7	0.1
Other manufactures	89.2	26.9	14.3	18.3	15.1	3.3	7.2	2.6	0.5	1.0
Chemicals	32.4	12.0	5.5	3.2	5.1	3.3	1.8	0.8	0.6	0.1
Food, etc.	24.3	3.3	6.8	2.1	3.8	3.7	1.1	1.9	0.9	0.7
Raw materials	5.9	1.4	1.0	0.7	0.9	0.8	0.3	0.5	0.1	0.2
Fuels	17.1	1.4	1.7	2.2	8.4	1.7	1.0	0.4	0.0	0.3
Total	303.0	98.3	52.0	43.2	58.7	19.1	17.0	9.4	2.9	2.4
Imports										
Machinery	58.4	16.3	10.1	4.9	14.5	4.9	3.6	1.7	1.3	1.1
Other manufactures	70.2	22.8	10.1	6.6	16.2	4.9	5.7	2.6	0.7	0.6
Chemicals	16.2	4.4	3.2	2.4	2.5	1.5	1.1	0.7	0.2	0.2
Food, etc.	34.3	8.4	6.0	4.2	7.0	4.8	2.2	1.1	0.3	0.3
Raw materials	30.2	8.1	4.3	5.4	5.6	2.7	2.6	0.8	0.2	0.5
Fuels	97.3	17.9	21.5	25.4	10.0	12.8	4.8	1.9	0.2	2.8
Total	328.5	85.2	55.4	51.7	64.8	32.2	21.2	9.5	2.8	5.7

Source: Eurostat, *Monthly External Trade Bulletin*, no. 6, 1984.
Notes: Totals include trade not classified by product group. Member countries: G: Germany; F: France; It: Italy; UK: United Kingdom; N: Netherlands; BL: Belgium–Luxembourg; Dk: Denmark; Ire: Ireland; Gr: Greece. Product groups: machinery and transport equipment (SITC 7); other manufactured goods (SITC 6,8); chemicals (SITC 5); food, etc. (food, beverages, tobacco, fats and oils) (SITC 0,1,4); raw materials (SITC 2); fuels (SITC 3); where SITC is Standard International Trade Classification.

Given the emphasis in the CCP on preferential treatment for selected non-member countries, the geographical patterns of trade of the member countries are of particular importance. Some idea of the degree of shared interest in the direction of trade of the member countries can be obtained by comparing the rank order correlation of their principal non-EEC trading partners. Tables 4.6 and 4.7 show that whilst some of the EEC countries have closely similar export and import patterns (e.g. Germany and the Netherlands), other countries have very little in common (e.g. the UK and Italy or Greece).

Table 4.6   Sources of EEC imports, rank order correlations[a] of member countries' trade partners[b], 1982

		Dk	Ire	UK	B	G	N	F	It	Gr	EC
D	Denmark										
Ire	Ireland	.88									
UK	United Kingdom	.75	.78								
B	Belgium	.69	.54	.78							
G	Germany	.70	.67	.72	.78						
N	Netherlands	.55	.47	.58	.74	.78					
F	France	.40	.38	.60	.74	.64	.78				
It	Italy	.14	.04	.20	.54	.45	.47	.60			
Gr	Greece	.37	.44	.40	.37	.61	.34	.35	.60		
*EC	EEC (10)	.55	.46	.76	.84	.85	.80	.81	.65	.60	
*S	Spain	.04	−.06	.16	.50	.26	.60	.65	.64	.15	.56
*P	Portugal	.52	.49	.59	.63	.46	.50	.60	.53	.33	.60

Notes: [a] A coefficient of +1 would indicate that the order of importance (by value of trade) of two countries' export markets was identical; a coefficient of −1 would indicate that the orders of importance were exactly reversed (the most important export market for country A was the least important for country B, etc.). [b] Based on the top 32 non-EEC destinations for EEC (10) exports, except for rows marked * for which the same destinations excluding Spain and Portugal were used.

The EEC member countries can be divided into three groups in relation to the direction of their trade:

(i)   a 'core' group of the Netherlands, Belgium, Germany and France whose direction of trade bears the closest similarity to the pattern of EEC trade as a whole,

(ii) the three countries which joined the Community in 1973 (the UK, Ireland and Denmark) who share similar rank orderings of trade partners but deviate quite strongly from some of the core countries (e.g. Danish and UK exports in relation to French exports) and

Table 4.7 Destinations of EEC exports, rank order correlations of member countries' trade partners[†] 1982

		UK	B	D	N	G	F	Ire	It	Gr	EC
UK	United Kingdom										
B	Belgium	.66									
D	Denmark	.72	.56								
N	Netherlands	.60	.68	.79							
G	Germany	.52	.64	.73	.86						
F	France	.48	.62	.47	.74	.65					
Ire	Ireland	.68	.47	.69	.69	.62	.68				
It	Italy	.25	.36	.41	.57	.57	.56	.57			
Gr	Greece	.26	.40	.36	.54	.58	.49	.53	.82		
*EC	EEC (10)	.71	.74	.75	.89	.88	.75	.77	.66	.65	
*S	Spain	.07	.13	.11	.33	.37	.49	.43	.63	.49	.36
*P	Portugal	.47	.58	.74	.69	.70	.53	.59	.39	.27	.70

Note: [†] See note b to Table 4.6.

(iii)   Greece and Italy whose direction of trade is similar but contrasts with that of the northern EEC countries (Spain is potentially a third member of this group, but not Portugal).

This analysis suggests that a common EEC trade policy which is geographically discriminatory and which is shaped according to the importance of non-member countries in overall EEC trade will be less appropriate for Greece, Italy, the UK and possibly Ireland and Denmark than it is for the other member countries.

There are many common threads which serve to bind the member countries' trade interests together, for example, the heavy dependence of most EEC countries on imported fuel supplies. There are also elements of diversity, such as the very different geographical trade patterns of the UK and Greece. Perhaps the only firm, if unsurprising, conclusion that can be reached is that the extent of the 'shared interest' depends on the particular trade issue in question.

This Chapter has outlined the main features of EEC trade patterns in relation to commodity structure and partner countries, and has reviewed the problems of measuring the effects on EEC trade patterns of the formation of the customs union. Patterns of trade also played an important part in the discussion of the shared interest of EEC countries in a common trade policy. The general nature of that policy and the main instruments employed are the subject of the next three chapters. Later chapters explore the EEC's trade arrangements with its principal partner countries—the 'pyramid of privilege'.

5   The Free Movement of Goods Within the EEC

At the heart of EEC trade policies is the customs union. As was seen in Chapter 2, a customs union has two complementary aspects: the free movement of goods between the member countries (which should lead to the creation of an integrated internal market), and the imposition of a common external tariff on imports from non-member countries. This chapter is concerned with the steps taken by the EEC to abolish tariffs and quotas on trade between the member countries (section 5.1), the problems experienced by the EEC in trying to create a genuinely integrated internal market (section 5.2), and the steps taken to tackle these problems (section 5.3). Chapter 6 focuses on the rules governing trade with non-member countries.

The economic rationale for an integrated EEC internal market rests heavily on the argument that, with barriers to trade between the member countries removed, the market mechanism will be able to operate more effectively; this will lead to a better use of the Community's limited resources, so enabling more goods and services to be produced. High-cost producers will be forced through increased competition either to raise their efficiency or to go out of production. Their lower-cost rivals will have the opportunity to expand in a bigger home market, possibly lowering their costs further through the fuller exploitation of economies of scale.

A number of serious reservations must be entered about this 'recipe' for European economic improvement, which was put forward at a time when government involvement in the western European economies was less pervasive than it is now. First, there is the general problem that the market, acting on the basis of private costs and benefits may not always produce the best results when social costs and benefits are also considered. This was recognised in the Treaty of Rome, for example, in the rules concerning competition and state aids. Secondly, the theory of customs unions does not suggest that the creation of a single market for two or more countries will always lead to a better use of the union's resources: where trade diversion occurs, domestic resources will be attracted into high-cost production. Thirdly, it is now clear from EEC experience that the removal of barriers to trade between the member countries of a customs union is an even more difficult task than the founders of the Community envisaged.

With these very important reservations in mind, we can now turn to the actual steps taken by the EEC countries to create a single Community market.

5.1 The abolition of tariffs and quotas on trade between the member countries

The Treaty of Rome calls for an end to virtually all government-imposed restrictions on trade between the member countries. Article 9 of the Treaty prohibits import tariffs, export taxes (of which there were relatively few) and 'all charges with equivalent effect' on *all* goods traded between EEC members. This includes not only products originating in the member countries but also imports from outside the EEC on which tariffs have been charged in another member country. Once such a good has entered the EEC, and the customs duty at the point of entry has been paid, it should then enter into free circulation within the Community: like EEC-made products, it should cross internal EEC borders duty-free.

Import quotas (quantitative limits on imports) were widely used in the 1950s to control trade, mainly for balance of payments reasons, but were clearly incompatible with the creation of a unified EEC market. Article 30 of the Treaty therefore calls for their total abolition on trade between the member countries. This was achieved in January 1962 for industrial goods, soon after all of the member countries' currencies became fully convertible, thus invalidating the general use of quotas on balance of payments grounds. Similarly, adjustments to the practices of state trading monopolies were required by Article 37 to ensure that there was no discrimination in trade between the member countries. The only permitted exceptions to the free movement of goods are those 'justified on grounds of public morality, public order, public safety, the protection of human or animal life or health, the preservation of plant life, the protection of national treasures of artistic, historical and archaeological value or the protection of industrial and commercial property' (Article 36). As will be seen later, national governments have tried increasingly to use this exceptions clause as a legal justification for protectionist measures on intra-EEC trade.

Manufacturers and traders within the Community were given a transitional period of twelve years (Article 8) in which to adjust to the freer movement of goods. If this appears to be rather a generous arrangement, it should be noted that the tariff and quota restrictions on trade were substantially higher than they are today, and also that the EEC was to some extent entering uncharted waters in attempting to abolish all institutional barriers to trade between a group of major industrial countries. In the event, it proved possible—spurred on by what was happening in the rival EFTA group—to speed up the timetable of changes set out in Article 14 (see Table 5.1), and the duty– and quota–free movement of goods between the member countries was achieved on 1 July 1968, 18 months ahead of schedule. Furthermore, member states had little recourse to the safeguard measures permitted under Article 226 of the Treaty, which allowed member countries to take action to deal with serious difficulties in a particular industry or region, as authorised by the EEC Commission.

Table 5.1   Internal tariff reductions of the EEC

Reduction effective from:	Individual reduction	Cumulative reduction
	(% of 1 January 1957 level)	
1 January 1959	10	10
1 July 1960	10	20
1 January 1961 (acceleration)	10	30
1 January 1962	10	40
1 July 1962 (acceleration)	10	50
1 July 1963	10	60
1 January 1965	10	70
1 January 1966	10	80
1 July 1967	5	85
1 July 1968	15	100

Source: Commission of the EC, *GR*, 1967, p. 34.

The apparent ease with which tariff and quota restrictions on trade between the EEC countries were swept away appears surprising in view of the general reluctance of governments to cut, let alone eliminate, tariffs. Strong pressure may be exerted by producer interests in import-competing industries against a loss of protection. Consequently, in international trade negotiations, it usually takes several years of tough bargaining to secure often quite modest tariff reductions. So how can the relatively trouble-free experience of the EEC be explained? The general answer appears to be in a combination of good timing and a change in the instruments of protectionism. More specifically:

(a) Rapid economic growth during the 1960s quickly absorbed resources released from firms unable to meet increased foreign competition; the market was growing so rapidly that the loss of protection often meant slower growth rather than actual cutbacks.

(b) Much of the increased specialisation was intra-industry in nature: rather than whole industries being shut down as might have been anticipated, adjustments to product ranges and scale of operations tended to occur within industries; hence adjustment costs have been less than expected.

(c) Tariff cuts affected both imports and exports, with the result that the net effect on the balance of payments and unemployment was small.

(d) The level of protection in the EEC was already fairly low following work in the OEEC to get rid of quota restrictions, and after several sets of negotiations to cut tariffs in the framework of the GATT; hence, major differences in the costs of production between the EEC countries were uncommon and the removal of tariff restrictions had no dramatic effects.

(e) Even at the end of the transition period, trade was heavily restricted by non-tariff barriers of many kinds; thus to some extent there was a change in the nature of protection rather than a decrease in its level. Non-tariff barriers are the key targets in the current attempts to fully integrate the EEC internal market.

The favourable experience of the six original EEC countries—EEC (6)—in establishing the customs union ahead of schedule and without too much trauma was reflected later in the length of the transition period given to new members of the Community: the UK, Denmark and Ireland became full members of the EEC customs union in under five years. The first tariff cuts on their trade with the original EEC countries were made in April 1973 and customs duties and quotas were eliminated by July 1977. Once again, relatively few problems were encountered which could be attributed directly to trade liberalisation, even though economic growth was much slower during the 1970s than it had been in the previous decade. Greece's transition period to full membership, beginning in 1981, is also five years for most products. However, this understates the period which Greece has had to adjust to freer trade, since tariffs had previously been reduced during Greece's lengthy Association Agreement with the EEC (see section 9.4).

5.2 Current problems of the internal market

Despite the achievements of the EEC in sweeping away customs duties and quotas on internal trade, and in widening the Community so that it now embraces almost 270 million people, the aim of creating a single EEC market is very far from realisaton. Substantial barriers to trade between the member countries exist, and firms regard exports to other EEC countries just as much as foreign transactions as trade with non-member countries. The EEC states are failing to grasp what should be one of the main prizes of EEC membership—the creation of a large unified home market comparable in size with that available to US firms. What is more, the situation appears to be deteriorating, though it is hard to quantify this. With high rates of unemployment hanging over all the European countries, governments are resorting to a whole range of non-tariff devices to protect their national industries. Short-term considerations prevail, but this could prove to be a costly mistake if the division of the EEC market undermines the competitiveness of European firms in world markets.

The division of the EEC market on national lines is highlighted by the behaviour of prices. Even during the initial period of EEC formation, there was no evidence that the removal of tariffs and quotas on internal trade led to a general convergence of prices. Indeed, a sample study showed that, for a considerable proportion of consumer goods, pre-tax price differences between EEC member countries grew larger and in some cases exceeded 100 per cent, far more than could be accounted for by transport costs.[1] Similarly a Commission-sponsored survey in October/November 1978 showed that for a group of 100 selected electrical goods (electrical appliances, hi-fi and video products) the average prices in Denmark, for example, were some 50 per cent above those in Italy.[2] The gap between average prices in France and Italy—neighbouring countries with more than twenty years' membership of the EEC behind them—was 30 per cent. In one area at least (cars) there is growing public awareness of the price differentials that exist between EEC countries for identical goods. These can be illustrated by the case of the British Leyland Mini Metro which in July/August 1981 was selling at a pre-tax price of £2666 in Britain compared with the equivalent of £1591 in West Germany.[3] Differences in car prices have received publicity in the media, but similarly wide variations are found for a whole range of goods.

These different prices can coexist only because there remain substantial barriers to trade between the EEC member countries, and for this their governments must be held largely to blame. Manufacturers go along with this arrangement because it gives them greater short-term security in their home market, and it enables them to practice price discrimination, thereby improving their profits through a greater exploitation of consumers. Price discrimination involves charging different prices to consumers in different markets for an identical good when those price differences exceed what could be accounted for by transport, distribution and other costs.

If price discrimination is to be carried out successfully there must be differences in price sensitivity (elasticity) of demand in two or more markets, and the markets must be separable. Assume that a firm has two separable markets for its product: a home market in which demand is inelastic (perhaps partly as a result of extensive advertising to increase consumer loyalty) and an export market in which demand is elastic. The firm can increase its sales volume by lowering the price of its product; but how much, if any, extra revenue this will generate will depend on the elasticity of demand for the product. At any given level, the extra revenue generated by an additional unit sold (marginal revenue) will be higher in the export market than in the home market. Therefore the firm can increase its profits by switching some sales from the home market to the export market, and will maximise its profits at any given level of output by switching sales such that marginal revenues in the two markets are equal. But these new levels of sales will clear the markets at different prices—a high price in the home market, a low price in the export market.

Meyer has argued, however, that price differences between markets are not generally the result of deliberate price discrimination.[4] Rather, exporters tend to respect the existing prices in their export markets and to compete for sales on the basis of product design and other non-price factors. In the case of cars, the price levels in different markets appear to be determined by the costs of the largest domestic producers. Existing prices are respected because undercutting might produce a protectionist response, whilst higher prices might encourage distributors to look for alternative sources of supply. Whether price differentials are due to deliberate price discrimination or merely to the observance of existing prices, firms will not be able to maintain these separate prices unless they can prevent entrepreneurs buying in low-price national markets and re-selling in higher price markets ('parallel imports'—so-called because this trade occurs alongside the official transactions between firms and their overseas distributors). There are various devices that can be employed to deter parallel imports, such as tight control of distributors, the use of different brand names in different markets, and small differences in product design. But firms are greatly aided in this by barriers created and maintained by governments.

Some indication of the range of barriers that exist is given in Table 5.2, which is drawn from a Commission publication based on actual cases reported. It is very difficult to assess the impact of these non-tariff barriers on trade, but it appears to be very substantial. The Commission has estimated, for example, that the cost of formalities at the internal frontiers could be equivalent to 5–10 per cent of the value of the goods affected.[5] By inhibiting trade, these costs deny some of the benefits from international specialisation. Where economies of scale are particularly important, non-tariff restrictions on access to other EEC markets may put EEC producers at a disadvantage on world markets compared with their US and Japanese rivals whose home markets are much more integrated.

In principle, the single market applies as much to agricultural products as to industrial goods, but there are additional complications in practice. Under the CAP market prices are manipulated by restricting imports from non-EEC countries and by fixing minimum prices (intervention prices) at which the EEC authorities are willing to purchase any supplies which are offered to them (see section 7.1). The intervention prices are expressed in terms of ECUs (based on a 'basket' of EEC currencies), converted into national support prices by 'green exchange rates' which are more stable than the market exchange rates and hence give farmers greater stability of prices in terms of their own currencies. A key problem with this arrangement is that if the green exchange rates are out of line with market exchange rates then the intervention prices in the member countries will differ. The result of this is that the country with, temporarily, the highest intervention price attracts supplies from all the other countries. In order to prevent this from happening the EEC has set up a system of border taxes

Table 5.2   *Examples of trade barriers and constraints in the EEC internal market*

Barriers/constraints	Example
General barriers and constraints	
A. National preference	Preference to national products in public contracts.
B. Legal uncertainty resulting from amendments to rules without adequate transition periods.	
Frontier barriers	
A. Formalities and inspections	Many complex customs, tax and statistical formalities.
B. Import restrictions	Imports subject to opinion of committee in which national manufacturers are represented (e.g. fire-fighting equipment).
C. Administrative matters	Limited number of approved crossing-points.
D. Other	Requirement to use customs agent or a guarantor.
Rules concerning technical safety and public health	
A. Preparation of the rules	Plethora of rules, lack of clarity, frequent changes, influence of national producers.
B. Substance of the rules	Trade standards which penalise imports.
C. Application of the rules	Lengthy and expensive checks.
Other barriers and constraints	
A. Transport conditions	Checking the weights and dimensions of vehicles.
B. Taxation	Tax schemes for alcoholic drinks which favour local producers.
C. Aid	Aid made subject to purchase of national products.
D. Price rules	Fixing a low price of gas in some countries.

Source: Commission of the EC, 'Assessment of the function of the internal market', *COM*, (83) 80 final, Brussels, 24 February 1983, pp. 29–32.

and subsidies *(monetary compensatory amounts)* which exactly offset the national price differences. In this way, the problem of trade flows generated by the green exchange rate system is largely solved, but at the cost of reinforcing the frontier barriers between member countries. Since the monetary compensatory amounts are adjusted weekly if necessary, traders have been faced with considerable uncertainty; this uncertainty was however reduced by the introduction in 1979 of the European Monetary System which led to more stable market exchange rates between most of the EEC currencies. In March 1984, the Council of Ministers took the decision to phase out monetary compensatory amounts over three years and to tie farm support prices to the strongest EEC currency.

Apart from the system of monetary compensatory amounts, many other restrictions on intra-EEC trade in agricultural products remain.[6] For example, ostensibly on the grounds of protecting the British poultry industry from fowl pest, the UK government introduced a ban on all poultry and egg imports from September 1981. Similarly, the French government has obstructed imports of wine from Italy on the pretext that import documents were incorrectly drawn up and that the origin of the wine could not be proved. In both of these cases, and in many more besides, the principal concern of the governments is clearly to protect the incomes of their own farmers.

5.3 Community action to integrate the internal market

With so many different types of restriction on intra-EEC trade, it is clear that movement towards a more integrated EEC market will require action on a broad front, much of it outside the scope of trade policy as such. Some of the more important areas where action is currently being undertaken are reviewed in this section.

HARMONISATION OF TECHNICAL STANDARDS

All modern governments attempt to protect the health, safety and welfare of their citizens through passing legislation making it compulsory for all products sold on the national market to conform to prescribed safety standards, construction methods, etc. The problem for the EEC is that if each member country adopts its own rules and regulations, without reference to those in other EEC countries, some of the advantages of the single market are lost because manufacturers have to produce different versions of their products for each national market. An example quoted by the Commission is the building regulations for lifts: in Belgium all lifts must have a 'stop' button, whereas in the UK such a device is expressly forbidden.[7]

One way around the problem of different national regulations is to create European regulations which are binding on all member states. Using the powers given to it under Article 100 of the Treaty, the Council has in fact agreed some 150 Directives of this kind. They are mostly concerned with motor vehicles and methods of measurement, though others relate to such diverse areas as tractors, cosmetics, textiles, toxic substances and pharmaceuticals. The chief difficulty with this approach is that it is so time-consuming and slow: the Community is obliged to work at the pace of the least willing member country. Those countries like Germany which have well-developed national measures are inclined to take the view that their system is best and are unwilling to compromise in order to reach a Community solution.

If all technical regulations were to be put onto a Community basis, several thousand Directives would be needed, along with a large increase in Commission staff. In present circumstances, there is no chance of this happening. Furthermore, it would still leave the problem of diverse national standards which are being drawn up by national standardisation authorities at the rate of dozens every week. The standards are intended to serve such desirable ends as: rationalisation of production, improvement of product quality, protection of workers, users, consumers or the environment, and more economic usage of energy. However, they may hamper the development of trade by giving national firms certain advantages. In particular, since national firms are involved in drawing up the specifications not only can they influence them in ways which benefit their own products but also they have more advance notice of new standards than do foreign firms.

Initially, the Commission tried to combat the problem of proliferating national standards by supporting the establishment of two European standards institutes and encouraging them to fix European standards. However, the results after twenty years are disappointing: there are too few European standards and they sometimes incorporate national deviations that rob them of much of their impact.[8]

In response to the snail-like progress with European-wide technical regulations and standards, the Commission advocates two lines of action.[9] The first is to continue with the harmonisation Directives where these are likely to serve an important purpose in facilitating trade. The Commission would like the Council to delegate some of the decision-making in order to speed up work on less controversial aspects. This already happens when harmonisation Directives are being revised: the Commission works with a committee representing the national interests and has some limited powers on uncontentious matters. Alongside the continuing effort on harmonisation Directives, the Commission urges an expanded work programme for the European standards organisations.

The second line of action is to try to prevent the erection of new barriers to trade by improving the circulation of information on proposed changes in national regulations and standards. To this end, the Council adopted an important Directive in March 1983 requiring the circulation to all EEC countries of the annual work programmes of standards institutions in the member countries, together with draft standards, and draft technical rules drawn up by the member governments. Other governments are given three months to examine these drafts, and six months if they have reasoned objections; if the Commission proposes to submit an EEC Directive dealing with the issue, a delay of one year can be imposed.[10]

SUPPRESSION OF NATIONAL BARRIERS TO TRADE

The rights of the EEC member governments to legislate on technical standards, health and hygiene regulations, etc. are increasingly being used as a cover for protectionist measures. Either deliberately or because of a general neglect of non-national interests, legislation is often drawn up in a way which discriminates against imports and has an effect equivalent to that of quantitative restrictions. As such, it is contrary to Article 31 of the Treaty of Rome. The Commission, in its role as guardian of the Treaty, has been taking action on an extensive and increasing scale to combat the more blatantly discriminatory measures, especially since 1978. There has also been a jump in the number of cases brought to the European Court of Justice, from about two a year in the mid-1970s, to about 50 a year in 1981 and 1982.

Following an important test case in 1978 (*Cassis de Dijon*), the Court ruled that:[11]

(a) if a product has been lawfully produced according to the rules of one member country, it must in principle be allowed to be imported into another member country;

(b) this principle implies that member countries must not take an exclusively national viewpoint in drawing up technical rules;

(c) only under very strict conditions does the Court concede exceptions to this principle; barriers to trade resulting from differences between commercial and technical rules are only admissible if the rules are necessary in order to meet mandatory requirements like public health, serve a purpose which is important enough to justify a departure from the fundamental rule of the free movement of goods, and are essential for such a purpose to be attained.

On this basis, the Court took the view that, to take one example, national legislation to prohibit the sale of vinegar which was not made from wine infringed the Treaty and must be withdrawn.[12] The Commission has asked for substantial additional resources to mount a bigger campaign against national protectionist measures. At present, the sheer volume of complaints to the Commission means that there is often a long delay before action is taken, to the advantage of countries which infringe the rules. In 1981, for example, over 400 complaints and infringements were under investigation.[13]

SIMPLIFYING FRONTIER FORMALITIES

Although tariffs and quotas on intra-EEC trade have been abolished, the Commission has acknowledged that 'the formalities at the internal borders of the customs union remain almost intact, and are as complex as those applying to imports from non-member countries.'[14] Part of the problem is that there is no common customs code, that is, a comprehensive set of community rules governing the customs procedures in the member countries. Instead, there has been a piecemeal adaptation of national legislation to Community requirements, which tends to be a very slow process because national customs legislation has been drawn up according to different economic concepts and in relation to different general legal systems. Until customs procedures have been harmonised there is wide scope for protectionist practices.

Since 1970, a Community transit system has been in operation in an attempt to streamline intra-Community trade. Goods can be transported through to a customs office in the country of destination without any further customs formalities on crossing the frontier—a modest enough achievement for a customs union. In a further attempt at simplifying formalities, EEC Ministers planned to reach agreement in 1984 on a single customs document to apply to all intra-EEC trade and to replace the 70 or so documents used at present. This would not mean an end to hold-ups at the frontiers, however, since tax adjustments (see below) and checks in connection with technical regulations would still be required. Frontier delays were a major factor in the massive blockades of French and Italian motorways by protesting lorry drivers in February 1984.

In the case of freight moving by rail, transit documents are not required when internal EEC frontiers are crossed; transport operations are monitored solely by means of international waybills.[15] The European Parliament has urged that the simplification of frontier formalities should be carried further: thus industrial goods in free circulation should be exempted from all frontier formalities, and the recording of trade and collection of VAT should be based on companies' normal accounts, supplemented by spot-checks by the customs authorities at the departure point.[16]

OPENING UP GOVERNMENT PURCHASES TO FOREIGN SUPPLIERS

Government purchases represent about 15 per cent of Community GNP including purchases of military and space equipment. Much of this large market is closed to foreign supplies. The Council of Ministers agreed to try to open up the public procurement market by insisting on wider publicity for forthcoming contracts, but the Commission reported that this has had 'very disappointing results. Although the scope for Community action has been limited, one is bound to conclude that the procedures, even when formally applied, have seldom been correctly implemented, and purchasing departments have generally resorted systematically to the restricted procedures, which in the spirit of the Community directives ought to have been used in exceptional circumstances only.'[17] Government 'buy national' policies remain the norm for many capital goods and advanced technology products with the result that in relation to, for example, electric power stations and telecommunications equipment intra-Community trade is small.

COMMUNITY ACTION IN OTHER POLICY AREAS

The integration of the EEC internal market is intimately affected by the slow progress in harmonising a broad range of Community policies, but especially in relation to taxation, company law, competition and exchange rates. For example, wide differences in company law between the member countries obstruct cross-frontier collaboration within the Community with consequential effects on trade. EEC competition policy is more developed, since it is a specific requirement of the Treaty. Thus the Commission has used its powers under Article 86 to combat price discrimination between national markets by firms which occupy a dominant position. It has also successfully attacked the practice of territorial protection of distributors whereby the distributor of a particular product in one area was not allowed to sell in the marketing area of another distributor. This was one of the devices employed by firms to prevent parallel imports. However, the wide price differences between EEC markets (section 5.2) indicate that companies are still able to find ways around the EEC rules.

The introduction of VAT in 1967[18] was an important step in the integration of the EEC market since it displaced the cumulative taxes on turnover previously employed: rebates on turnover taxes had been used extensively and deliberately to subsidise exports. The EEC's *indirect taxes* remain firmly based on the destination principle—that is, goods are subject to the indirect taxes of the country in which they are consumed. This necessitates an adjustment on the internal frontiers of the Community, even though customs duties have been abolished. Only if the member countries agreed to adopt an origin system, with goods carrying the taxes of their country of manufacture could the fiscal frontier be truly eliminated.[19] However, if the EEC countries could agree to collect VAT not at the frontier post when goods are being imported but as part of the normal tax payments by firms, border delays would be greatly eased. This system has been used by the UK and on intra-Benelux trade, but so far the Commission has been unable to persuade all of the member states to adopt it because of concerns over a one-off loss of tax revenue and resistance from customs staff.

CONCLUSIONS

The Community can point to some concrete achievements in integrating the internal market, for example the abolition of tariffs and quotas and the introduction of a common system of indirect taxation. However, this progress is under threat. Intra-EEC trade as a proportion of the member countries' combined GDPs has tended to decline in the wake of the oil price shocks of 1973 and 1979, and the Commission complains of a 'retreat from a Community-oriented approach'[20] as governments allow short-term protectionist considerations to take precedence over maintaining, let alone extending, the integration of the EEC market.

The current economic problems of high unemployment and slow growth pose a fundamental dilemma for EEC members in relation to the Community's internal market. On the one hand, it is recognised that to be competitive on world markets EEC industries need to have access to the large integrated home market that the Community potentially could provide. On the other hand, it is feared that this unified market would become even more attractive to Japanese and other exporters; at the same time, the member countries would no longer be able to protect their home markets with the present variety of non-tariff devices.

As ever, France's attitude is crucial to the direction which EEC policy is to take, though they have no shortage of protectionist partners within the Community. The French government, alarmed at the inroads which foreign manufactures were making into the French market (import penetration rose from 22 per cent in mid-1978 to 28 per cent in mid-1982) and the consequent large trade deficit, launched a new programme aimed at the 'reconquest of the domestic market' in 1981. The programme included targets for reducing import penetration in six industries (e.g. in the machine tool sector cutting imports from 60 to 30 per cent of the market) backed up by government aid. Import regulations have also been tightened up (e.g. import documents must be in French, and goods must be labelled with the country of origin, as indeed they already were in some other EEC countries). Nevertheless, the government recognises the importance of the EEC market for French manufacturers and would back a move towards further integration, but only if tougher measures were taken against damaging surges of imports, especially from Japan—a movement towards a 'Fortress Europe' strategy.

At their summit meeting in Copenhagen in December 1982, the EEC heads of state and government came down in favour of new moves to strengthen the internal market and to prevent it from being fragmented by national protectionism. However, progress remains slow, and the dilemma over the integration of the internal market remains unresolved.[21]

6 The Common Commercial Policy

The Treaty of Rome commits the member countries of the Community to establishing common EEC policies in three areas: agriculture, transport and trade. These policies can be seen as essential elements in the Treaty's *ad hoc* balance of national interests with, for example, France expecting to obtain under the CAP better access to markets in other European countries for its food exports, and the Netherlands anticipating new opportunities in the EEC for its efficient transport industry through the Common Transport Policy. Similarly, a common trade policy was essential to the successful operation of the customs union which, it was envisaged, would benefit German industry in particular. Moreover, the trade policy was to be the central element in the Community's relationship with non-member countries. Through it, the smaller nations (Benelux) could secure more leverage in world affairs, Germany could recover an influence in international deliberations more in keeping with its economic stature, and France could help to shape a distinctive European position on world issues, less dependent on the US and closely aligned with French foreign interests.

A common EEC policy must entail some loss of national freedom of action for the member countries. What general arguments, then, can be made for pursuing economic policies (and, specifically, trade policies) at the EEC level, rather than leaving them in the hands of the national governments? This type of issue is addressed by 'level of government assignment analysis'[1] which suggests a number of criteria that can be used to assess the case for EEC–level policies. They include: externalities/spillover effects of national policies, economies of scale from joint action, the interlocking of various sets of policies, the requirements of democratic control, and the degree of political cohesion between the jurisdictions involved. Using these criteria, the MacDougall study group[2] concluded that there is a strong case for a common EEC trade policy on the grounds that (i) it increases the bargaining power of the member countries in international trade negotiations, helping to shape a world trade environment in conformity with European interests; (ii) spillover effects of national trade policies are important—for example, subsidies bestowed by one member government on its exports to non-member countries may affect the competitive position within the EEC market of firms in other member countries; and (iii) the existence of a technically uniform system (common external tariff, negotiating procedures) is essential to the efficient functioning of a trade bloc—and trade and aid policies will be more effective if pursued at the same level of government. The group also took the view that democratic control would not be weakened by conducting trade policy at the EEC level,[3] and that there existed sufficient political homogeneity for the Community to be responsible for this area of policy.

A common trade policy was thus an integral part of the balance of national interests on which the Community was founded, as well as being underpinned by important political and economic advantages for the member countries. Accordingly, the Treaty of Rome called for a Common Commercial Policy (CCP) to be established which, from 1970 would require not only that the rules on the conduct of external trade be uniform as between the member countries, but also that any negotiations on trade with individual non-member countries, groups of countries or international organisations should be handled jointly through the Community institutions. The CCP commits the member countries to work together in the field of external relations. It could thus become the starting-point for an integrated EEC foreign policy,[4] with implications for broader political cooperation and even political union.

Closer to earth, the first priority in the development of the CCP was to establish a common external tariff (section 6.1). Since it was formed, the EEC has negotiated a series of reductions in the level of its common external tariff, in exchange for tariff reductions by other GATT members (section 6.2). If the common external tariff is to be uniformly applied, then there has to be agreement between the member countries of the EEC on detailed tariff rules, for example on how goods are to be classified for customs purposes (section 6.3). The EEC has made considerable progress in putting the member countries' trade policies onto a uniform basis, but there remain a number of key areas—such as safeguard arrangements—where the member countries have been reluctant to hand over their remaining powers to Community control (section 6.4). Trade agreements are now negotiated exclusively at the Community level (section 6.5), and an elaborate hierarchy of EEC trade agreements has evolved (section 6.6).

6.1 The Common Customs Tariff (CCT)

A customs union must, by definition, operate a common external tariff: that is, product by product, the member countries must agree to charge the same rate of customs duty on their imports from non-members. The EEC's common external tariff is known as the Common Customs Tariff (CCT). In general, it was determined not by negotiation between the member countries over the rate of duty to be charged on each product but by the application of a standard formula, as set out in Article 19. This required the CCT to be fixed 'at the level of the arithmetical average of the duties applied in the four customs territories covered by the Community' (i.e. France, Germany, Italy and Benelux). The average was to be calculated for each product on the basis of the duties applying on 1 January 1957. For a few sensitive products, where adjustment difficulties were anticipated, the rates of duty were determined by negotiation.[5]

Before the EEC was formed, there were wide differences in the general level of protection in the member countries: for example, the French tariff on manufactured goods averaged 24 per cent, whilst the Dutch tariff was only 8 per cent.[6] Consequently, the alignment of national tariffs on the CCT brought substantial changes in the levels of protection; the averaging formula meant that most French and Italian duties had to be lowered whilst German and Benelux duties were raised. The member countries were given a long transition period to phase in the CCT: Article 23 set out a three-stage timetable for adjusting to the new tariffs by 1970. Some flexibility was written into the Treaty to allow a slower or faster move to the CCT, and it turned out that the member countries were able to adopt the full CCT 18 months ahead of schedule in July 1968 (see Table 6.1).

The level at which a customs union's common external tariff is fixed is likely to have an important effect on the trade experience of the member countries. In particular, the higher the tariff, the greater will be the potential for trade diversion. Even where the average level of tariffs in the member countries does not change, the harmonisation of the rates of duty between the member countries will have an economic impact. Consider the customs

Table 6.1   The introduction of the Common Customs Tariff

Adjustment effective from:	Industrial products		Agricultural products	
	Individual adjustment	Cumulative adjustment	Individual adjustment	Cumulative adjustment
	(% of difference between national tariff and CCT)			
1 January 1961 (acceleration)	30	30		
1 January 1962			30	30
1 January 1963 (acceleration)	30	60		
1 January 1966			30	60
1 July 1968	40	100	40	100

Source: as Table 5.1.

union formed by the two countries shown in Figure 6.1. The common external tariff is fixed as the average of the different national rates, and both countries import the focus good. The country whose duty is raised through tariff harmonisation (Figure 6.1, left) will experience a price rise which will have three consequences: (a) domestic production will increase by q_1q_2, (b) consumption will fall by q_3q_4, and (c) imports will decline from q_1q_4 to q_2q_3 (trade suppression). The whole process operates in reverse in the formerly high tariff country (Figure 6.1, right), leading to external trade creation, as imports from non-member countries increase from q_6q_7 to q_5q_8.

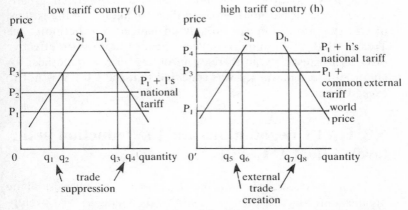

Figure 6.1   The trade effects of tariff harmonisation in a customs union

Thus for the individual member countries in a customs union, tariff harmonisation effects could modify the general trade diversion impact on trade with non-member countries. In particular, in the countries which formerly had high national tariffs (France and Italy in the original EEC), external trade creation could offset the trade diversion effect. By contrast, in the low tariff countries (Germany and the Netherlands in the original EEC) trade suppression would add to the loss of imports from non-member countries resulting from trade diversion. In the case of the EEC, there is some empirical evidence to support this interpretation (see section 4.2).

Although the alignment, or harmonisation, of the external tariffs in the original EEC had a substantial effect on national levels of protection, its impact on the structure of protection seems to have been less pronounced. This was because, under the national tariffs in 1957, the products on which relatively high duties were charged tended to be the same in each of the member countries, and these products therefore averaged out with high duties under the CCT. In the same way, the products with relatively low duties in the national tariffs generally attracted low duties under the CCT.[7]

Changes in the (nominal) rates of duty give only a limited picture of the impact of tariff harmonisation on producers, since their position is also affected by changes in the tariff treatment of the raw materials and components which they use. For a given nominal rate of duty, the *effective protection*[8] given to manufacturers will be greater the lower are duties on raw materials and components. As observed above, the structure of nominal tariffs in the EEC countries does not appear to have been greatly affected by tariff harmonisation, so that it is likely that the pattern of effective protection was broadly unchanged. Furthermore, the Treaty tried to cushion producers against a loss of effective protection caused by an increase in duties on raw materials: for about 80 raw materials it was specified that the CCT was not to exceed 3 per cent.

6.2 GATT negotiations and the reduction in the level of the CCT

To head off criticism that the EEC was an inward-looking organisation whose formation would be damaging to the development of world trade, the member countries of the EEC declared in the Treaty that they would be prepared to negotiate reductions in the CCT 'below the level which they could claim as a result of the establishment of a customs union between themselves' (Article 18). The US Under-Secretary of State for Economic Affairs, Mr Dillon, took up the offer and proposed a tariff conference of GATT members. In place of the usual item-by-item bargaining, the EEC offered to cut its CCT on most industrial goods by 20 per cent provided that suitable reciprocal concessions were made by the US and the UK. The Dillon Round negotiations began in May 1961 and bilateral agreements were signed between the major participants in March–May 1962; under the most-favoured-nation rule the tariff cuts were extended to all GATT members. The EEC, in fact, anticipated the Dillon Round cuts—its January 1961 tariff alignment (see Table 6.1) was based on a CCT provisionally reduced by 20 per cent. Taking account of the products which were not included in the negotiations, the effect of the Dillon Round was to reduce the average level of the CCT from 12.5 per cent in 1958 to 11.7 per cent in 1963.[9]

Further cuts in the level of the CCT were agreed before it was fully implemented. In 1962, President Kennedy called for a new approach to US relations with a united Europe, based on equal partnership and free trade. His trade proposals were designed to forestall a division of the western world into regional trading blocs, and were made more urgent by the UK decision to apply for EEC membership. Under the Trade Expansion Act 1962, the President was given powers to negotiate the total abolition of tariffs on trade between the US and the EEC, where this trade amounted to 80 per cent or more of the free world total. For other products, the target was to be a halving of the rates of tariff. US industries were to be offered government aid where changes in protection levels gave rise to serious adjustment problems.

The Kennedy Round opened in Geneva in May 1964. The failure of the first UK attempt at EEC membership meant that the ambitious target of tariff-free trade for some goods, such as aircraft, had to be abandoned. There was protracted bargaining over products to be exempted from the 50 per cent cut, differences in the range of US and EEC tariffs, and measures to deal with agricultural trade. A package agreement was finally reached in May 1967, with tariff cuts averaging 32 per cent for the EEC and the US, and 35 per cent for the UK. By 1 January 1972, it was estimated that the EEC's CCT would average 8.1 per cent compared with about 12 per cent for the US tariff and 11.5 per cent for the UK tariff.[10] The tariff cuts were to be made in five equal instalments, with the EEC making its first two cuts together on 1 July 1968 at the time of the final alignment of national tariffs on the CCT.

As a result of the Dillon and Kennedy Rounds, the average level of the CCT was reduced by 35 per cent. Whereas it had been expected that taking part in the EEC would force up tariffs in Germany and the Benelux countries, in fact few duty increases were needed. In France and Italy there was a double reduction in tariffs: the national tariffs were aligned on the lower CCT which was itself reduced. These adjustments to the CCT played an important part in limiting the trade diversion effect of the formation of the EEC.

The CCT was further adjusted following the enlargement of the Community on 1 January 1973 to include the UK, Ireland and Denmark. The alignment of the new members' tariffs on the CCT resulted in some tariff increases and some cuts—the UK's tariff for industrial goods, for example was on average 1.5 to 2 percentage points higher than the CCT.[11] Where the gains and losses failed to balance out for a non-EEC country, negotiations were held under Article XXIV (6) of the GATT to make a compensatory reduction in the CCT.

During the 1970s, the latest of the major GATT negotiating rounds—the Tokyo Round—took place. Most of the discussions were concerned with non-tariff issues (see section 13.1), but a general reduction of over 30 per cent was agreed for industrial tariffs. These reductions will be implemented by stages during the 1980s and, when implemented, will leave the nominal level of tariffs under the CCT at about 6 per cent. This would appear to have very important implications for the EEC's CCP because the CCP has to a large extent been based on the discriminatory tariff treatment of various groups of countries. As the level of the CCT diminishes, the importance of discriminatory tariff treatment, and the leverage of the CCP, will be eroded.

There is, however, some controversy over the extent of protection afforded by the present nominal level of the CCT. Using the standard formula,[12] it has been estimated that even the present generally low level of nominal tariffs nevertheless provides substantial effective protection for some sectors. For example, 14 out of 35 industrial sub-sectors in Italy were found to have effective rates of protection under the CCT in 1975 of 13 per cent or more, and four sub-sectors (plastic products, knitwear, clothing and primary chemicals) appeared to have rates of 19 per cent or more.[13] These findings suggest that the CCT is still an important instrument of EEC trade policy.

The standard methods of calculating effective rates of protection have, however, been criticised recently by Deardorff and Stern.[14] They argue that when proper account is taken of the effect which tariffs have on the level of world prices, the imperfect substitutability of home-produced and imported goods, the impact of foreign tariffs, and adjustments in exchange rates, then the effective rate of protection turns out to be much lower than previously suggested. The difficulty is that taking account of these factors requires a model of the entire world trade system, which poses formidable conceptual and data problems. The significance of tariff protection in the EEC, as in other industrial countries, therefore remains contentious.

6.3 Rules for the uniform application of the CCT

Agreement on common rates of duty is only one step towards the uniform application of the CCT. If imports are to receive identical tariff treatment in each member country of the EEC, there must also be agreement between the member countries on tariff nomenclature (i.e. precisely how goods are to be classified for the purpose of determining the rates of duty); agreement on how goods are to be valued for customs purposes; agreement on special duty suspensions and reductions; and standardised rules of origin. Without a high degree of consistency on each of these points, customs treatment could vary between the member countries and the customs union would be incomplete. The EEC's task has been made more difficult by the lack of precise guidelines in the Treaty of Rome. Article 27 calls on member states to 'take steps to approximate their legislative and administrative provisions in regard to customs matters', but only 'in so far as may be necessary'. Nevertheless considerable progress has been made towards uniformity of treatment.

CUSTOMS NOMENCLATURE

In all countries, the precise way in which goods are classified for customs purposes is important because it may affect the rate of duty charged, and any vagueness or inconsistency may lead to arbitrary decisions by the customs authorities. But in the EEC, tariff nomenclature is especially important for two further reasons:

(i) some categories of goods, especially textiles, are restricted by quota, so that customs classification may affect not just the rate of duty, but whether or not a particular consignment is admitted at all; and (ii) the EEC gives specially favourable treatment to goods from certain countries, but only if it can be shown that they were wholly or largely made there. The rules of origin used in this connection rely heavily on the tariff classification of the goods and any imported materials which they may contain (see *Rules of origin,* below).

The nomenclature used in the CCT had to be distilled from the classifications used previously by the member countries. Some 19,000 different national tariff headings were reduced to 3000 for the CCT, which was introduced in 1960, but the number has since risen to about 3700. Under the CCT, the tariff headings are divided into 99 main sections ('chapters'); chapters 1–24 cover agricultural products and the remaining chapters deal with fuels, raw materials and manufactured goods. The CCT provides the basis for the more detailed Nomenclature for External Trading Statistics (NIMEXE) which identified some 6500 types of good, and allows the EEC to monitor imports in a detailed way. A laborious, but important job of the Commission is to up-date the NIMEXE regularly to take account of new products, and technological developments affecting existing products.[15]

CUSTOMS VALUATION

Once an imported good has been classified by the customs authorities, the relevant rate of duty can be ascertained; where the duty is of a percentage *ad valorem* kind the actual customs charge will also depend on the value of the good. This is sometimes manipulated by an importing country to make a customs duty more penal—for example, the US used to base its customs duties for certain chemicals not on their import price, but on the US domestic price (the American Selling Price) which was often much higher, and therefore resulted in a larger customs charge.

Following international negotiations in the GATT, the EEC adopted a new set of rules concerning customs valuation in July 1980. The basis of the valuation is now 'the price actually paid or payable' for the imported goods, including insurance and freight charges (that is, cif). In certain cases, for example where the buyer and seller belong to the same company and the customs authority has grounds for believing that this has influenced the price, the valuation for customs purposes can be based on the prices of identical or similar imported goods, or an equivalent price for such goods sold in the EEC. Failing these, a valuation can be based on the estimated costs of production and marketing.[16]

DUTY SUSPENSIONS AND REDUCTIONS

Thus far, it has been implied that there is a single rate of duty for each good under the CCT. There may, however, be alternative rates, or duties may be suspended or reduced, often according to the country in which the goods have originated. Some of the principal reasons for variations in the customs rates applied are:

(i)   For many products, the Community has two sets of duties: *autonomous duties*, resulting from the initial averaging of the customs duties in the original member countries, and *conventional duties* which have been negotiated and fixed under the GATT. On trade with the GATT countries, or countries which also get most-favoured-nation treatment, conventional duties are applied unless the autonomous rates are lower.

(ii)   There are many countries with which the EEC has preferential trade agreements under which some or all the EEC's imports are partially or wholly exempted from duties. These preferential arrangements are an important element in the EEC's trade policies towards certain groups of countries and will be considered in detail in later chapters.

(iii)   The EEC temporarily suspends duties on some goods because of a shortage of supplies in the EEC and also so as not to hamper the introduction of new technology. In recent years, the number of tariff suspensions has averaged about 1000 p.a. and has affected mainly chemicals, plastics, medical supplies, electronic products, and aircraft, together with some agricultural and fisheries products.

(iv)   Duties may be partially or totally lifted under *outward processing* or *inward processing* arrangements. Because of the high wage rates in the Community, there is an incentive for firms to cut costs by undertaking the more labour-intensive parts of their manufacturing process in countries where labour is cheap. The EEC has encouraged outward processing to some extent by introducing rules which permit, with the consent of the member state, the re-importation of the processed goods at zero or reduced duties. There are similar arrangements for inward proces-sing, whereby goods are imported into the EEC for certain manufacturing operations before being re-exported.[17]

(v)   As part of its trade arrangements with Mediterranean countries, for example, the EEC uses *tariff quotas* on certain products (wines, vegetables, and textile products); imports are duty-free only up to a certain annual quantity, and if they exceed this amount duties are re-imposed on imports until the end of the year.

(vi)   For a few products (mainly agricultural items, raw materials and newsprint) there are global tariff quotas, operated on the same basis as those described under (v) above, but open to all countries. In 1982, eleven tariff quotas were opened under GATT agreements, and a further fourteen on a unilateral basis to improve the Community supply position for certain products. The tariff quota represents a less open-ended commitment than tariff suspension but does involve more administrative controls.

(vii) In some of its trade arrangements, for example the Generalised Scheme of Preferences (GSP), the EEC uses *tariff ceilings* which are similar to tariff quotas except that once the quota limit has been reached the reimposition of the tariff is not mandatory.

RULES OF ORIGIN

Rules of origin play a vital role in the EEC's trade policies, notably in determining which goods can benefit from the Community's various preferential trading arrangements with non-member countries, and in the administration of country-specific quotas. On trade within the Community rules of origin are largely redundant except in the relatively few cases where there are national quotas on imports from non-member countries. In relation to the EEC's preferential trade agreements, the main purpose of the rules of origin is to prevent producers in non-preferred countries from sending their goods to the EEC via a country which has a preferential trade agreement with the Community and then claiming preferential terms of access for them *(trade deflection)*.

It is easy to define the origin of a good where it has been entirely produced ('wholly obtained') in one country, but the more usual situation is that an exported good contains some, and maybe a large element of, imported raw materials or components; further, the manufacturing operations may be divided between countries. As yet, there is no internationally accepted definition of the origin of goods in these more complicated circumstances, nor even a single definition within the Community. The general EEC approach is however that a good must be wholly obtained or *substantially transformed* in a particular country for it to be regarded as originating there. Substantial transformation is usually determined in relation to particular working or processing operations: the *process rule*.

Since it would be extremely cumbersome to have to list all of these processes for every traded good, the EEC uses a *change-of-tariff heading* test in its preferential trade agreements. Under this test, a transformation is considered sufficient to confer originating status when it causes a product to change its classification under the Brussels Tariff Nomenclature—that is, the product must have a different tariff heading from all of its imported components or parts. But, as Vaulont observes,

> the change-of-heading rule is too blunt an instrument to give the right result in every case, so, where greater precision is needed, the descriptive method is retained, setting out additional criteria in two lists. The first of these, List A, includes products where the change-of-heading itself is not sufficient to confer origin, so that supplementary criteria are given; List B, on the other hand, specifies certain working or processing operations which are regarded as conferring origin though not resulting in a change of tariff heading.[18]

The change-of-tariff heading system, backed up by Lists A and B, is used for all of the Community's preferential tariff schemes, including the GSP, as well as the textile voluntary export restraint schemes. In the case of the EEC's preferential agreements with the EFTA, Mediterranean and Lomé Convention countries, the rules of origin are set out in protocols annexed to those agreements. These rules are not identical, but are broadly similar. Proof of a good's origin is given by a *movement certificate* endorsed by the authorities in the exporting country, and there are various controls to deter fraud.

The main alternative to the process rule for determining the origin of goods, is the *value added rule* whereby a product is considered to originate in a specified country if more than a certain percentage of its ex-factory price is represented by the value added in that country. The EEC does make limited use of this rule (e.g. in relation to list A) but is under pressure to apply it more generally, especially in relation to trade with the EFTA countries. Because of its applicability to complicated manufacturing processes it is particularly suited to trade between highly industrialised countries.

6.4 Common trade rules

The Treaty of Rome offers only rather sparse guidance as to how the CCP should be conducted. Article 113 requires that the CCP should be based on 'uniform principles'—that is, the rules governing trade with non-member countries must be essentially the same in each member state. This Article also lists, in an illustrative rather than an exhaustive fashion, some areas where a common approach would be needed. These are:

- tariff amendments,
- existing import quotas,
- protective commercial measures, including measures to be taken in cases involving dumping or subsidies,
- export policy (e.g. export credits),
- the conclusion of tariff or trade agreements.

As usual, the Commission is charged with drafting proposals for common measures, but decision-making rests with the Council of Ministers.

TARIFF AMENDMENTS
It is obvious that a customs union would quickly disintegrate if the member countries could take unilateral action to alter their tariffs on imports from non-member countries, and, right from the outset, the EEC countries' ability to adjust their tariff rates was restricted. Once the CCT was in full operation (July 1968), tariff changes could be made only by agreement between all the member countries through the Council. Many of the duty rates in the CCT are fixed by international agreement under the GATT, and any attempt by the EEC to change them unilaterally would risk retaliation from the principal countries affected. The Community may negotiate in the GATT to 'unbind' a duty rate but may be required to offer compensation to the affected partner.

IMPORT QUOTAS
The EEC has inherited a substantial number of national import quotas from the pre-Community period when quotas were widely used to control trade flows. Although quantitative restrictions were banned on intra-EEC trade, the member states were permitted to retain existing quotas on imports from outside the Community. The Treaty of Rome calls only for an 'alignment' of the liberalisation list—that is, the list of products not subject to quotas. The member states have, however, been very reluctant to

abandon quota controls unilaterally, and when the liberalisation list was consolidated in 1979 about 10 per cent of tariff headings were still subject to quotas in one or more member countries. In 1982, some 500 quota restrictions were in operation against imports from non-member countries; about a half of these were Community measures affecting imports of textiles, and the remainder were national measures (see Table 6.2).

Table 6.2 Quota restrictions operated by member countries against non-EEC products, 1982

	Quota restrictions applying to imports from:				
	More than one non-member country			Japan or Taiwan only	Total
	Community textile quotas	National textile quotas	Other national quotas		
France	47	6	62	4	119
Greece	47	1	43	0	91
Italy	27	36	7	66	136
UK	50	12	1	0	63
Benelux	50	0	2	11	63
Denmark	31	0	7	5	43
Germany	23	1	4	1	29
Ireland	0	2	9	4	15
Total	275	58	135	91	559

Source: Derived from *Official Journal of EC*.

The retention of import quotas varies considerably between the member countries. Table 6.2, based on the quota list for 1982, indicates that the Benelux countries, UK, France and Greece make extensive use of the common rules for restricting textile imports, negotiated in the bilateral agreements with over twenty non-member countries under the Multi-Fibre Arrangement (see Chapter 7). Italy also has a substantial number of quota restrictions on textiles, more than half of which are national measures. Many Japanese goods are subject to quotas in Italy, and it is no coincidence that whereas in 1982 Japan ranked between second and sixth as a source of imports for all the other EEC countries, in Italy its position was only fourteenth. France and Greece alone control imports of a range of agricultural and industrial products by quotas applying to more than one non-member country.

Of course, in a customs union national import quotas would be largely ineffective unless indirect imports via another member country could be blocked. In the EEC, this blocking is permitted under Article 115. A two-stage process is involved in which a member country must first apply to the Commission for authority to require free circulation licences for a particular product. If this is granted, then an application from a trader for a licence can be refused only with the consent in each case of the Commission. At both stages, the member country has to provide supporting evidence for its application (e.g. of the economic difficulties that might arise if imports of the product concerned took place). The Commission considers that Article 115 may only be used where formal quotas exist; it cannot be used to back up voluntary trade restraints or other informal agreements.[19]

Over 200 requests for the 'non-application of Community treatment' were reported in the *Official Journal* in 1982, of which about two-thirds were approved by the Commission. As with the national quotas, textiles were the main product group affected (see Table 6.3), and the countries making most use of the controls for textiles in 1982 were France, Ireland and Belgium. In addition, Italy backed up its national import quotas against Japanese industrial goods by blocking indirect imports via Article 115: France similarly restricted imports of a wide range of manufactured goods from Japan, Hong Kong, South Korea and Taiwan, and accounted for almost half the successful applications made under Article 115 in 1982. The frequency with which controls under this Article are used can be regarded as a barometer of protectionism within the Community. On this basis, protectionism is strongest in France, followed by Italy. Denmark, the Netherlands and Germany emerge as the countries with the most liberal approach to trade. It should, however, be added that many national restrictions on imports from non-member countries, including some of the most important, take the form of 'understandings' between governments or between associations of national manufacturers and are not recorded in the quota lists. For example, Japanese exports of cars and televisions to the UK have for a long period been controlled by such 'understandings'.

ANTI-DUMPING DUTIES AND COUNTERVAILING DUTIES

Where products are sold at a lower price (net of taxes) in the export market than their normal price in the home market, GATT rules allow an importing country to impose *anti-dumping duties,* not greater than the difference between the two prices. Similarly where a subsidy, either direct or indirect, has been bestowed on

Table 6.3 Cases of 'non-application of Community treatment' under Article 115, 1982

Controls on:	Textiles			Other manufactured goods			Agricultural products	Total
Originating in:	Developing countries[a]	State trading countries[a]	Mediterranean countries	Developing countries[a]	State trading countries[a]	Japan		
EEC country[b]								
France	26	13	4	21	0	8	0	72
Italy	4	3	0	0	3	16	2	28
Ireland	26	0	1	0	0	0	0	27
Belgium–Luxembourg	11	8	0	0	1	0	2	22
UK	5	2	0	0	2	0	2	11
Germany	0	2	0	0	0	0	0	2
Total	72	28	5	21	6	24	6	162

Source: Derived from index to Official Journal of the European Countries, 1982.
Notes:
[a] The countries most frequently affected were Hong Kong (27), South Korea (25), Taiwan (22), China (16) and Romania (9).
[b] No cases were reported for Denmark and the Netherlands; Greece retained controls on imports from other EEC countries under its accession arrangements.

the manufacture, export or transport of a product, an importing country may impose a *countervailing duty* not greater than the incidence of the subsidy. In both cases, it must be shown that the imports cause or threaten to cause material injury to the industry in the home country. The determination of injury has to take into account changes in the volume of imports, their prices in comparison with those of home-produced goods, and the condition of the home industry (Article 4 of the Community's rules sets out a list of 'relevant economic factors' including production, utilisation of capacity, stocks, sales, market shares, prices, profits, return on investment, cash flow and employment).[20]

EEC anti-dumping regulations came into effect in July 1968, but the first use of these measures was not made until November 1976 when the EEC imposed a duty on Taiwanese bicycle-chains! The regulations were revised in the light of the GATT Tokyo Round negotiations and the new rules were introduced in January 1980. The procedure set out in these rules allows for an initial consultation between member countries when a complaint that imports have been dumped or subsidised in the exporting country has been made. The Commission may then initiate investigations which may be terminated if investigations show that the complaint is unfounded, and/or the Community may accept an undertaking by the exporters to adjust their prices/end the use of subsidies. Pending the outcome of the investigation, provisional anti-dumping or countervailing duties may be imposed by the Commission for a period not exceeding six months, after which the duties must be terminated or made definitive by the Council. Duties or undertakings are subject to review at the instigation of a member country, the Commission, or any other interested party.

Table 6.4 summarises the anti-dumping and countervailing duty measures taken in 1982. In general the EEC appears to have used anti-dumping duties in two main circumstances: (i) against exporters in the USA and other developed countries, especially for chemicals (proceedings have usually ended with price undertakings being given by the exporters); and (ii) against exporters in state-trading countries, against whom a substantial number of anti-dumping duties were imposed. The 'normal price' for these goods is usually taken to be the price of a comparable good in another market economy country, or its estimated costs of production plus a profit margin in that country. It is noticeable that the Community has taken very few anti-dumping actions against Japanese products or goods from the NICs, presumably because the competitiveness of these items arises out of the low

Table 6.4 Anti-dumping cases reported in the Official Journal of the EC, 1982

	State-trading countries	Developing countries	Mediterranean countries	United States	Other developed countries	Total
Procedure						
initiation	23	7	5	7	13	55
acceptance of undertaking	2	—	—	—	5	7
terminate with undertaking	20	—	2	5	4	31
terminate	18	—	3	2	1	24
re-open	5	—	—	—	—	5
Provisional duties						
impose	27	1	2	2	—	32
extend/prolong	4	1	1	1	—	7
definitive collection	3	—	—	—	—	3
cancel	1	—	—	—	—	1
Definitive duties						
impose	5	1	1	1	—	8
notice of review	1	1	—	6	—	8
termination of review	1	1	—	—	—	2
repeal	1	—	1	—	—	2

Source: Index to Official Journal of the EC, 1982.

costs of production rather than a manipulation of prices.

SAFEGUARD MEASURES

Even where imports have not been subsidised in the exporting country or dumped, the EEC may still take action to protect its own producers against a surge of imports, either through *surveillance*—the monitoring of imports through the use of import licences, issued freely, and a statistical check on the flow of imports; or through *quotas* at the Community or national level. Although under Article 113 safeguard measures should be based on 'uniform principles', the Commission, as guardian of the Treaty, has faced an uphill struggle to persuade member goverments to give up independent quotas against imports from non-member countries. In 1979, the Commission wrote that 'From 1982, the power to reintroduce national restrictions on imports will lie exclusively with the Community institutions, in accordance with the normal safeguard procedure.'[21] However, the revised rules introduced in 1982 still permit national governments to introduce quotas where domestic producers face serious injury or threat thereof.[22] The Commission can revoke or amend the measures, but the member country has a right to refer the matter to the Council which normally must adjudicate within one month, and at most three months. Since the Council is to act by qualified majority, the member country which introduced the quota could be over-ruled. Before the end of 1984, the powers of member countries to introduce national quotas will be reconsidered.

The 1982 rules lay down a Community procedure to deal with problems caused by a rapid growth in imports of a particular product. This involves a similar investigation procedure to that used in anti-dumping cases, namely an initial consultation, a formal announcement of an investigation, an inquiry into the nature of the import threat and the damage caused or threatened to domestic industry, and the imposition of penalties, in this case national or Community surveillance or quotas. In 1982, only one Community investigation of this kind was made, concerning tableware exports from South Korea and elsewhere to France and the UK. Community surveillance was introduced or renewed on certain major Japanese exports including motor vehicles, motorcycles, videotape recorders, televisions and machine tools (see section 13.3).

Under the GATT rules, any safeguard measures other than surveillance must not discriminate between contracting parties. The EEC has pressed hard for a change in the rules to permit it to take selective action against particular suppliers who are 'disrupting' the EEC market, but this has been resisted, especially by the NICs and Japan against whom such measures would be largely directed. In the absence of a revision of Article XIX of the GATT, the EEC has made little use of official safeguard measures,[23] preferring instead to negotiate voluntary export restraints with the exporting countries. These restraints are most widespread for textiles and clothing (see section 7.3). They are voluntary only in a very limited sense, since those who do not 'volunteer' are likely to have restraints forced on them through quotas, as Turkey discovered in 1981 in relation to its cotton textiles exports to the Community.[24]

COMMON RULES FOR EXPORTS

Although some progress has been made towards the establishment of common rules for exports,[25] there remain considerable differences between the member countries in their detailed arrangements. A few, generally minor, national export quotas still survive, whilst Community export restrictions are confined to a single export quota (on copper scrap) and the possibility of levies on the export of some agricultural products. The most important facet of export policy concerns *export credits*,[26] the terms of which can play a major role in influencing capital goods exports, especially to developing countries. Export credit terms are governed by the 1978 OECD Arrangement, in which the EEC participates as a bloc. There are, however, wide differences of view between the EEC countries on export credits. France, for example, has favoured the use of mixed credits (a combination of aid and export credits) as a form of development assistance, whereas Germany has opposed the use of export credit guarantee arrangements to subsidise interest rates.

THE 'NEW TRADE POLICY INSTRUMENT'

The EEC took a further step towards the completion of the CCP in April 1984 when it adopted the 'new trade policy instrument' to speed up the EEC's response within the GATT rules to unfair trading practices by other countries. Although the Commission has the power to initiate actions, the less protectionist member countries insisted that any final decisions should rest with the Council of Ministers. Thus, for example, the Commission's mandate to negotiate compensation from third countries applying safeguard measures under GATT rules will be determined by the Council, if necessary on a majority vote, within 30 days of receiving a Commission proposal.

6.5 EEC trade agreements

By locking the trade arrangements of the member countries together through the customs union and the CCP, the Treaty of Rome aimed to establish the EEC as a single trading entity, able to speak with a powerful voice in international trade affairs. An integrated approach to trade left no room for national trade agreements involving individual EEC countries and these had to be abandoned after the end of the transition period. As the world's largest trading bloc, the EEC is a prime focus for trade negotiators from non-member countries anxious to secure the best possible trading conditions with the Community. The legal basis for EEC trade agreements is provided by Article 113. Arrangements which are more comprehensive, involving for example financial aid, may be negotiated in the framework of Association set out in Article 238. In the case of 'simple' trade agreements, Articles 113 and 114 set out a negotiating procedure, as follows:

- The Commission makes recommendations for negotiations to the Council.
- The Council authorises the Commission to open discussions.
- The Council establishes a framework for negotiations, and appoints a special Committee to 'assist' the Commission.
- The Commission conducts negotiations in consultation with the Committee.
- An agreement is concluded by the Council.

As usual, ultimate power rests with the Council which, in practice, keeps a very tight control over the Commission's conduct of negotiations with non-member countries, both through the watchful eyes of the Committee and by giving the Commission a very detailed negotiating mandate. The Commission may find its hands so tied by this that it is reduced almost to the status of a go-between, sometimes having to return repeatedly to the Council for fresh instructions in order to break a negotiating deadlock. The Commission's position may be made even more trying by leaks from the Council giving non-member countries advance notice of the Community's negotiating position.

Article 113 provides a basis for negotiating preferential trade agreements with non-member countries which offer specially favourable terms of access to the EEC market; it may also be used for non-preferential agreements. The point of negotiating non-preferential agreements is that there are some countries which are not members of the GATT and do not therefore qualify automatically for most-favoured-nation treatment; and that the Community makes increasing use of cooperation agreements with non-member countries which establish 'mixed committees' (i.e. involving representatives of the EEC and its trading partner).[27] These committees provide a valuable forum in which trade issues of mutual interest can be discussed.[28]

Article 238 permits the Community to enter into a wide-ranging agreement with non-member countries, known as *association*. Article 238 is vague as to the nature of association, referring only to 'reciprocal rights and obligations, joint actions and special procedures'. It could range from little more than a straightforward trade agreement to not far short of full membership. In practice, Article 238 agreements are restricted to countries which hope eventually to become full members of the EEC and to developing countries which receive special trade and aid terms from the Community. Since agreements under Article 238 (usually styled 'cooperation agreements') may incorporate elements like financial aid which are not reserved exclusively for Community action, the member states must also participate in the negotiations, which tend therefore to be cumbersome. In contrast to the position for agreements under Article 113, the European Parliament has the right to be consulted. Decision-making power however rests with the Council.

Article 229 gives the Commission responsibility for 'ensuring all suitable contracts with organs of the United Nations, GATT and other international organisations'. In recent years, the Community has been involved as a single entity in the 'North–South dialogue' in the Paris-based Conference for International Economic Co-operation, UNCTAD negotiations for a 'New International Economic Order' (including negotiations on international commodity agreements), various rounds of trade negotiations in the GATT and the World Food Conference associated with the UN's Food and Agriculture Organisation.

Finally, it may be noted that in addition to negotiated agreements, the EEC also grants autonomous trade concessions to certain countries, for example under the GSP.

6.6 The EEC's hierarchy of trade agreements

The EEC member countries are contracting parties to the GATT, and hence have an obligation to adopt a non-discriminatory approach to trade with other contracting parties, except where there is special provision for preferential arrangments. This suggests that the EEC should have three forms of trade relationship:

(i)   within the EEC customs union: preferential, tariff-free trade;
(ii) with GATT contracting parties: mutual most-favoured-nation treatment, based on conventional duties negotiated in GATT;
(iii) with countries which are not parties to GATT: most-favoured-nation treatment, or worse, based on bilateral agreements.

Since the bulk of the EEC's non-oil trade is with GATT members, bilateral trade agreements, on this basis, should not be of major importance. Three issues have, however, made for a more complex system of trade arrangements: (a) the EEC's colonial legacy, (b) the past and prospective enlargement of the EEC, and (c) the trade problems of developing countries.

The colonial legacy.   When the EEC was formed, several of the member countries still had colonies in Africa and elsewhere with which they had special trade relations. France, in particular, was strongly opposed to breaking its preferential trade links with its colonies, and insisted on a Community arrangement involving association. Even when these colonies became independent, the special trade link was retained, and indeed was extended to some Commonwealth countries following British entry to the Community in 1973. The colonial legacy has exercised a powerful influence on the EEC's trade relations with developing countries, including those bordering on the Mediterranean.

EEC enlargement.   Under Article 237, any European state may apply for membership of the Community. In the early 1960s, Greece and Turkey became 'associated' with the Community with a view to eventual full membership. The special trade terms which they were then granted, plus the favoured position of the former French colonies in North Africa, led other Mediterranean countries to apply for trade concessions from the Community. The EEC responded with an *ad hoc* and then global approach to its Mediterranean trade relations which helped to consolidate another tier in the EEC's increasingly hierarchical trade arrangements.

The UK's membership of the Community created a similar problem in relation to the northern and west-central European countries which were partners with the UK in the European Free Trade Association (EFTA). Rather than re-erect barriers to trade between Britain (and Denmark) and the other EFTA countries, the Community chose to establish in effect an industrial free trade area covering virtually all of western Europe.

Trade problems of developing countries. During the 1960s the developing countries successfully campaigned for the rich countries to admit imports of Third World manufactures tariff-free as a method of encouraging industrial growth in developing countries and boosting their export earnings. The EEC implemented its version of the GSP in 1971, thereby creating another category of trade treatment.

As a result of these various factors, the EEC has evolved a complicated and hierarchical pattern of trade arrangements—the 'pyramid of privilege' referred to at the beginning of Chapter 2. It is a changing pattern, however. Spanish and Portuguese membership of the EEC, for example, will radically alter the relative position of the non-member Mediterranean countries. As noted in section 6.4, *Safeguard Measures,* the EEC has been pressing for revisions to the GATT safeguard rules which would permit it to take selective action, especially against exports from the NICs. If successful, this would enable the EEC to differentiate further its trade relations with developing countries, creating a new rung in the hierarchy.

The layering of EEC trade preferences is shown in Table 6.5. As the table indicates, the EEC has tried to avoid a conflict with other GATT contracting parties by casting its preferential trade arrangements within the framework of customs unions or free trade areas, or by utilising the GATT dispensaton for generalised preferences in favour of developing countries. The outcome is that the full CCT applies only to the US, Canada, Japan, Australia, New Zealand, South Africa and the Eastern bloc countries.

The complexity of the tariff preferences is greatest for agricultural products, where four different tariff rates are common, usually the CCT, two lower rates for Mediterranean countries and a zero rate for Lomé Convention countries. Five rates are used for a range of products including new potatoes, broad beans, garlic,

Table 6.5   The hierarchy of EEC trade relations

Form of trade relationship	Countries concerned	Trade and aid[3] conditions	Population 1981/2 (millions)	Percentage of world exports[6]
Customs union	EEC	AMR	272	32
Free trade area	EFTA	MR	42	6
Mixed[1]	Mediterranean	aMr £	234	5
One way prefs.				
special	ACP[2]	aM £	348	3
generalised	Other Third World	m £q[4]	2900	21
MFN	US, Japan, etc.	q[5]	393	24
Other	East European	Q	380	9

Notes:
[1] Customs unions, free trade areas, reciprocal and non-reciprocal (one-way) tariff preferences.
[2] African, Caribbean and Pacific countries.
[3] A: covers agricultural trade; M: covers trade in manufactures; R: reciprocal (i.e. partner must offer concessions on EEC members' exports); £: EEC provides financial aid; Q: EEC imports are controlled by quotas or voluntary export restraints (VERs). Upper case letters signify full, lower case partial, application of the measure.
[4] VERs on NICs' exports, quotas on textiles, tariff quotas/ceilings on other goods.
[5] National quotas on some imports from Japan; some products subject to VERs.
[6] 1981/2: percentages for Mediterranean and Other Third World countries include OPEC trade whose combined share was 15 per cent.

Definitions of trade regimes in Table 6.5

Customs union: tariffs and quotas are eliminated on trade between members and they apply a common external tariff on imports from non-members (see pp. 16–7).

Free trade area: tariffs and quotas are eliminated on trade between the members, but there is no common external tariff; on trade with non-member countries, national tariffs are applied (see pp. 116 and 21–7).

One-way (non-reciprocal) preferences: the EEC reduces/ eliminates its tariffs on imports from the partner country but obtains no reciprocal (reverse) concessions on its exports; general-ised preferences apply to all developing countries, special prefer-ences to a selected group (see pp. 163–9).

Most-favoured-nation (MFN) treatment: trade is subject to the (non-discriminatory) tariffs negotiated and bound in GATT (see pp. 39–40).

wine and preserved vegetables, fruit and fish. The most complex arrangements are found for canned sprats and frozen prawns where, including differences in rates between EEC member countries seven different rates apply. In many cases, the tariff differentials are ludicrous—there are four tariff rates for locust beans with a CCT of only 2 per cent, and three rates for conifer resins with a CCT of 0.5 per cent! For industrial products, the position is usually simpler with a CCT rate, a reduced rate for Spain and a zero rate for the EFTA, Mediterranean and Lomé Convention countries. Other developing countries benefit from a zero rate for many manufactured products under the GSP.

At this point, two general observations seem appropriate. First, the CCP has become a very complicated system of preferential arrangements with the preferences in some cases more of symbolic than commercial significance. This differential treatment of trading partners runs in opposition to the general non-discriminatory approach enshrined in the GATT. Secondly, although the EEC has achieved considerable success in meeting the tasks set out in Article 113 in relation to tariffs, anti-dumping measures, etc., these traditional elements of commercial policy are now of diminishing significance in the conduct of world trade. As the level of tariffs, for example, declines further from its already generally low level, the relevance of an EEC trade policy which focuses on preferential tariff rates is called into question. As Dahrendorf pointed out some time ago, 'There is an almost absurd disproportion between the expectations of the European Community's partners in the world, and the instruments which the Community has at its disposal in order to respond to these expectations.'[29]

There has been some attempt to deal with this problem by bringing the newer instruments of trade policy, such as voluntary export restraints, under Community control but this has met with only limited success. The EEC has also broadened the nature of its trade agreements, especially with developing countries. Cooperation agreements now include elements such as technical assistance, industrial joint ventures, and the exchange of technological information, which were not envisaged by the EEC members in their original formulation of a common commercial policy.

7   EEC Sectoral Policies and Trade

Under the Common Commercial Policy, a set of tariff-based rules has been developed by the EEC countries for the conduct of their external trade. However, in a number of sectors where EEC producers are in difficulties these general rules have been replaced by special rules which are more restrictive towards imports and which place more emphasis on non-tariff instruments. These special rules will be reviewed in this chapter in relation to agriculture (section 7.1), the steel industry (section 7.2) and the clothing and textiles industries (section 7.3).

The economic recession which began in the mid 1970s exacerbated the structural problems facing a number of European industries. In order to stave off as far as possible uncoordinated national interventions which might lead to the break-up of the single market, the EEC countries have agreed—some of them very reluctantly—to implement Community measures. The purpose of these measures is to provide support in the short term and to facilitate structural adjustment in the long term. Although imports were not in most cases the fundamental source of the problems facing Europe's declining industries, without action to curb imports it was felt that the support measures envisaged would have been ineffective. The Commission has used the prospect of restrictions on imports from third countries as an inducement to the member countries to agree to a common intervention policy.

For the most part the import controls have not taken the form of higher tariffs because these would have involved the Community in a complex series of negotiations to compensate the affected trade partners, without a guarantee that the increased tariffs would have the desired effect in restricting imports. Instead, the EEC has preferred in several cases to negotiate arrangements with its principal suppliers whereby these countries voluntarily restrain their exports (as with steel and textiles). Since many of these countries have very little bargaining power and for them the EEC represents a vital market, these agreements are 'voluntary' only in name. The increasing use of non-tariff trade measures to protect weak industries runs counter to GATT principles. Moreover, the restrictions are difficult to tackle in international negotiations (see section 13.1, *Negotiations on non-tariff barriers*) because of their diversity and their susceptibility to different administrative interpretations. In any case, unless and until the underlying industrial problems can be overcome, there seems to be little likelihood that the growing tide of non-tariff measures—the 'New Protectionism'—will be reversed.

7.1 Trade arrangements for agricultural products

The establishment of the EEC customs union involved a considerable dismantling of industrial protection in France and Italy. Not only were they obliged to make substantial cuts in their tariffs on trade with non-member countries in order to bring them into line with the CCT, but they were also obliged to abolish completely their duty and quota restrictions on imports from other EEC countries, including their most powerful competitor, Germany. The French government was apprehensive that these changes might be very damaging for French industry which in many sectors was fragmented and weak. In the negotiations before the EEC was formed, it insisted that in return for duty-free entry to the French market for their manufactured goods, the other EEC countries should open up their markets for French agricultural exports.

This raised a fundamental difficulty in that for many years European governments had been manipulating their market prices for agricultural products with the aim of supporting the incomes of farmers. Because of the strategic and social importance of farming, and the sector's powerful political influence, it was inconceivable that the EEC countries would abandon their agricultural protection. Hence, if agricultural trade between the EEC countries was to be freed from restrictions, then the manipulation of market prices would have to be undertaken jointly by the member countries: there would have to be a common approach to agricultural support policy.

This became a central element in the Treaty of Rome. Article 38 called for a common agricultural policy (CAP) to be established and the following Article outlined some unexceptionable aims for the CAP (to increase agricultural productivity, to improve farm incomes, to stabilise markets and to ensure regular supplies to consumers at reasonable prices). The Treaty was entirely vague as to how these aims were to be achieved; decisions on policy instruments were left until after the EEC was established. Since the member countries had previously used widely differing measures to support their farmers' incomes, agreement on a uniform EEC system required immensely complicated and protracted negotiations. In December 1961, a common support system was drawn up for grains and several other major products, and arrangements for other items were agreed in following years.

Once the common support mechanisms had been agreed, decisions had to be made on the level of support prices. The grain price was especially important, not only because many farmers relied heavily on cereals production but also because cereals were used as feeding–stuffs for livestock and hence affected the costs of livestock farmers. The price decision was difficult because grain prices in Germany, Italy and Luxembourg were much higher than those in France and Belgium. A compromise deal was agreed in December 1964 and the common prices were introduced in July 1967.

The general aim of the common support system under the CAP is to keep EEC market prices above the world market level so as to raise farm incomes, at the expense of consumers and, increasingly, taxpayers. The instruments employed in pursuit of this aim vary between products according to their economic characteristics and to the EEC's international obligations under the GATT. For some products (fruit and vegetables, oilseeds, wine and tobacco) protection is provided against imports in the same way as for manufactured goods, that is through customs duties, reinforced in some cases by quotas. The duties on wine are specific (i.e. fixed without reference to the import price), otherwise they are *ad valorem* or a combination of *ad valorem* and specific.

For the remaining products covered by the CAP (cereals, rice, sugar, pigmeat, eggs, poultry, dairy products, olive oil and beef) border protection is given by means of *variable import levies;* in the case of beef, a combination of levies and duties may be used. The variable import levy is an import tax which varies inversely with the price of imports, so that the higher the price at which goods are offered to the EEC, the lower the variable import levy. The objective is to ensure that the imports do not enter the EEC below a fixed *threshold* (minimum import) *price.* The levy is calculated, usually on a daily basis, as the difference between the world market price and the threshold price, which is generally well above the world level. The levy acts as an insulating device in that world market price fluctuations affect the size of the variable import levy, but not the price at which imports are available inside the EEC (see Figure 7.1(a)). Consequently, the price received by EEC farmers is not affected by changing world market conditions, as long as the EEC is an importer of the product concerned. This is so even if world prices rise above the threshold level, in which case a variable import subsidy replaces the variable levy.

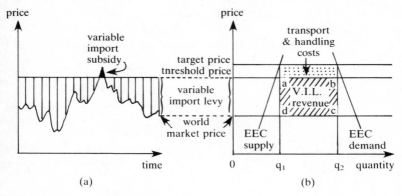

Figure 7.1   The variable import levy system

In Figure 7.1(b), the threshold price plus the transport and handling charges for imports within the EEC set the maximum price which EEC farmers can charge for what they produce (the *target price*). At this price, the deficit between EEC production (Oq_1) and consumption (Oq_2) will be met by imports of q_1q_2 from non-member countries on which levies will be charged. The total revenue from the levies is equivalent to the shaded area (a b c d). The levies are collected by the customs authorities at the point of entry to the EEC, and handed over to the European Budget. In addition to the variable levies, imports may also be subject to monetary compensatory amounts (see section 5.2).

By keeping out low-priced imports, EEC market prices will be supported at about the target price level as long as the EEC is less than self-sufficient; that is, as long as consumption exceeds production. But once demand at the target price can be met by EEC production, then imports will cease, and the EEC market price will depend on the interaction between EEC supply and EEC demand. However, in order to prevent market prices falling to a level that would be ruinous for the many small farmers in the Community, the EEC sets a floor price or *intervention price* which it is prepared to defend if necessary by taking supplies off the market. The difficulty with this approach is that, unless the fall in market prices is temporary, the EEC is left with supplies in store that cannot be sold on the Community market without undermining the floor price. Sometimes it is possible to find extra markets inside the EEC through secondary uses, such as distilling surplus wine into industrial alcohol, but for the most part surpluses are disposed of on the world market. Since world market prices are normally well below the EEC intervention price, sales have to be subsidised at great expense to the European Budget (i.e. European taxpayers) by *export restitutions*.

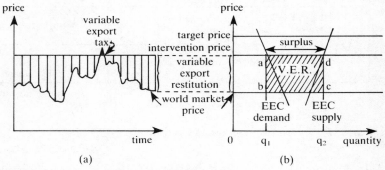

Figure 7.2   The export restitution system

As with the import levies, the export restitutions vary inversely with movements in the world market price (Figure 7.2(a)), since the intervention price, apart from the regular monthly increments, is fixed for a year at a time by the Council of Ministers. In Figure 7.2(b), the surplus to be disposed of with the aid of export restitutions amounts to q_1q_2, the difference between EEC production and consumption at the intervention price. The size of the restitution is usually fixed weekly or fortnightly, and the total cost of the restitutions is represented in Figure 7.2(b) as the shaded area (a b c d).

The support system employed by the CAP has drawn hostile criticism from governments outside the EEC, especially from the USA, Canada and Australia which have important agricultural export interests. They claim that:

(i)   the high level of protection given to EEC farmers denies efficient non-European producers a valuable export market in Europe;

(ii)   the damage to export interests is compounded by competition in third country markets like those in Asia from heavily subsidised EEC produce;

(iii) EEC policy, by insulating market prices in the EEC from movements in world prices, has destabilised the world market by throwing the whole burden of shifts in demand and supply onto the non-EEC market; and

(iv)   the EEC's use of export subsidies breaches the understanding reached in the GATT that they would not be used to secure more than an equitable share of world markets.

The EEC responds to these criticisms by stressing the difficulties faced by European agriculture, especially the low level of farm incomes. The Community tried in the 1960s to find a basis for compromise with the US by offering to fix the margin of support given to EEC farmers and to cooperate in organising world markets so as to secure higher prices for exports.[1] However, without a fundamental reorganisation of European agriculture in the direction of fewer but larger farms, (structural reform), it is difficult to reconcile US demands for better market access with the EEC's commitment to support the incomes of its farmers. Measures to promote structural reform were originally intended to be a major element in the CAP, but partly because of the rising cost of short-term price supports, such long-term measures have been largely left to national governments.

Pressures for reform of the CAP itself have built up both within and outside the Community. The external pressure arises from the willingness of countries like the US to engage in an export subsidy war to force the EEC to curb its exports by making the cost of export restitutions to the Community unacceptably high. The internal pressure is generated by the mounting cost of the CAP to the European Budget which comes on top of massive consumer support to agriculture. Under the present, largely open-ended support arrangements, output-increasing technological progress in European agriculture on the one hand and a stable demand for food on the other lead inexorably to larger and more costly surpluses.

The funds available to the European Budget are limited to the proceeds from the agricultural import levies and the customs duties plus contributions based on a notional VAT, first set at a maximum rate of 1 per cent throughout the Community. The increasing cost of agricultural support, however, pushed the Budget to exhaustion, and in March 1984 the EEC took the first step towards a major reform of the CAP through the introduction of milk quotas limiting the amount which dairy farmers can sell at the support price. And at the European Summit in June 1984, it was agreed to raise the VAT limit to 1.4 per cent in a deal which also provided a substantial rebate to the UK on its large net contribution to the Budget.[2]

7.2 The steel crisis and EEC trade

The period of slow or zero growth which began in the early 1970s has posed particularly severe problems for a number of long-established industries in the EEC. Foremost amongst these has been the steel industry. Until about ten years ago, the European steel industry had experienced a fast and sustained growth of output and was formulating ambitious plans for further capacity expansion. The buoyant home and world markets, however, obscured the widening gap in efficiency between the European industry and innovative rivals like the Japanese. When demand for steel fell in the wake of the oil price increase of 1973, it was for a long time believed by European steel firms that it was only a temporary fluctuation and that economic activity would soon pick up again. In fact, demand for steel has remained depressed, so that capacity utilisation has been low, and heavy losses have been sustained by most of the leading European producers. Furthermore, it is clear that structural changes are taking place in the world steel industry with the transfer of production to the NICs.[3]

The problem facing the European steel industry is that to respond to the challenge of foreign competition, the steel industry must cut its labour force at a time when unemployment in the steel areas is already very high, and must spend large sums on modernising its plant. However, the industry has not been generating the profits which could finance this, and in any case modernisation might aggravate the over-capacity problem. In the absence of Community action, there is a danger that the member countries will resort to national solutions based on competitive subsidies and that this will lead to the break-up of the single market for steel and perhaps also for other goods. To avert this danger, the Davignon Plan proposed a twofold Community approach based on raising prices and profitability by getting agreement between EEC producers on minimum prices and output restrictions, and cutting capacity and modernising the remaining plants. This restructuring of the industry would be accomplished by controlling national aids and by using European Coal and Steel Community funds. The plan was introduced in 1978 but, even after production quotas were made compulsory in 1980, had only mixed success. The introduction of mandatory minimum prices on about 40 per cent of EEC steel production in 1984, backed by a stiff penalty system, seems initially to have been more effective. As in the case of agriculture, it has proved easier to get governments to agree on short-term measures than to tackle the longer-term structural problems. 'Temporary' measures of support soon become entrenched.

The authors of the Davignon Plan appreciated that the fundamental problems of the EEC steel industry could not be ascribed to imports, which took only about 10 per cent of the Community market. However, if the price-raising plans were not to be undermined by an upsurge of imports, some measure of import control was seen to be necessary. The EEC has therefore negotiated 'arrangements' with the dozen or so of its principal suppliers. If these countries exercise voluntary export restraint by keeping within their annual quotas and not undercutting EEC prices, their share of the EEC market will be preserved. Other supplying countries are also obliged to observe the EEC's basic prices, on pain of anti-dumping measures. Such action was taken, for example, against Spain in February 1984. Despite the growth of controls over EEC production and imports the problems of the EEC steel industry remain acute, and have been exacerbated by the dispute with the US over EEC steel exports (see Chapter 13).

7.3 EEC textile imports and the Multi-Fibre Arrangement

The unfavourable treatment given to textiles under the GSP reflects the very restrictive approach of the EEC to textile imports from the developing countries. Under the umbrella of the Multi-Fibre Arrangement (MFA), the EEC strictly controls these imports through voluntary export restraints negotiated with the principal developing country suppliers. The background to the MFA is that the developing countries substantially increased their share of world exports of textiles and clothing during the 1950s and 1960s. Textile production tends to be labour-intensive and, even allowing for differences in labour productivity, this has given textile producers in low-wage developing countries a substantial cost advantage over producers in the rich countries.[4] Low-cost exports were mainly directed to the developed countries, whose home-producers already faced serious adjustment problems. These producers lobbied their governments for selective protection against imports from developing countries. Selective action was incompatible with GATT rules on trade, but in 1962 rich and poor countries agreed in the GATT on a Long Term Arrangement on the Cotton Textile Trade (LTA). This committed the developed countries to end their import restrictions and to allow a progressive increase in low-cost imports. In return, the developing countries agreed to apply voluntary export restraints in order to give a breathing space in which the textile industries of the rich countries could adjust to their changing circumstances. However, despite substantial change, adjustment problems persisted and the LTA was extended until 1974, when it was replaced by the present Multi-Fibre Arrangement which extends the trade restrictions to textiles manufactured from wool, synthetic fibres and other materials.

The MFA sets out a framework within which bilateral agreements for voluntary export restraint can be negotiated with the main developing country suppliers but bans all unilateral quota restrictions. The bilateral agreements aim to strike an acceptable balance between the interests of the low-cost exporting countries in a rapid opening-up of their export markets, and the interests of producers in the rich countries who want protection whilst they continue to rationalise and modernise. With the main power in the hands of the rich countries, at the renewals of the MFA in 1978 and 1982 the arrangements have become increasingly protectionist.

The first MFA in 1974 provided for an annual 6 per cent increase in the quantity limits, but in 1978 at EEC insistence a new clause was added permitting 'reasonable departures' from this growth rate for short periods and in emergencies. This clause has been used to hold down the growth of imports in recent years. Also, in 1982, the EEC was successful in adding to the MFA a provision controlling import surges caused by exporters making fuller use of a previously under-utilised quota.[5] The current MFA rules will operate for 4½ years until 31 July 1987.

BILATERAL AGREEMENTS AND VOLUNTARY EXPORT RESTRAINTS

The EEC has negotiated bilateral agreements under the current MFA with 25 countries in Asia, Latin America and Eastern

Europe;[6] in addition, all of the Mediterranean countries (except Turkey) agreed in 1982 to restrict their exports to the EEC for two or three years. The bilateral agreements restrict EEC imports of most categories of textiles and clothing by quotas (on volume rather than value). They are 'voluntary' in the sense that the exporting countries have, reluctantly, signed agreements to that effect, but they have done so under strong pressure from the EEC and in the knowledge that if they refused to limit their exports to the extent demanded then the EEC might well impose restrictions. The EEC would, of course, much prefer not to do this since selective action of this kind would be considered as contrary to GATT principles by many of the contracting parties and might be seen as a dangerous escalation of protectionism. Voluntary restraints give the exporting countries some scope for bargaining over the all-important details of the restrictions, such as the precise product coverage, the right to shift between quota categories and carry-overs of quotas into succeeding years.[7]

There is a further advantage to the exporting countries agreeing to restrain exports rather than have import quotas or tariffs imposed. When trade is restricted, a wedge is driven between the price that the consumer in the importing country pays and the foreign supply price. In Figure 7.3, EEC demand (D_{EEC}) is met partly by home production (S_{EEC}) and partly by imports (S_m). If the EEC were to impose a tariff of amount t on imports, the price of the focus good to EEC consumers would be Op_1, and consumption would be Oq_2, of which q_1q_2 would be imports. The stippled area represents the tariff revenue accruing to EEC taxpayers. A similar situation would occur if the EEC restricted imports by an import quota equal to q_1q_2, except that there would be no tariff revenue. The stippled area would be a windfall gain either to importers or to exporters, depending on their bargaining strength and the system of administering the quota, or to taxpayers if the government auctioned the quotas. Alternatively, if exporters agreed through a voluntary export restraint to restrict their exports to q_1q_2 then they would be in a good position to capture the scarcity premium, represented in Figure 7.3 by the stippled area. Their ability to do this would be improved if a government agency or a trade association sanctioned by the government is responsible for allocating export quotas. Hence, an attraction to exporting countries of voluntary export restraints is that they may receive higher prices for their goods than if other forms of trade restriction are used.

The bilateral agreements which were negotiated in 1982 cover

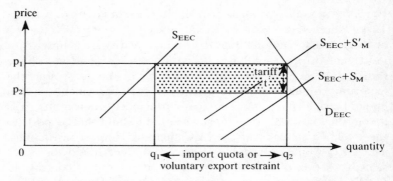

Figure 7.3   Voluntary export restraints, import quotas and tariffs

EEC textile imports in 1983 to 1986. Some 123 categories of textiles are identified, and annual quotas are fixed for the main developing country suppliers of each product. In some cases the quotas are fixed for all EEC imports, in other cases only for certain EEC countries. Where quotas are fixed for all EEC imports, these are allocated between the member countries on the basis of past trade patterns and the need for 'improved burden-sharing between the Member States'.[8] Quotas are not fixed for all countries in all products, only for the most important trade flows. However, if a country develops a fast-growing new line of exports not yet covered by a specific quota, the EEC can implement 'voluntary quantity ceilings' through the painful-sounding 'basket extractor mechanism'. Other provisions of the bilateral agreements include: procedures for flexible operation to allow better use of the quotas, a system of double-checking quotas by importing and exporting countries, and rules to deter misrepresentation of a good's country of origin in order to exceed the quotas.

EVALUATION OF THE EEC'S TEXTILE IMPORT ARRANGEMENTS

Although the first MFA represented a departure from GATT principles in that quantitative limits were fixed for particular exporting countries, it did permit a fast rate of growth of imports to the EEC—about 25 per cent a year between 1973 and 1976. However, with the onset of recession and the application of the 'reasonable departures' clause, the growth of imports was cut back sharply in the second MFA (1978–82) to about 2.4 per cent a year. Very little further growth in imports is permitted in the bilateral agreements negotiated under the current MFA, especially for the 'sensitive products' (cotton yarn, woven fabrics of cotton or man-made fibres, T–shirts, jerseys, trousers, blouses and shirts). It is estimated that for the UK the growth in textile import quotas between 1983 and 1986 will be substantially below 1 per cent a year. Hong Kong, Macao, South Korea and Taiwan fare particularly badly in that their quotas on the five sensitive clothing categories were reduced in 1983 by 7–8 per cent on average from their 1982 levels.[9] These cuts are represented by the EEC as an attempt to make room for more supplies from the poorer developing countries.

The increasingly restrictive nature of the Community's textiles trade arrangements must be seen in the context of recession and rising unemployment in the EEC and elsewhere. The European textile industry has lost more than a million jobs over the last decade (from 3.1 millions in 1971 to 2.1 millions in 1981) and employment in the UK industry, for example, halved between 1978 and 1982. Many factors contributed to these job losses, in particular a static demand in the EEC coupled with rising labour productivity which has lifted output per person employed by about 50 per cent since 1973.[10]

Increased imports from developing countries have probably been only a relatively minor source of textiles job losses in the EEC. Indeed, EEC imports from other developed countries (especially the US and Portugal) which were not subject to quantity controls grew much faster than imports from most developing countries during the 1970s. Much of the producer benefit from EEC trade restrictions under the MFA may have accrued to manufacturers in other developed countries and not to the EEC interests which were supposed to be protected.

Figure 7.4 illustrates this proposition.[11] With no controls on trade the EEC price level is Op_1 and EEC production amounts to Oq_1. Import demand (D_m) is met by supplies of Oq_2 from other developed countries (S_p) and q_2q_3 from developing countries (S_w). If then voluntary export restraints are negotiated which reduce developing countries exports to q_2q_4, the EEC price level will rise to Op_2 to the obvious detriment of EEC consumers. EEC production will increase by q_1q_5 (trade suppression) and there will be an associated gain in producers' surplus of area A. But there will also be a rise in imports from other developed countries of q_2q_6 (trade diversion) with an associated gain in producers' surplus of area B. Depending on the initial quantities supplied, and the slopes of the supply curves, area B could even exceed area A.

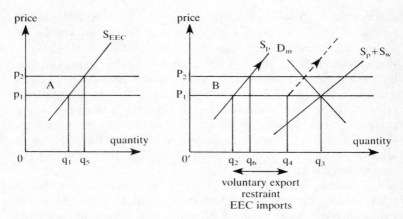

Figure 7.4   The effects of voluntary export restraints on non-restricted suppliers

Over the last two decades, the international textile agreements have changed from instruments of liberalisation to highly restrictive and discriminatory devices for managing part of the world textile trade.[12] The focus of EEC policy appears to have shifted from adjustment of the European industry to import containment and burden-sharing. Views within the EEC on textile policy vary considerably between countries with the UK, France and Italy advocating a restrictive approach, and Germany,[13] the Netherlands and Denmark favouring a more liberal regime. The former have argued successfully that to cut protection at a time of recession would add to the pool of unemployment, increase imports, destabilise the home industry and undermine its attempt to modernise. However, a more liberal approach—perhaps through a return to the use of tariffs only and their progressive reduction to the CCT level—could bring substantial benefits: reduced inflation through lower textile prices, export gains in other industries (e.g. chemical dyes, textile machinery and specialist fibres) and a valuable contribution to the economic development of the Third World.[14]

In this chapter, EEC trade measures in relation to agriculture, steel and textiles have been reviewed. These measures reflect the power of protectionist producer lobbies. The success of the measures in relation to their stated objectives is, to say the least, questionable. For example, in spite of the immense cost of the CAP to both consumers and taxpayers, the Community has not succeeded in resolving the income problems of Europe's small farmers, though larger producers and landowners may have benefited. Short-term support measures have been emphasised at the expense of structural reform measures, and as the problems facing the declining industries become more entrenched, so the Community has tended to be drawn into more and more intervention, as with the introduction in 1984 of milk quotas in agriculture and mandatory minimum prices for steel. The associated trade measures are a constant source of friction with non-member countries (see section 13.2) and are highly damaging to the GATT open trading system.

*   *   *

Having considered the EEC's general provisions for trade with non-member countries in Chapters 6 and 7, we now turn to the differentiation of the Common Commercial Policy with respect to the Community's principal trading partners (see section 6.6). This differentiation relates to product coverage, the extent of preferential treatment, the return concessions demanded of the partner country and the legal framework of any agreement. With the EFTA countries (Chapter 8) the EEC has established a series of free trade areas for manufactured goods, whilst in relation to the Mediterranean countries a mixture of customs unions, free trade areas, reciprocal and non-reciprocal preferences is envisaged (Chapter 9). The EEC's approach to the rest of the Third World is two-tiered: most developing countries benefit from generalised tariff preferences on their exports (Chapters 10 and 12), but the African countries (Chapter 11) receive special preferences. EEC trade with the principal developed countries outside Europe (including the US and Japan: Chapter 13) is subject to most-favoured-nation treatment under the GATT, whilst the entry of East European goods to the EEC market is controlled by quotas (Chapter 14). Together, the varied and sometimes conflicting measures surveyed in Chapters 8 to 14 constitute an elaborate hierarchy of trade treatment—the EEC's 'pyramid of privilege'.

8 The EEC–EFTA Free Trade Agreements

The seven EFTA countries (Austria, Finland, Iceland, Norway, Portugal, Sweden and Switzerland) have a special relationship with the Community: 'The EFTA countries as a group are the principal trading partners of the EEC, the market for a quarter of the EEC's external exports while the EEC is the destination of three-fifths of their exports. Geographical closeness, shared values, traditional commercial links, similarities in economic and legal systems also create natural bonds.'[1] Unlike most other industrialised countries, the EFTA members receive specially favourable terms of access for their exports to the EEC market through a series of industrial free trade area agreements. This special access places them, alone among the more developed economies, near to the top of the Community's 'pyramid of privilege'.

How the EFTA countries came to occupy this position can only be understood in relation to the origin and successful record of EFTA as an industrial free trade area, and to the transition of Britain and Denmark from EFTA to EEC membership. These issues are discussed in sections 8.1 and 8.2. Section 8.3 reviews the current trade arrangements between the two groups, and section 8.4 examines the changing pattern of EEC–EFTA trade. The final sections deal with the impact of the Second Enlargement of the EEC (section 8.5), and the future for EEC–EFTA cooperation (section 8.6).

8.1 Industrial free trade areas—the EFTA experience

From the perspective of EEC trade policy, the most important aspect of the EFTA experience[2] up to 1973 was the demonstration that a free trade area between highly industrialised countries was both practicable and potentially beneficial to the countries taking part.

In some ways, the membership pattern of the EFTA was unhelpful to the successful creation of a cohesive regional trade group: apart from the Scandinavian countries (Denmark, Norway and Sweden) and Finland,[3] the membership was geographically rather dispersed (the other members, being Austria, Portugal, Switzerland, the UK, and later Iceland). Moreover, there were major disparities in the populations of the member countries, notably between the UK and the rest. On the other hand, the EFTA countries, except for Portugal, all had highly developed economies with a similar range of modern industries, suggesting some scope for intra-industry trade creation.

Another factor favourable to the EFTA experiment was the timing of its formation. In 1958, the EEC countries had rejected, after lengthy discussions, the proposal for a pan-European free trade area in which the EEC customs union would have been one element. A group of European but non-EEC countries then conceived the EFTA as a temporary arrangement which could be used to provide a basis for negotiating a favourable trade deal with the EEC (whose customs union was already taking shape). EFTA began life in May 1960 when the Stockholm Convention took effect, and adopted a programme for dismantling tariffs on trade between the member countries which paralleled the EEC timetable. Internal free trade on industrial goods was generally achieved ahead of schedule, by December 1966.

The largely trouble-free experience of trade liberalisation within EFTA can be attributed in part to the buoyant economic conditions of the early 1960s. In addition, the EFTA countries skirted the major problem area of agricultural trade. They did so because of the widely varying agricultural support systems in the member countries, the major adjustment problems that free trade in foodstuffs would have caused, and the assumed temporary nature of EFTA. However, agricultural trade could not be entirely ignored because of its export importance for some of the member countries. The solution—in line with EFTA's pragmatic approach—was to establish a series of bilateral agreements giving Danish and Portuguese food exports preferential access to other EFTA markets. Similar arrangements were made for fish exports from Norway and Denmark.

The exclusion of agricultural products from tariff-free treatment raises the question of the compatability of EFTA with the GATT Article XXIV rules on the formation of free trade areas. Whilst the timetable for tariff dismantling in EFTA seems to meet the GATT requirement that a free trade area be speedily established, the product coverage of EFTA is more problematic. The GATT rules require that 'substantially all trade' within the area must be freed. According to Curzon,[4] the exclusion of agricultural products, together with a slower timetable for Portugal, restrictions on some textiles trade and the retention of certain revenue duties (e.g. on Norwegian car imports) meant that only about 88 per cent of intra-EFTA trade was tariff-free in the late 1960s. However, this was close to EFTA's target of 90 per cent, with which the GATT contracting parties did not openly disagree.

The crucial operational problem of the EFTA experiment was how to deal with a possible *deflection of trade* in the absence of a common external tariff. The freedom of member countries to pursue independent trade policies towards the outside world was a major attraction of the free trade area approach: it reduced the encroachment on national sovereignty and permitted a decentralised mode of operations with only a small institutional superstructure. The decision-making body in EFTA, the Council, comprises representatives of the governments of the member countries and meets two or three times a year.

Trade deflection occurs when imports from outside the free trade area are imported via the member country with the lowest tariff and are then redistributed free of further tariff charges to the other member countries. In this way, the higher tariffs in these countries are evaded and the free trade area becomes, in effect, a customs union with a common external tariff set at the level of the lowest national tariff. In order to combat trade deflection, all free trade areas are equipped with rules of origin which allow goods to move tariff-free between the member countries only if they have been wholly or largely produced within the area. A balance has to be struck between rules which require such a high local content that few goods are eligible for tariff-free treatment, and rules which are too liberal to prevent trade deflection. Under the Stockholm Convention, tariff-free treatment on intra-EFTA trade was given to all goods which contained less than 50 per cent in value of non-EFTA parts and components—the *'value' criterion*. Alternatively, manufacturers could opt for the application of the *'process' criterion* on their goods, whereby exemption from tariff was obtained if certain manufacturing processes had been carried out in the EFTA countries. The rules allowed cumulation, that is, the value and process criteria were applied in relation to the EFTA countries as a group, not just for each country separately. The EFTA experiment showed that a free trade area could be operated between industrial countries on the basis of relatively simple rules of origin, without being suffocated by a mountain of paperwork or time-consuming border formalities, and with little fraud.

Even where rules of origin can be devised which prevent trade deflection, the possibility of *indirect* trade deflection may still raise doubts about the viability of the free trade area approach. Suppose that a high tariff country and a low tariff country, H and L respectively, form a free trade area, equipped with effective rules of origin. For protected goods, H's prices will tend to exceed those in L, and the formation of the free trade area will encourage L's producers to direct more of their sales tariff–free to H's market, possibly lowering H's market price. At the same time as L's producers switch their sales towards H, L's consumers will buy more goods from outside the free trade area, subject to L's low tariff. Thus, some of the effects of trade deflection may be reproduced, even though imports from outside the area are prevented from reaching H's market tariff-free via L through the rules of origin. In particular, there may be increased imports from non-area countries into L, the low-tariff country, (indirect trade deflection) and a lowering of prices in H, the high tariff country. As Shibata has shown,[5] the impact of the formation of the free trade area on prices in the high tariff country will depend on the relationship between demand in that country and the joint supply in the two countries. It is quite possible that in a free trade area price differences could persist between the member countries, whereas in a customs union under similar assumptions (specifically, no transport costs and perfect competition in all industries) this could not happen. In practice, the problems associated with indirect trade deflection do not seem to have aroused much concern in EFTA, perhaps because of the general similarity of the member countries' external tariffs and the influence of the oligopolistic structure of industry on product prices.

Although the EFTA experiment demonstrated that the free trade area approach was a practicable alternative to a customs union, the economic benefits to the member countries depend on the extent to which increased intra-group trade is generated, especially through trade creation. A number of attempts have been made to measure the effects of the EFTA on the trade of its member countries using a variety of residual imputation techniques (see section 4.2). For example, a major study by the EFTA Secretariat[6] examined the shares in each EFTA country's consumption of home-produced goods, goods imported from other EFTA countries, and non-area goods. By extrapolating the trends in these shares during the 1950s (i.e. before EFTA was formed) through to the 1960s the study was able to suggest, product by product, what the EFTA countries' imports might have been in the absence of the free trade area. By comparing these hypothetical levels of imports with the levels of imports actually recorded, the Secretariat concluded that the trade effect of EFTA was substantial: by 1967, intra-EFTA trade had increased by 40 per cent, or $2.2 billions a year. A similar order of magnitude was obtained by Williamson and Botrill[7] using a different approach, although other estimates put the trade effect rather lower.[8]

There is disagreement in the empirical studies of EFTA trade over the crucial issue of the relative size of trade creation and trade diversion. The EFTA Secretariat's study suggested that some 60 per cent of the extra trade between the EFTA countries was attributable to trade creation,[9] but other researchers have concluded that trade diversion was two to three times as great as trade creation.[10] Trade diversion seems mainly to have been at the expense of the EEC (especially Germany and the Netherlands); similarly, the formation of the EEC had caused trade diversion against the EFTA countries. This reciprocal trade-diversion effect provided an incentive for the EEC as well as the EFTA to reach an agreement on liberalising industrial trade between the two groups.

The EFTA free trade area experiment was important for EEC trade policy in two respects: (i) it demonstrated that through the use of relatively simple rules of origin it was possible to have tariff-free trade between industrial countries some of which shared common borders without the need for harmonising their external tariffs; and (ii) it showed that such an arrangement could provide a useful stimulus to trade. Thus the EEC was much more receptive to the idea of a free trade link with other western European countries in 1973 than it had been in 1958. The trigger for such a link was provided by British and Danish membership of the EEC, the background to which we explore in the next section.

8.2 Origins of the EEC–EFTA Free Trade Agreements

The achievement of EFTA's original objective of securing a favourable trade arrangement with the EEC was initially frustrated by the failure of attempts at bridge-building between the two groups at the beginning of the 1960s. Western Europe began to divide into two separate trading blocs, and the 'temporary' EFTA came to have a life of its own. The EFTA countries continued to search for better conditions of trade with the EEC, but abandoned joint ventures in favour of an individual country approach. They pledged solidarity with each other in the London Communiqué of June 1961 so that they would all be able to 'participate from the same date in an integrated European market'.[11]

The new approach was spearheaded by Britain which, following a major reappraisal of policy, applied for full EEC membership in July 1961. Britain's change of heart reflected a number of considerations, especially the expansion of British trade with Europe, the declining importance of the Commonwealth as a unit in world affairs, and the initial economic success of the EEC which contrasted sharply with the parlous state of the British economy.

At this early stage in the life of the Comunity, Britain hoped that the Treaty of Rome could be fundamentally revised to accommodate UK interests. However, discussions on British entry to the EEC were broken off in January 1963 because of opposition from the French government. There was a renewed bid for British membership in 1967, but it was not until after the resignation of President de Gaulle in 1969 that negotiations began in earnest with a Community which was by now fully established. After overcoming, or at least postponing, some major difficulties, negotiations were completed in June 1971 and the terms of EEC entry were accepted by the UK parliament in October of that year. A new phase in European trade relationships was about to begin.

The entry negotiations raised many thorny problems, notably about how Britain would switch over to the EEC system of farm price support, about the size of Britain's contribution to the European Budget, and about trade arrangements. The main trade issues concerned the treatment of exports from developing countries in the Commonwealth, and especially the sugar-exporters (see section 11.2 *Special treatment for CAP products*), the assurance to New Zealand of continued access to the UK market for its exports of temperate agricultural products and, what is of particular concern here, arrangements for trade between an enlarged EEC and the remaining EFTA countries.

These arrangements were vital to the EFTA countries, because not only was their organisation losing its largest member— Britain—but also two other founder members—Denmark and Norway—had similarly negotiated for full EEC membership, along with Ireland. The remaining EFTA countries would be dependent on the newly enlarged EEC market for about a half of their export earnings, and the loss of tariff-free access to the

British and Danish markets on top of continued discrimination against their exports in the original EEC market would have been very damaging for their trade prospects. Accordingly, each of these countries, which mostly for political reasons felt unable to apply for full EEC membership, requested association or some other form of trade link with the Community. They were supported in this by the applicant countries who were anxious to prevent the erection of trade barriers between themselves and their former EFTA partners.

The original EEC countries were sympathetic to the establishment of a special trade arrangement between themselves and EFTA given the dependence of the EFTA countries on the EEC market, the opportunity that enlargement gave to end the division of Europe into two trade blocks, and indeed the importance to the EEC countries of their export markets in EFTA. Thus it was agreed in 1969 that once enlargement negotiations were under way, the EEC would hold discussions with the other EFTA countries over the future of their mutual trade arrangements.

In June 1970, the Commission suggested that these arrangements should take the form of a series of free trade areas for industrial products. A customs union between the EEC and the EFTA countries had been ruled out by the Community on the grounds that decisions affecting the common external tariff would have to be shared with countries who were not full members of the Community. The harmonisation of external tariffs would also have been unpalatable to the EFTA countries because of the political implications. As Curzon puts it, the free trade area formula 'was the only one which could accomplish the triple feat of integrating the whole of Western Europe, without sacrificing the unique and exclusive nature of the CET and without compromising the neutrality of the neutrals.'[12] Moreover, the EFTA experiment had shown that a free trade arrangement was feasible.

Negotiations on the basis of the Commission's formula took place in 1970–71 and resulted in the signing of bilateral trade agreements between the EEC and Austria, Iceland, Portugal, Sweden and Switzerland.

These agreements took effect from 1 January 1973, to coincide with the entry of Britain, Denmark and Ireland to the EEC. Norway's application for full EEC membership was withdrawn following rejection of EEC entry in a national referendum. Norway later negotiated a free trade agreement with the Community which took effect from 1 July 1973. Finland followed later with a similar agreement effective from 1 January 1974. As a result of these agreements the seven remaining EFTA countries not only maintained their free trade links with Britain and Denmark, but also received tariff-free access to the markets of the original EEC countries and Ireland.

8.3 The content of the EEC–EFTA Free Trade Agreements

The bilateral trade agreements between each of the EFTA countries and the EEC did not change the nature of the EFTA arrangement, which continues to operate as an industrial free trade area, albeit with a reduced membership and with intra-group trade cut by two-thirds. Similarly, the EEC customs union remains, but with an enlarged membership. The agreements do however end tariffs on most industrial trade between the EEC and EFTA countries, and in that sense the division of Europe into two separate trade blocs was terminated in 1973. The present arrangements correspond quite closely to what the EFTA countries tried to achieve in the 1950s, except that Britain and Denmark are part of the central customs union rather than the free trade area periphery.

Summary of the main features of the EEC–EFTA Free Trade Agreements[13]

(a) the Agreements set up a series of free trade areas between the EEC and the EFTA countries (Switzerland, Sweden, Austria, Norway, Finland, Portugal and Iceland);

(b) they provided for tariff-free treatment of most industrial goods from 1 July 1977, with a slower timetable for certain 'sensitive' goods; agricultural trade was excluded from the arrangement;

(c) the rules of origin for the free trade areas were to be those already used elsewhere by the EEC under the Yaoundé Convention;

(d) restrictive business practices and state aids which affect trade are deemed 'incompatible' with the proper functioning of the Agreements;

(e) safeguard arrangements were provided to deal with balance of payments problems or adjustment difficulties in particular industries or regions;

(f) Portugal, as the least developed EFTA country and as a

candidate for full EEC membership, received special terms;
(g)   each Agreement was to be administered by a joint commit-
      tee.

THE BILATERAL NATURE OF THE FREE TRADE AREAS

The EEC negotiated trade agreements with each of the EFTA
countries separately rather than with the EFTA countries as a
group for several reasons. The bilateral approach may have been
speedier, making it easier to meet the January 1973 deadline set
for EEC enlargement. In addition, a series of bilateral agreements
was seen by the Community as the best way to prevent any dilution
of its separate identity and to minimise the constraints on its
freedom of action. The provisions of the Free Trade Agreements
are closely similar, and the most important consequence of their
bilateral nature is probably the constraint on cumulation under the
rules of origin (see *Rules of origin,* below).

PRODUCT COVERAGE

The Agreements deal mainly with free trade in industrial goods.
Full inclusion of agricultural products would have involved EFTA
countries in the mechanisms of the Common Agricultural Policy
and would then have raised difficult questions about the influence
of non-member countries in shaping EEC common policies. The
EFTA countries resisted EEC pressure that they should offer
concessions on EEC agricultural exports, but were able to get
special arrangements for Portugal, Norway and Iceland which
depend heavily on agricultural and fisheries exports. The EEC
agreed to reduce or eliminate its tariffs on imports of certain
fisheries products from these countries and on two agricultural
products (tomato concentrates and wine). Processed agricultural
products receive few trade advantages under the Agreements, in
contrast to the intra-EFTA arrangements where considerable
progress had been made in eliminating tariffs.

Building on the earlier experience of the EEC and EFTA
countries, the transition period to free trade was a short one for
most products: tariffs and quotas were phased out between 1 April
1973 and 1 July 1977. The timetable was synchronised with that for
British and Danish accession to the EEC, thus avoiding problems
of trade deflection caused by different rates of tariff reduction. For
some sensitive products where adjustment difficulties were anticipated, longer transition periods, up to a maximum of eleven years,
were permitted and reinforced in some cases by the use of tariff

quotas. The industries concerned are mainly those where natural conditions in the EFTA countries give EFTA producers an important comparative advantage (e.g. paper and cardboard, and aluminium, where Nordic producers have access to relatively cheap hydro-electric power). In turn, EFTA countries whose exports were affected by this slower phase-out of tariffs were permitted to delay their tariff cuts on certain imports from the EEC. Except for Portugal (see *Safeguard arrangements,* below), the timetable for tariff removal was largely adhered to despite the unfavourable world trade conditions during the transition period.

With regard to the GATT rules for the formation of free trade areas, the speed with which the provisions of the EEC–EFTA Agreements were implemented seems satisfactory as, in general, does the coverage. Only about 6 per cent of EEC–EFTA trade consisted of agricultural and fisheries products, though the proportion was much higher than this for Iceland. The inclusion of agricultural products in the Agreements would have been mainly trade-diverting, to the detriment of other GATT contracting parties.

THE RULES OF ORIGIN

Both the EEC under the Yaoundé Convention, and the EFTA countries had experience of operating rules of origin in a free trade area. The EFTA countries would have much preferred to retain their dual process/value system in the Free Trade Agreements with the Community, but were obliged to accept the EEC's process system (see section 6.3, *Rules of origin*) which for simplicity they now apply also to intra-EFTA trade. After sustained pressure from the EFTA countries, the EEC agreed to modify the origin rules for certain engineering goods from April 1983.[14] Since then, engineering companies have had a choice between alternative grounds for claiming duty-free treatment—either the standard EEC rules or on the basis that no more than a certain percentage (in most cases 40 or 30 per cent) of the ex-works value of the product is accounted for by input materials or components from third countries. The changed rules affect approximately 25–30 per cent of EEC–EFTA trade.

Under the pre-1973 EFTA system, the rules of origin made *cumulation* of origin status possible, that is, a production process which would give origin status could be divided between two EFTA countries and if the finished product were then exported to another EFTA country, it would be admitted tariff-free as an EFTA-origin product. Under the bilateral EEC–EFTA Agreements such cumulation is not permitted, though the EFTA countries have campaigned for the rules relating to cumulation to be changed. The present rules provide only that if a product has achieved origin status in one EFTA country and is then exported to another EFTA country, it could be re-exported to the EEC tariff-free.

RULES OF COMPETITION

Restrictive business practices (such as market-sharing agreements between firms), the manipulation of markets by monopolies and state aids which distort competition are outlawed by the Agreements, in so far as they affect trade between the EEC and individual EFTA countries. Whilst, for its part, the Commission has taken some action concerning restrictive business practices—for example, over alleged collusion on pricing between pulp producers—it is clear that the competition rules on EEC–EFTA trade have fewer 'teeth' than the corresponding rules within the EEC which have, of course, the ambitious aim of creating a fully integrated market.[15] Similarly, although there have been bilateral exchanges of information on state aids between the EEC and EFTA countries, this does not seem to have had any noticeable effect on government practices. Another area where governments have a major influence on trade—public procurement policies—is not mentioned in the Agreements even though both the EEC and EFTA have their own rules in relation to intra-group trade.

SAFEGUARD ARRANGEMENTS

The Agreements contain a safeguard Article which permits a country that 'is in difficulties or is seriously threatened with difficulties as regards its balance of payments' to 'take the necessary safeguard measures' but that country is required to 'inform the other Contracting Party forthwith'. Iceland, Finland and Portugal have each availed themselves of this provision to bring in general import controls, usually in the form of surcharges.[16]

Where 'an increase in imports of a given product is or is likely to be seriously detrimental to any production activity', countries may be permitted to take protective measures. However, the increase must be due to *both* tariff reductions under the Agreements *and* differences in tariffs on raw materials and intermediate products between the two trading partners. Finland was permitted to introduce an import deposit scheme for furniture in 1979, but in general there has been little resort to safeguard measures for specific products. Where such measures have been applied, the partner country in the Agreement has the sanction of withdrawing tariff concessions. For instance, when the EEC failed to persuade Sweden to withdraw the quotas imposed on imports of EEC footwear in 1975,[18] it introduced higher restrictions on Community imports of Swedish paper and paperboard until the dispute was ended in July 1977.

SPECIAL ARRANGEMENTS FOR PORTUGAL
Most of the safeguard actions under the Agreements have been responses to specific difficulties but in the case of Portugal, and to a lesser extent Iceland, adjustment problems have been more general and persistent. Soon after the Agreement came into effect there was a radical change in the political regime in Portugal. The rapid end of the colonial era brought an influx of refugees from Mozambique and Angola, and there was a sharp increase in Portugal's trade deficit with the EEC. The new government in Lisbon asked, in 1974, for closer links with the Community and especially for finance for Portuguese industrial development. The Community responded by providing exceptional emergency aid in the form of loans from the European Investment Bank of 180 million u.a.s, and, in January 1976, the Council authorised negotiations with Portugal under the 'evolutionary clause'[19] of the Free Trade Agreement. The results of these negotiations were set out in an additional protocol to the 1972 Agreement.[20]

In relation to trade, the main features of the protocol were that:

- Portugal could slow down its timetable of tariff cuts on some industrial products imported from the EEC;
- the preferential margin on Portuguese exports to the EEC was increased;
- tariff quotas on Portuguese wines, textiles and clothing were increased; and
- the EEC agreed to bring forward tariff reductions on Portuguese industrial exports (duty-free entry was given from 1 July 1976).

In addition, improvements were made in the working conditions of Portuguese migrant workers in the EEC, and further low interest rate loans of 200 million u.a.s were made available through the European Investment Bank (EIB).

The protocol was followed in 1977 by a formal application by Portugal for full membership of the EEC. Substantive negotiations began in 1980, when the Community also provided pre-accession aid of 275 million EUA (of which 125 million EUA was in the form of grants).[21] This aid has been used to finance measures intended to ease Portugal's adjustment to EEC membership (e.g. improvements in transport infrastructure). In December 1982, the Commission proposed that a further loan of 150 million ECU should be made to Portugal.[22]

Special protection was given to some Portuguese industries under the Free Trade Agreement, including a slower timetable of tariff dismantling, extending to 1985 in some cases. This timetable was further delayed in 1982. In addition, the Agreement authorised Portugal to introduce (or re-introduce) tariffs until 1979 to protect or develop new export industries. This measure has been extended until 1984 (or until Portugal becomes a member of the Community). The protective effect of the tariff measures has been supplemented by Portugal's use of the safeguard clause in the Agreement to introduce import surcharges on a wide range of products and import quotas on some consumer goods, including cars.

These actions may be seen as evidence of the Community's flexibility in responding to particular problems as well as its earnestness in seeking Portugal's accession. At the same time, doubts must be entertained over Portugal's ability to adapt to full EEC membership over a short transition period, bearing in mind the EFTA and FTA experiences. After more than twenty years as a member of EFTA, Portugal has still not achieved free trade with its partner countries, though it has certainly benefited from what has been closer to a one-way preference system than a free trade area created by mutual tariff disarmament.

ADMINISTRATION

Each Free Trade Agreement is administered by a joint committee, consisting of representatives of the EEC and the relevant EFTA country, which meets twice a year. The committee can take decisions about the details of operation of the Agreements and acts as a forum for consultation over, for example, the use of safeguard measures and the application of the rules of competition. In the event of a disagreement between the two sides, there is no procedure for dispute settlement; this gives the EEC a decided advantage since it can never be overruled and is by far the stronger party. The EFTA countries have tried to improve their weak bargaining power by coordinating their positions ahead of each round of committee meetings.

In 1980, Norway and Sweden, which have been anxious to

widen their cooperation with the EEC beyond matters of trade, decided to replace one of the joint committee meetings each year by talks at Ministerial or State Secretary level.

8.4 The trade effects of the Free Trade Agreements

The introduction of the Free Trade Agreements has been accompanied by a substantial expansion of trade between the EEC and the EFTA countries. The Agreements have allowed the damaging effects of the division of western Europe into two separate trade blocs to be reversed. In particular, the Agreements may have brought about three types of adjustment in the pattern of European trade in industrial goods:

(a) a reduction of trade *within* the previous preference groups (EFTA(9), EEC(6)),
(b) an increase in trade *between* these groups, and
(c) a fall in trade with the *rest of the world*.

These possible trade effects can be explored further, with the aid of a four-country example, in which France and Germany represent the members of an existing preference group, Sweden is a member of another trade group to which preferences have been extended, and the US represents the rest of the world.

The *intra-group effect* (a) is caused by a reversal of those factors which had previously increased trade between the member countries of the customs union or free trade area. Thus exports from Germany to France increased after the EEC was formed partly through trade diversion against non-member countries like Sweden. The Free Trade Agreements stop tariff discrimination against Swedish exports and allow Swedish exports to regain their lost markets in France. This process may be called *trade reversion*. Within an orthodox customs union framework, the replacement of higher-cost German exports by lower-cost Swedish exports is welfare-improving for France, for Sweden and for the world.

A second aspect of the intra-group effect is what may be termed *super trade creation*. Thus the formation of the EEC may have caused French consumers to switch from a higher-cost, home-produced good to lower-cost imports from Germany (trade creation). Now, if it happens that Sweden is a still lower-cost producer of the good than Germany, then the Free Trade Agreements may lead to the French consumers switching from the

German to the Swedish products (super trade creation), with beneficial welfare effects for both France and Sweden. As with trade reversion, trade within the previous preference groups declines, and there is a corresponding increase in trade between the groups.

As described, trade reversion and super trade creation will both contribute to the second trade effect (b): *the increase in trade between the previous preference groups*. In addition, there will be a trade creation effect as, for example, low-cost (and now tariff-free) Swedish goods displace French goods in the French market. Trade diversion may also help to boost trade between the previous preference groups at the expense of rest of the world supplies, which are still subject to tariffs. In this way, higher-cost Swedish goods may supplant lower-cost US goods in the French market after the EFTA–EEC trade agreements come into effect.Finally, effect (c), *rest of the world* exporters are likely to lose markets as a result of the spread of trade preferences in western Europe, through the process of trade diversion already mentioned. There will also be adjustments in trade with Denmark and the UK as these countries adopt the EEC's Common Customs Tariff leading to external trade creation where tariffs are lowered to the CCT (in the UK) or trade suppression where tariffs are raised (in Denmark).

Summarising, Figure 8.1 shows the direction of the trade effects that might be expected following the introduction of the EEC–EFTA Free Trade Agreements.

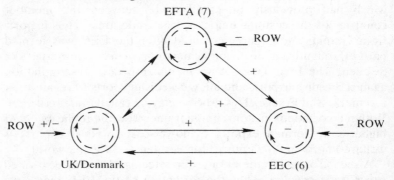

Figure 8.1   The effects on EEC–EFTA trade of the introduction of the Free Trade Agreements

Notes: Arrows indicate the direction of trade between groups; broken arrows are used for trade flows between members of the original preference groups; + indicates positive and − negative expected effects on the volume of trade; intra-group effects are shown inside the circles. ROW signifies rest of the world.

Some indication as to whether or not actual trade flows have been affected in the ways hypothesised may be obtained by examining data on changes in import shares. The import-shares approach has the major drawback that it does not permit the separate identification of trade creation/diversion/reversion, etc. and it also suffers from the usual residual imputation problems (see section 4.2). In mitigation, it can be argued that we are here concerned particularly with the direction of the trade effects rather than their magnitude and, in particular, the relative impacts on intra- and inter-preference group trade.

The Free Trade Agreements are largely confined to trade in industrial products, which under the Standard International Trade Classification (SITC) are grouped into four sections—SITC 5: chemicals, SITC 6: manufactures classified chiefly by material, SITC 7: machinery, and SITC 8: miscellaneous manufactured articles. For each of these, the import shares of each of the trade flows identified in Figure 8.1 were calculated for the EEC(6), EFTA(7) and the UK/Denmark for 1972 (the last year before the Agreements took effect) and 1980 (by which time virtually all the tariff barriers on industrial trade between the EEC and EFTA had been removed). Figure 8.2 shows the import shares in 1980 as a percentage of the corresponding share for 1972, for each of the product groups.

The results of this import shares analysis suggest that trade flows have developed broadly as hypothesised in Figure 8.1; that is, the share of EEC(6) in the EFTA increased, and vice versa, and that there was also an increase in import shares of the EEC(6) in the UK and Danish markets, and vice versa. These were the trade flows directly affected by the removal of tariff barriers. The remaining intra-European trade flows, where trade preferences were reduced, all had declining import shares. If any trade diversion against rest of the world suppliers occurred, it was in general submerged by other factors like the increased competitive strength of Japanese exports. Clearly, during the 1970s many factors other than the Agreements influenced the development of market shares. Nevertheless, the differential performances of the EEC(6), UK/Danish and EFTA(7) exporters in their own and other markets suggest that the Free Trade Agreements have had an important effect on intra-European trade flows.

There is some evidence that the impact of the Agreements has been greater amongst the southern EFTA countries than for the Nordic group (see Table 8.1).[23] The formation of the EEC and EFTA groups appears to have led to a redirection of the European

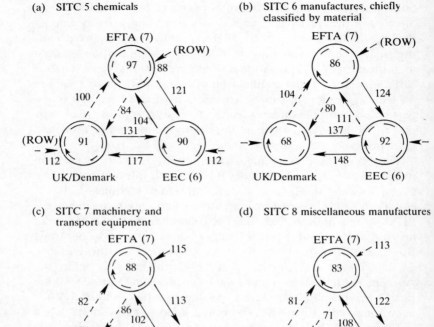

Figure 8.2   Changes in EFTA and EEC trade flows in manufactured goods, 1972–80

export trade of the southern group (Austria, Switzerland and Portugal) away from the EEC, but to have had less impact on the direction of their imports. By 1981, the pattern of this trade had returned to its pre-EFTA position. In the case of the Nordic countries, the direction of both exports and imports appears to have been affected by the formation of the regional trade blocs, but except for Swedish exports there has been only a modest tendency for the direction of trade to revert to its pre-EFTA pattern.

Table 8.1   Changes in the direction of intra-European trade, 1959–81

Importing country	Source of imports (in %) EFTA (7)			UK & Denmark			EEC (6)		
	1959	1972	1981	1959	1972	1981	1959	1972	1981
Austria	10	15	12	7	10	4	83	75	84
Switzerland	6	13	10	13	12	12	81	75	80
Portugal	11	17	16	23	26	17	66	57	67
Finland[a]	24	37	35	24	21	18	52	42	47
Sweden	12	26	25	24	26	22	64	48	53
Norway	29	37	37	21	24	22	50	39	41
Iceland	27	29	38	37	31	26	36	40	36
EFTA (7)	14	22	20	19	19	14	67	59	65
UK	30	33	23	1	4	2	69	63	75
Denmark	24	38	33	20	15	11	56	47	56
EEC (6)	17	10	11	15	9	12	68	81	77

Source: OECD, Statistics of Foreign Trade Series C, Imports volumes 1959, 1972 and 1981.
Notes: The figures refer to the percentage shares of imports of manufactured goods (SITC 5, 6, 7 and 8) in 1959, 1972 and 1981 from European countries (EFTA (7), UK, Denmark and EEC (6) only).
[a] For Finland in 1959, figures based on partner countries' export data.

8.5 EFTA and the Second Enlargement of the EEC

The general impact of the Second Enlargement of the EEC on the trade of the EFTA countries, except for Portugal, is likely to be modest. This is because there is relatively little overlap between the exports of the EFTA countries and the 'candidates', and also because many of the relevant trade flows have already been liberalised. When *Greece* became a member of the EEC in 1981, the EFTA countries abolished their tariffs on most Greek industrial products, and by the end of 1985 industrial tariffs and quotas on EFTA–Greece trade in both directions will be eliminated. Greece has enjoyed tariff-free access to the Community for manufactured goods for some years and so the balance of advantage vis-à-vis EFTA exports will be unchanged. On agricultural products, Greek membership of the Community has affected trade flows, but of the EFTA countries only *Portugal* is directly affected, and Portugal is of course a candidate for full EEC membership. Again, Portuguese membership of the Community is unlikely to affect the other EFTA countries' trade much because Portugal is a member of EFTA and has tariff-free access to the EEC market under a Free Trade Agreement.

Spanish entry to the EEC is more likely to affect the EFTA countries, since Spanish goods would be admitted to the EEC market duty-free in place of the present preferential access. Through an extension of the Free Trade Agreement, Spanish industrial goods would also get tariff-free access to the EFTA markets, and vice versa. The EFTA countries have already anticipated this to some extent: in 1980 they implemented a preferential trade agreement with Spain which is very similar in its provisions to the 1970 EEC-Spain agreement.[24] Perhaps the most interesting feature of the 1980 agreement is the arrangement for freeing trade between Spain and Portugal. If both Spain and Portugal become members of the EEC then they will be committed to free trade between themselves, but in any case the 1980 agreement lays down a target for free trade between the two. Over a period of eight years Spain has undertaken to eliminate virtually all restrictions on its imports from Portugal, whilst Portugal has agreed to treat Spanish goods no less favourably than imports of similar goods from the EEC.

8.6 Conclusions

Both the EEC and the EFTA countries have expressed their general satisfaction with the operation of the Free Trade Agreements. The distortions of trade brought about by the previous division of Europe into two separate trade blocs have gradually been removed to the advantage of both groups, and especially for countries like Austria and Switzerland which share a frontier with the Community. In terms of the analysis of customs union effects in Chapter 2, the Agreements appear to have offered considerable scope for intra-industry trade creation, given the similarly advanced level of industrial development in the two blocs, and this may help to explain the largely trouble-free introduction of the Agreements. Adjustment problems caused by inter-industry trade creation were in some cases side-stepped (notably by the exclusion of agricultural products) or moderated by a long transition period (e.g. for the paper industry) or a slower national timetable (e.g. for Portugal). Inter-industry trade creation has also been held up by non-tariff barriers, like the heavy government subsidies to papermakers in a number of EEC countries.

EFTA criticisms of the Free Trade Agreements have focused on the rules of origin, and the EEC has recently agreed to make some changes to the rules, though not yet as regards cumulation. Other complaints, particularly from Austria, concern the exclusion of most agricultural products from the Agreement. However, it is most unlikely that the EEC will make any major concessions in this direction given the massive problems already facing the CAP and the additional burdens which Spanish and Portuguese membership of the Community will entail.

Non-tariff barriers to trade between the EEC and the EFTA countries have come into prominence as a result of the elimination of tariff restrictions and of the general rise in protectionism. The problems involved are similar to those afflicting the EEC internal market. As reviewed in Chapter 5, the EEC has been making attempts to tackle non-tariff barriers on intra-Community trade, and if this is not to lead to a re-emergence of the EFTA–EEC trade division there is a need for cooperation between the EEC and the EFTA countries. Both parties have expressed an interest in working together, and in January 1980 an EFTA memorandum to the EEC made some specific proposals, including the mutual recognition of national product-testing and inspection, increased cooperation in international standards-writing bodies such as CEN and CENELEC, and a system of advance notification of new national technical regulations.

There are, however, a number of general difficulties for EEC–EFTA cooperation. The aims of the EFTA group are less far-reaching than those of the EEC, and the EFTA countries are anxious to preserve their national independence of action. 'Coordinated autonomous actions' and cooperation through 'spontaneous consensus' may not be sufficient to tackle non-tariff barriers to trade. At the same time, the EEC is unwilling to allow non-member countries to take part in decision-making affecting common EEC policies. In any case the process is already cumbersome enough with ten member countries. The danger for the EFTA countries is that they will be obliged to accept rules affecting the conduct of their trade with the EEC which they have not helped to determine. This problem could eventually push some EFTA countries into seeking full EEC membership.

9   Trade Policies Towards the Mediterranean Countries

Trade relations with the countries which border the Mediterranean Sea[1] have always been of special interest to the Community, and particularly to its Mediterranean members, France, Italy and Greece. Several of the Mediterranean countries (e.g. Libya and Algeria) are important suppliers of oil to the Community, and the region as a whole absorbs about 10 per cent of EEC exports, which puts it on a par with the United States as an export market for the Community. The Mediterranean trade relationship is asymmetrical, however, because the EEC receives about a half of the Mediterranean countries' exports, and the EEC's trade policies are hence of vital concern to them.

Two issues in the EEC–Mediterranean trade relationship are of particular importance, and are explored in this chapter. One concerns the attempt by the EEC to adopt a unified policy approach towards the Mediterranean countries in the face of the considerable political and economic diversity of the area. The armed conflict and political turbulence in the southern Mediterranean countries, and the danger that the two superpowers might become directly involved, have led the Community to try to strengthen and coordinate its economic relations with the Mediterranean world. The underlying hope is that by assisting the economic development and stability of the region, political turmoil can be reduced and the military threat de-escalated. The EEC has been obliged to rely mainly on measures affecting trade—the most developed aspect of Community external relations policy—and aid. The use of tariff preferences for this purpose has, however, created many problems, not least because the Mediterranean countries are rival suppliers for many products, especially certain foodstuffs, clothing and textiles.

The other principal issue concerns the Second Enlargement of the Community. Greece became a full member in 1981 and negotiations are in progress regarding the entry of Portugal and Spain. Unless adjustments are made, the Second Enlargement will alter the balance of the EEC's Mediterranean trade arrangements to the substantial detriment of the non-member Mediterranean countries.

9.1 The 'mosaic' of Mediterranean trade agreements

The Treaty of Rome made no special mention of the EEC's trade relations with the Mediterranean region and, during the early years of the Community, trade arrangements developed in a very *ad hoc* fashion. By the beginning of the 1970s, the EEC found itself with a diverse and uncoordinated 'mosaic' of Mediterranean trade agreements.[2] Individual agreements differed in *legal structure*—some were Association Agreements under Article 238, and others were simple trade agreements under Article 113; in *economic form*—the agreement with Greece was intended to set up a customs union, whilst with Tunisia and Morocco the objective was a free trade area, and the early agreements for Lebanon and Israel offered only MFN treatment; in the *degree of preference offered*—on manufactured goods, for example, the EEC offered duty-free access to Greek products from 1968, compared with a 60 per cent tariff reduction for Spain's exports; and the *extent of reciprocity required*—from very little in the case of Morocco, to eventual full reciprocity from Greece. Since the Mediterranean countries tended to export a broadly similar range of products, the mosaic was a recipe for trade diversion and commercial conflict; it threatened to become more of a political liability than an asset.

How had such a variety of trade agreements arisen in relation to such a limited geographical area? The explanation seems to involve a combination of factors:

The need to assimilate trade arrangements inherited from the member countries. France was permitted to retain preferential trade links with its former North African colonies (Morocco, Tunisia and Algeria[3]) after 1958 under a protocol attached to the Treaty of Rome. The price for phasing out these national preferences in the 1960s was the introduction of Community preferences in the shape of Association Agreements for Morocco and Tunisia.

The desire of some Mediterranean countries with relatively backward economies to join the EEC. Soon after the EEC was formed, Greece and Turkey applied for EEC membership, but it was clear that a long period of gradual adaptation to free trade with the Community would be needed; to this end, Association Agreements were negotiated giving special trade concessions to Greece and Turkey in the framework of eventual customs union.

The circumvention of GATT rules.   GATT rules in general prohibited the introduction of new trade preferences in favour of selected countries and this initially inhibited the proliferation of EEC preferences in the Mediterranean; however, from about 1967, the EEC found that it could exploit the GATT provisions for customs unions and free trade areas as a screen for the introduction of selective and varied tariff preferences by presenting each preferential agreement as the first stage of an eventual customs union or free trade area.[4]

The 'drag' or 'knock-on' effect.   As each preferential agreement was granted, other Mediterranean countries lobbied the Community for more favourable treatment both to forestall trade diversion and to gain new advantages. In order to maintain political balances both between non-members and within the Community (because the various Mediterranean countries had different allies within the EEC) the Community was obliged to respond.

9.2 The global approach to Mediterranean trade policy

Even before the mosaic of Mediterranean trade preferences was completed, pressure for a more coordinated EEC approach began to build up. The increased military tension in the area drew attention to the need on security grounds for a more broadly-based policy towards the Mediterranean countries, particularly in view of the growing presence of the Soviet navy in the Mediterranean. The Mediterranean countries themselves wanted to improve their agreements with the EEC in order to counteract the damaging effects of the CAP on their exports, or else to be included in the EEC's GSP. For its part, the Council of Ministers found the mosaic of preferences increasingly difficult to justify. Moreover, a more coordinated set of agreements would make it easier for the Community to adopt a coherent position in the proposed new round of GATT negotiations (the Tokyo Round). In any case, changes would have to be made to the Mediterranean trade arrangements in view of the accession of Britain, Denmark and Ireland to the EEC in 1973.

After discussions within the various Community institutions, in June 1972 the Council asked the Commission to produce concrete proposals for a 'global approach to the Community's entire relations with the Mediterranean countries'.[5] The Commission's plan, presented in September 1972, envisaged the creation of an industrial free trade area in the Mediterranean, with duty-free access to the EEC market by July 1977, coupled with substantial EEC concessions on Mediterranean agricultural exports, and measures of cooperation, including financial aid. It proved extremely difficult, however, to translate the broad policy outlines into detailed and mutually acceptable arrangements. In particular, there were problems about the degree of reciprocity to be expected from the Mediterranean countries, and the safeguard provisions necessary to protect European farm interests. The negotiations, which the Commission had hoped to conclude within a year, dragged on until 1977. By November 1978, however, the main elements of the new policy were in operation. They can be summarised as follows:

(a)   tariff-free access for industrial exports to the EEC, subject to quotas or ceilings for some products;

(b)   tariff concessions on a high proportion of each Mediterranean country's agricultural exports to the Community;

(c)   no reciprocity demanded for the Mahgreb (Algeria, Morocco and Tunisia) and Mashreq (Egypt, Jordan, Lebanon and Syria) countries, nor for Yugoslavia; and

(d)   provision of aid and other forms of cooperation (e.g. collaboration on science and technology, environmental matters and migrant labour problems).

TRADE ARRANGEMENTS FOR MANUFACTURED GOODS

By 1972, tariff-free access to the EEC market had already been granted to imports of manufactured goods from Greece (with effect from July 1968), Morocco, Tunisia and Turkey as Associates. Under the global approach, this facility was extended to Algeria, Portugal, Egypt, Syria, Lebanon, Jordan, Israel and Malta (see Table 9.1); Yugoslavia received similar treatment from July 1980. Spain has not negotiated with the EEC under the global

Table 9.1 The EEC's Mediterranean trade agreements

Mediterranean countries	Form of agreement[a]	Date signed	Effective from	Trade arrangement[b]	Industrial free trade from	GSP status
Mahgreb	Cooperation	Apr. 1976	July 1976	OWP	Sept. 1969	yes
Mashreq	Cooperation	Jan. 1977	July 1977	OWP	July 1977	yes
Israel	{Free Trade	May 1975	July 1975	FTA	July 1977	no
	Coop. protocol	Feb. 1977	Nov. 1978			
Portugal	p. to Free Trade[d]	Sept. 1976	Nov. 1976	FTA	July 1976	no
Malta	p. to Assoc.[e]	Mar. 1976	June 1976	CU	Jan. 1974	no
Cyprus	p. to Assoc.[f]	Sept. 1977	June 1978	CU	July 1977	yes
Yugoslavia	Cooperation	Apr. 1980	July 1980	OWP	July 1980	yes
Turkey	Association	Sept. 1963	Dec. 1964	CU	Sept. 1971	no
Spain	Trade	Oct. 1970	Oct. 1971	PA	—	no

Notes: p. = protocol; [b] OWP = one-way preference; FTA = free trade area; CU = customs union; PA = preferential agreement; [e] effective May 1977; [d] effective Jan. 1973; [e] effective April 1971; [f] effective June 1973.

approach, preferring instead to concentrate its efforts on achieving full EEC membership; in the meantime, its trade relations with the EEC continue to be regulated by a 1970 preferential trade agreement under which its industrial exports receive a 60 per cent tariff preference in the EEC market.

The benefits to the Mediterranean countries of being able to industrialise on the basis of preferential, tariff-free access to their single most important export market are potentially large. However, in assessing these benefits it should be recalled that the industrial export capacity of most Mediterranean countries, especially the Mahgreb and Mashreq, is still very small; that the margin of advantage for the southern Mediterranean countries should be calculated in relation to the GSP which gives exports from all developing countries tariff-free access to the EEC market, though in limited quantities; and that even under the Mediterranean agreements, tariff-free treatment is limited by quota or ceiling for a number of the principal export products like cotton textiles and refined petroleum. Tariff quotas have been phased out for the southern Mediterranean countries, but they continue to affect exports from Spain, Portugal and Cyprus. More flexible ceilings apply in the case of Malta and Yugoslavia. Even so, in 1981 for example, tariffs were reimposed on about one-third of the considerable range of Yugoslav products subject to ceilings.

For many of the Mediterranean countries, textiles and clothing account for an important part of their export earnings. Under the global approach, exports to the EEC have been treated more favourably than if they had been subject to the full rigours of the Multi-Fibre Arrangement (see section 7.3). For example, under the second Multi-Fibre Arrangement, Morocco, Tunisia and Malta had quotas which were set sufficiently high to be safety margins rather than effective restrictions, Portugal successfully pressed for an increase in its quota, and Greece was not penalised for substantially exceeding its informal quota in 1978. During the late 1970s, several of the Mediterranean countries were able to increase their share of the EEC clothing and textiles market at the expense of the big low-wage exporters like South Korea and Taiwan.[6]

Since none of the Mediterranean countries has aligned its external tariffs on the CCT, and most do not have any obligations to do so, the possibility of trade deflection arises. As usual, this has been tackled by the use of rules of origin, similar to those used in the EEC–EFTA agreement (see section 8.3, *Rules of origin*).

EEC CONCESSIONS ON AGRICULTURAL IMPORTS

Without concessions on agricultural products, the Mediterranean trade agreements would have had little to offer the poorer countries in the region. However, such concessions were strongly opposed by farmers in southern parts of the EEC whose range of products was similar to that of the Mediterranean countries (especially fruit and vegetables, wine, tobacco and olive oil). It was only after new safeguard measures for these farmers (e.g. distillation of surplus EEC wine) had been agreed in July 1975 that the agricultural aspects of the Mediterranean trade negotiations under the global approach were able to move ahead.

The detailed and individual arrangements with each Mediteranean country followed two main lines: (i) where the product concerned was not produced on any scale within the EEC, large tariff cuts were made (e.g. in Egypt, 80 per cent); and (ii) for competing agricultural products, measures were devised to minimise the adverse impact on European farmers, especially by exploiting the complementary seasonality of EEC and Mediterranean production. Tariff cuts were restricted to the off-season for European farmers, usually some interval between November and May. This device enabled the EEC to make concessions on products such as new potatoes, tomatoes, peas and raspberries which had previously been excluded from tariff preferences. However, the tariff preferences were usually less generous than on non-competing products, ranging between 30 and 60 per cent. For olive oil, the system of reducing the variable import levy for Mahgreb and Turkish exports under earlier agreements was continued, and the maximum permitted reduction was increased. Other safeguards to protect European farmers included import licences, minimum import prices and quotas.

The agricultural preferences negotiated under the global approach provide better export conditions for the Mediterranean countries than they had previously. In part, though, these have been obtained through trade diversion at the expense of developing countries outside the Mediterranean region. So long as the EEC continues to give top priority to the CAP and the support of European farmers, the opportunities that it can provide for Mediterranean farm exports are strictly limited. Something has been done to improve the prices received by Mediterranean suppliers at the expense of reduced tariff revenues for the EEC, but the gains in export volume are likely to be small. Furthermore, the general objective of more uniform trade arrangements for the Mediterranean countries has not been achieved. There continue to be wide variations in product coverage, the size of tariff cuts and in the timing of tariff concessions.

THE RECIPROCITY ISSUE[7]

In 1972, arrangements were being finalised for industrial free trade between the EEC and the EFTA countries, including Portugal. French Minister Schumann suggested that the same formula of free trade could be offered to Spain and Israel. This led on to the idea that all the Mediterranean countries should be invited to take part in a free trade area with the EEC, negotiated under the global approach. There were criticisms of the idea both within the Community and outside. The US had for long been opposed to special preference schemes in favour of selected countries. In the face of obvious EEC determination to pursue its global approach to Mediterranean trade policy, the US concentrated its attack on what it saw as the most objectionable feature: the reverse preferences in favour of EEC exports. The US took the view that the southern Mediterranean countries would never be able to dismantle all their restrictions on EEC goods, as would be required in a free trade area. The likely outcome was that the EEC would benefit from partial preferences to the detriment of both US exports and the GATT trading system. To strengthen its attack, the US warned that any Mediterranean country which offered the EEC reverse preference would be considered ineligible for the US version of the GSP.

It quickly became clear, in any case, that reciprocity would be too arduous for the southern Mediterranean countries: the dismantling of restrictions on EEC imports would worsen their balance of trade, destroy jobs and impose a setback on industrialisation plans. Consequently, the EEC settled for most-favoured-nation treatment from the Mahgreb and Mashreq countries and, later, Yugoslavia. From the more developed countries, and especially those with which it had negotiated customs union agreements (Greece, Turkey, Malta and Cyprus), the EEC continued in principle to demand full reciprocity. However, the agreed timetables for tariff dismantling have proved to be too ambitious, and postponements have occurred under the agreements with Portugal, Turkey and Israel, whilst Malta and Cyprus have had to delay moving on to the next stage in their Association Agreements (scheduled for 1976 and 1977, respectively) which would have required the total abolition of all tariffs on EEC exports.

In short, instead of the network of free trade area links

envisaged initially in the global approach, the EEC's Mediterranean trade agreements seem likely to involve full reciprocity only for Israel outside the EEC, and Greece, Spain and Portugal within. Partial reciprocity exists for Turkey, Malta and Cyprus, but for the other Mediterranean countries the global approach has created a one-way preference system.

FINANCIAL AID AND OTHER FORMS OF COOPERATION

The limited industrial base of the Mediterranean countries, their emphasis on products like textiles which are regarded as sensitive by the EEC, and the continued priority given to the maintenance of the CAP, all conspire to restrict the advantages that the Mediterranean countries can derive from purely trade agreements with the EEC. In the global approach, therefore, the Community tried to reinforce the trade measures with various forms of cooperation, especially financial aid. Indeed, the Mediterranean agreements are styled 'Cooperation Agreements'. The financial aid programmes ran initially for three to five years, and involved a mixture of commercial loans, loans on easy terms and grants. The programmes were renewed in 1981 (see Table 9.2), with some shift in emphasis towards subsidised loans through the European Investment Bank and away from soft loans organised by the Commission. EEC aid *per capita* in the recipient countries remains very small, and its distribution reflects the particular relationship of a country with the EEC rather than its degree of poverty; priority has been given to countries like Portugal that are potential members of the Community.

9.3 The recent development of the Mediterranean countries' trade with the EEC

The key trade issue in any assessment of the EEC's global approach to its Mediterranean policy is the extent to which bilateral trade developments have been influenced by the preferential trade agreements. Apart from Spain and Israel in the last few years, the non-oil exporting countries of the Mediterranean have had persistent, and often very large, deficits on their trade with the member countries of the EEC. These deficits arise particularly in relation to chemicals and machinery, where only Spain (in machinery) and Israel (in chemicals) have anything approaching a balanced trade with the EEC, even with the

Table 9.2   *EEC financial aid for the Mediterranean countries*

Mediterranean countries	Grants	Special loans	European Investment Bank	Total	Time period
		million ECU			
Mahgreb	132	82	275	489	1982–87
Mashreq	128	73	285	486	1982–87
Israel	—	—	40	40	1982–87
Total	260	155	600	1015	
Turkey	50	325	225	600	*
Malta/Cyprus	11	9	36	56	1978/9–1983/4
Portugal	—	—	200	200	1981
Yugoslavia	—	—	200	200	1980–85

Source: Commission of the EC, *Fifteenth General Report*, 1982, p. 267.
* Not yet implemented.

deliberately unbalanced tariff arrangements. For other types of manufactured goods, most of the northern Mediterranean countries are in balance or run a surplus on their trade with the EEC, and their position has improved considerably over the last decade, thanks largely to a big increase in their textiles and clothing exports. On food products, the EEC's trade concessions have been insufficient to prevent a deterioration in the relative trade position of the Mediterranean countries as a group; this is most notable for the Mahgreb countries. Only Israel, in a limited way, has managed to swim against the tide.

Without preferential treatment under the global approach, the Mediterranean countries' export performance in the EEC market might have been substantially worse. Some indication of this can be obtained by comparing the development of the Mediterranean countries' import share in the EEC market with their share in other developed country markets between 1970 and 1979, a period spanning the introduction of the trade agreements under the global approach. A superior performance in the EEC market may reflect in part the effects of the special trade preferences, though as ever the results of a residual imputation approach need to be treated with great caution (see section 4.2).

In view of the diversity of the Mediterranean countries it is helpful to consider separately Greece, Spain and Portugal; the Mahgreb and Mashreq countries; and Yugoslavia.

GREECE, SPAIN AND PORTUGAL
During the 1970s exporters in Greece, Spain and Portugal were

increasingly successful in the EEC market, which now absorbs two-thirds of their foreign sales. By 1977–79, their combined exports of food and manufactured goods to the EEC were some $2000 million a year (40 per cent) higher than if they had kept only the same share of the EEC import market as in 1970–72. In some cases (e.g. transport equipment), there was a similarly strong performance in non-EEC markets, suggesting a general improvement in competitiveness. In other sectors, and especially clothing and textiles, Greece, Spain and Portugal were much more successful in increasing their import penetration in the EEC than outside. This differential performance was particularly marked during the latter part of the decade. Overall, manufactured and semi-manufactured exports to the EEC were 58 per cent higher in 1977-79 than might have been expected on the basis of their performance during the decade in non-EEC developed country markets. The corresponding figure for food exports was a gain of 21 per cent (see Table 9.3). These results lend some support to the view that preferential treatment has helped the three countries concerned to increase their share of the EEC market, although they do not disclose whether this was due to trade creation or to trade diversion.

THE MAHGREB AND MASHREQ COUNTRIES
The combined exports from the Mahgreb and Mashreq countries are dominated by fuels and raw materials, and the most important factor affecting export earnings during the 1970s was the increase in oil prices. However, starting from a small base, exports of manufactured and semi-manufactured goods have grown rapidly, especially textiles and clothing. Their share of the EEC market has increased substantially, which would be consistent with a positive effect from EEC preferences. A different picture emerges for agricultural goods. The share of the Mahgreb and Mashreq countries in total EEC imports fell from 7.1 per cent in 1963 to 4.6 per cent in 1970, and further to 2.5 per cent in 1979, whereas in the non-EEC developed countries their import share was stable. This reflects, in part, the deliberate attempt by the Mahgreb countries to diversify their export markets away from their heavy dependence on France.

YUGOSLAVIA
Yugoslavia's share of the EEC's imports of agricultural and manufactured goods fell by 50 and 25 per cent respectively during the 1970s, and exports became more heavily concentrated in the

Table 9.3 Changes in the share of Mediterranean countries in EEC imports during the 1970s

Exporting country:	Annual imports of EEC(9), 1977–79			Share of EEC imports in 1977–79 as percentage of share in 1970–72				
	GPS	Y	M & M	GPS	Y	M & M	GPS	Y
	$ million			actual			adjusted[b]	
Product group[a]								
1 fuels & raw materials	900	270	5330	80	86	90	126	120
2 food	2 500	200	720	103	48	67	121	40
3 semi-manufactures	3 220	560	410	169	69	145	135	69
4 manufactures ex 5	2 240	660	440	132	69	194	172	47
5 machinery & transport equipment	2 380	410	100	173	124	173	142	229
Total	11 240	2100	7000	132	74	93	145	77

Source: Commission of EC, *EC World Trade: a statistical analysis 1963–1979*, Luxembourg, 1981.

Notes:

GPS: Greece, Portugal and Spain; Y: Yugoslavia; M & M Mahgreb and Mashreq.

[a] Import shares calculated on a disaggregated basis as follows: for GPS and Y (1) 2 groups: fuels and raw materials, (2) 2 groups: primary food and processed food, (3) 1 group, (4) 3 groups: non-durable, semi-durable and durable manufactures, (5) 4 groups, machinery, cars, other transport equipment, parts and accessories; for M & M (1) 2 groups fuel, raw materials, (2) 2 groups primary food and processed food; (3), (4), (5) 1 group each.

[b] Adjusted by weighted changes in import shares in USA, Japan and other industrial countries 1970–72 to 1977–79, with weights based on imports from relevant group of Mediterranean countries in 1970–72. Adjusted data are not given for the Mahgreb and Mashreq countries because, apart from fuel, their exports to industrial countries other than the EEC were very small.

COMECON market. There were some industrial sectors which achieved a greater penetration of the EEC market (e.g. parts and accessories for transport equipment) but the two main commodity groups, semi-manufactures and semi-durable consumer goods, both lost ground. Some blame can be laid on particular EEC import restrictions, (e.g. on beef from 1974 onwards) and Yugoslavia may have suffered trade-diversion losses in relation to more favourably treated exporters in other Mediterranean countries, though Yugoslavia itself was a GSP beneficiary. A more general problem seems to be that Yugoslav exporters on the one hand were unable to match the production and marketing skills of rival western European firms, but on the other hand were not able to adopt the arbitrary price-cutting tactics of East European state enterprises.[8] The growing trade deficit with the EEC prompted the negotiation of a preferential trade agreement with the Community in 1980.

The very tentative conclusion that may be drawn from this analysis is that the agreements under the global approach may have been of some benefit in the 1970s to the Mediterranean countries' exports of manufactures, especially textiles and clothing, but the impact on agricultural exports appears to have been less, and confined to Greece, Spain and Portugal. In the reverse direction, EEC exports for the most part obtained only most-favoured-nation treatment in the Mediterranean countries. However, where there were preferences for EEC goods (e.g. in Israel and Spain), there is no apparent evidence that EEC exports have fared any better in the latter part of the 1970s than, for example, US exports.

9.4 The Second Enlargement of the EEC and its implications for trade

During the course of the negotiations on the global approach, the relationship between the EEC and the Mediterranean countries stood to be fundamentally changed when first Greece in 1975 and then Spain and Portugal in 1977 applied for full EEC membership. The inclusion of these three more advanced Mediterranean countries would not only increase the size of the Community—the combined populations, for instance, would rise from 260 millions to 320 millions—but would also alter its internal balance, by strengthening the voice of the less-developed southern regions.

Each of the applicant countries had *per capita* incomes well below the Community average, though rapid industrialisation was narrowing the gap. Each would bring a large, semi-subsistence, Mediterranean-type agricultural sector into the EEC. Under the system of Community preference, there would be potentially trade-diverting consequences for other, non-member Mediterranean countries. The trade interests of the latter might also be threatened by the greater influence that the EEC's own Mediterranean population would have in shaping future EEC trade policies.

The motivation for the membership applications from Greece, Spain and Portugal was primarily political. Having recently thrown off right-wing dictatorships, EEC membership would confirm their position in the mainstream of western European political life, and help to underpin their newly reinstated parliamentary democracies. By joining the EEC, the applicants would gain a voice in determining policies which already had a powerful influence on their economies. Furthermore, in a world of resurgent protectionism, their future economic development might depend on having security of access to the huge EEC market, which currently absorbed more than half of the applicants' exports.[10]

THE TERMS OF ENTRY FOR GREECE

Greece became a full member on 1 January 1981, having served a twenty-years apprenticeship under its Association Agreement with the EEC. The Greek market had been partly opened up to EEC exports through the halving of tariffs, and most Greek goods had duty-free access to the Community market. Against this background, and with the example of the first EEC enlargement in mind, a short transition period of five years was fixed for full membership. By 1986, Greece would:

- abolish its remaining customs duties on EEC goods,
- align its external tariffs on the CCT,
- take part in the EEC's Generalised Scheme of Preferences,
- phase out its import deposit scheme (by 1984),
- remove the quotas on imports from the EEC (immediately).

In return, the Community agreed to eliminate its few remaining tariffs on Greek steel exports by the end of the transition period, and to extend the CAP to Greek agriculture. Farm support prices in Greece would be brought into line with those under the CAP within five years, with border taxes (accession compensatory amounts) being used to offset EEC–Greek price differences until parity was achieved. At the EEC's behest, a longer (seven-year) transition period applies to peaches and tomatoes, where Greek production is particularly competitive. As a result of the agricultural support measures, regional development assistance and other measures, Greece has become a net recipient of funds from the European Budget to the extent of 120 million ECU in 1981, 600 million ECU in 1982 and a forecast 800 million ECU in 1983.

In view of the economic recession and the backward state of much of the Greek economy, Greece's terms of entry to the EEC now appear over-optimistic, certainly in the light of the initial trade experience as a member of the Community. The trade deficit with the EEC widened, and the balance of trade in agricultural products switched from surplus to deficit. A new Greek government came to power in November 1981, threatening to take the country out of the EEC. In contravention of EEC rules, it took measures to restrict trade 'amounting indeed to a general control of agricultural imports, especially of livestock products'.[11] This was accompanied in March 1982 by a memorandum in which the Greek government claimed that EEC membership was either exacerbating the country's problems or making their solution more difficult, and called for increased financial aid and a temporary derogation for Greece from Community competition rules (e.g. on state aids, including export aids for small and medium sized firms).[12]

The EEC Commission has acknowledged the severe difficulties faced by Greece but has pointed out that many are of long standing, and that all member countries have to cope with the problems caused by the present economic crisis.[13] With full commitment from Greece, the Commission argued that a solution could be achieved within the framework of EEC rules, especially under the Integrated Mediterranean Programme. The Commission's proposals under this programme envisage a wide range of agricultural, infrastructural and small business measures, at a cost to the European Budget of 2542 million ECU.[14] In addition, the Commission put forward proposals in March 1983 for more immediate action which could be taken to help Greece, for example, aid for irrigation.[15]

ENTRY NEGOTIATIONS FOR SPAIN AND PORTUGAL

Negotiations over Spanish and Portuguese membership of the EEC began in 1979, but the negotiations did not get to grips with the key problems until 1984. The latter involved (i) how to curb the additional costs to the European Budget resulting from the extension of the CAP to the applicant countries; (ii) how to ensure that the livelihood of farmers in southern France and Italy is not undermined by a flood of low-cost produce from Spain; (iii) how to balance the claims of the EEC and the applicants for a rapid transition to free trade where their industries are strong and for a long period of adjustment where their industries are weak; and (iv) how to protect the interests of non-applicant Mediterranean countries. In June 1984, it was reported that agreement had been reached on outline terms for Spanish membership of the EEC in 1986. These included a ten-year transition for Spain's highly competitive fruit and vegetables, with no dismantling of EEC tariffs during an initial four-year period, and a six-year transition period towards tariff- and quota-free access for EEC industrial products into Spain.

THE EFFECTS OF THE SECOND ENLARGEMENT ON EEC (9) IMPORTS

For those countries which were members of the EEC before 1981—the EEC (9)—the most important effects of the Second Enlargement on their imports of *manufactured goods* would occur in relation to Spain. This is partly because of the much larger Spanish industrial sector but also because Greek and Portuguese goods already enjoy largely tariff-free access to the EEC market whereas Spanish goods still face customs duties (at 50 per cent of the CCT rates). The main problem for the EEC (9) is that Spain's considerable industrial strength lies in those sectors like textiles, shoes and steel where EEC (9) industry is in decline. Trade creation in these sectors would exacerbate the difficult adjustment problems currently faced by existing EEC producers, who have demanded a long transition period for Spanish entry with stringent safeguard measures. EEC industrial restructuring measures will be extended to the new members; Spain is under pressure from the EEC not to increase its steel-making capacity prior to joining the Community.

In the longer term, there is a fear that the comparative advantage possessed by Greece, Spain and Portugal (the three) in labour-intensive industries like textiles may not persist as wage rates rise towards the level of those in other EEC countries and as more developing countries embark on industrialisation. The EEC might then be faced with the same kind of costly adjustment problem in the new member countries as is now occurring in the northern parts of the Community,[16] and protectionist pressures in the Community would be intensified.

At the same time, the importance of EEC entry for Spain's industrial exports should not be overstated: Spain has achieved an impressive increase in its sales to the Community even with relatively unfavourable conditions of access compared with other European suppliers. Its likely future export successes in, for example, cars, appliances and electronics will probably owe much more to decisions by multinational companies about their global spread of operations and rivalry with other large companies than to the abolition of the remaining restrictions on Spain's trade with the EEC.[17]

Before 1981, none of the three had unrestricted access to the EEC market for their *agricultural products,* and their full participation in the CAP is expected to lead to important trade and agricultural policy effects.[18] Trade creation is likely for products such as fruit and vegetables, wine and olive oil, bringing benefits for consumers but depressing farmers' incomes, especially in Italy and southern France where these products account for a large share of farm output. Dutch horticulturalists growing crops under glass may also be affected. All these farmers fear that enlargement may, over a period of years, depress the prices that they receive for their products. Enlargement would increase the EEC's self-sufficiency in Mediterranean products, leading to costly export disposal measures and attempts to curb the Budget costs through price restraint. These products, in the view of Mediterranean farmers, already have a lower margin of support than that given to farm output in the northern part of the EEC.

For the European Budget, the most difficult enlargement problems would concern olive oil, where the present EEC is already self-sufficient; Spanish accession would double EEC production. The Commission has estimated that the extra cost of market support for olive oil in a Community of twelve countries would be 780 million ECU a year,[19] and this would intensify pressure for the EEC to restrict access to its market for imports of substitute oil and fats, a move which is strongly resisted by the US. There is concern amongst non-member countries, especially in the Mediterranean, that their agricultural exports to the EEC may be damaged by trade diversion as membership of the Community stimulates higher-cost marginal production in the three countries, and particularly in Spain (see *The effects of enlargement on non-EEC Mediterranean countries,* below).

THE EFFECTS OF ENLARGEMENT ON EEC EXPORTS TO GREECE, SPAIN AND PORTUGAL

Although Greece, Spain and Portugal have export surpluses of some foodstuffs, overall Spain and Portugal are net importers of *agricultural products,* and Greece is little more than self-sufficient. Membership of the EEC would lead the three countries to purchase substantially more of their food imports from the EEC, especially butter, certain cereals, meat and (except for Greece) sugar. These imports would be trade-diverting, displacing low-cost imports from third countries and they would inflate the food import bill of the three because payment would be at EEC, rather than world, prices. In turn, this would benefit the European Budget since exports to the three would not have to be subsidised, and the costs of export disposal from the EEC (9) would fall.

For *industrial exports,* the implications of enlargement are rather different since Greece and Portugal were already committed under existing agreements to admit EEC goods duty-free by 1984 and 1985 respectively, and, as Tsoukalis argues, Spain would have had to follow suit because the preservation of the *status quo* was unacceptable to the Community.[20] The three have maintained relatively high levels of tariff and quota protection, even on imports from the EEC which have benefited from partial cuts in tariffs. Deprived of this protection, many industries in the three could founder: in Greece fears have been expressed about the prospects for the transport equipment, electrical and mechanical engineering industries; and in Spain the vulnerable industries include electrical appliances, industrial and agricultural machinery, office equipment and chemical products.[21] A particular difficulty in the three may be the very fragmented nature of many industries, leading to production problems where economies of scale are important. Government financial assistance is being provided to help with restructuring, but this is likely to be a lengthy process. It should be added that small firms in the three are not necessarily inefficient and may prove to be highly adaptable; in any case, they 'often cater for local markets where the problem of import competition is not likely to arise.'[22]

Within the Community, industry in the three may face increased competition from non-EEC producers because tariffs in the three would have to be brought into line with the generally much lower CCT, leading to the possibility of external trade creation. Since the adjustment in tariffs on imports from third countries would be mainly downwards, trade diversion in industrial goods may be small, unlike the position for foodstuffs. The absolute margin of tariff preference enjoyed by EEC exports to the three could well decline.

THE EFFECTS OF ENLARGEMENT ON NON-EEC MEDITERRANEAN COUNTRIES

Although the Mediterranean countries have generally tariff-free access for their manufactures to the EEC market, their exports could be damaged by the ending of EEC tariffs on imports from Spain and by the possible introduction of new protectionist measures. The substantial clothing and textile exports from Tunisia could be at some risk as also might be exports from the Asian NICs.[23] However, the main effects of EEC enlargement would occur in relation to agricultural trade where 'the whole system of preferential agreements is likely to be disrupted.'[24] The disruption could even extend to markets outside the EEC, if enlargement led to the increased use of export subsidies to dispose of EEC surpluses. The main effects would be on exports from Israel, Tunisia and Morocco, but in relative terms the small countries like Cyprus and Malta could be hardest hit.[25]

The non-member Mediterranean countries have pressed the EEC for further trade concessions in order to offset the possible effects of enlargement. The EEC's response has been (i) to promise continued tariff-free access to its market for industrial products; (ii) to offer access for textiles as far as possible in line with the better treatment for Portuguese and Spanish goods; (iii) to adjust import regulations so as to maintain imports of Mediterranean fruit, vegetables and wine 'up to a ceiling corresponding to traditional trade flows'; and (iv) to develop other areas of cooperation. The EEC has little enough room for manoeuvre, bearing in mind its budgetary problems, the anxieties of its own Mediterranean farmers, and the trade advantages expected by the prospective new member countries. In the longer term, the Mediterranean world's relationship with the EEC will be strongly influenced by the three.

In concluding this review of the trade effects of EEC enlargement, special mention should be made of Turkey in view of its declared intention of applying for EEC membership. Turkey is concerned that its agricultural and textiles exports to the EEC may be threatened by the Second Enlargement. Its neighbour, Greece, with whom it is in dispute over a number of issues including the partition of Cyprus, is now a Community member and able to influence EEC policies directly. Turkey has been linked to the EEC since 1964 through an Association Agreement which was designed as a preparation for eventual full EEC membership. The Agreement was renegotiated in 1980, and in addition to unrestricted access for its manufactured exports to the EEC (except for quota controls on petroleum products and textiles), Turkey will obtain duty-free access for its agricultural products by 1987.

Following a military take-over in November 1980, relations between Turkey and the EEC are strained, financial aid has been suspended, and the Agreement is merely ticking over. Even without this latest difficulty, the EEC would seem to be in no shape to admit a thirteenth member whose full integration into the Community would pose formidable economic and political problems. Bearing in mind Turkey's membership of NATO and its strategic location on the USSR border, 'the case for a positive response to a Turkish application would have to rest almost entirely on military grounds.'[26]

9.5 Conclusions

During the 1970s, the EEC aimed to coordinate and to reshape its trade policies towards the Mediterranean countries under the global approach. Some success was achieved—for example, by making the treatment of the three Mahgreb and four Mashreq countries more uniform, by aligning the structure and timing of the financial aid programme and by adopting a more consistent approach to agricultural trade concessions—though considerable variation of treatment remains. In the present decade, the Second Enlargement of the EEC both facilitates and makes more difficult the task of the global approach. The entry of the three northern Mediterranean countries into the EEC would leave the non-member Mediterranean countries economically more homogeneous, thereby easing the construction of a more uniform approach. It may also help the EEC to integrate its trade agreements with the Mediterranean countries into the general framework of trade relations with developing countries. The Commission has floated the idea of a Convention for the Mediterranean countries along the lines of the Lomé Convention, though in the present political conditions this possibility seems remote. More immediately, enlargement will undermine the value of the existing Mediterranean preferences, as well as tying the hands of Community negotiators more securely: the pursuit of the global approach will become even more tricky.

The Second Enlargement, if and when completed, would have a

number of implications for EEC trade policies. In particular, it could:

- increase the importance of the EEC in world trade, and thereby its influence over world trade policies in such bodies as the GATT,
- reduce the Community's flexibility of response in relation to trade initiatives from non-member countries, since the three's interests have also to be taken into account,
- aggravate the EEC's trade relations with non-member Mediterranean countries,
- strengthen EEC protectionism in relation, for example, to the textiles trade, so as to provide trade benefits to the new members with least effect on production in the original member countries, and
- open up the possibility of stronger links between the Community and Latin America, through the influence of Spain and Portugal.

Enlargement can be expected to have important trade effects involving both trade diversion (especially at the expense of other Mediterranean countries) and trade creation. The three would be expected to increase their exports to the EEC of labour-intensive manufactures like textiles and clothing and Mediterranean-type agricultural products. In return, EEC producers expect to build up their exports of machinery and other technologically advanced manufactures. It seems likely that trade creation would be mainly inter-industry in nature, and could involve substantial adjustment costs. The Community faces possible dangers in this kind of specialisation since it may perpetuate a dualistic economic structure in the three and the EEC (9). First, the three may not represent—at least, not for long—least-cost sources for labour-intensive manufactures, and there is a longer-term danger that the EEC may become locked into protectionist pressures in order to preserve their industries. The problems of the EEC (9) would be repeated. Secondly, if the three are obliged to remove their import restrictions on all EEC goods over a short transition period, their production of more advanced manufactured products may be stunted. They may then be condemned to an unequal relationship with the rest of the Community.[27]

The evolution of the EEC's trade agreements with the Mediterranean countries seems to illustrate well one of the propositions advanced in Chapter 2 (see page 37). In the Mediterranean region there is considerable scope for inter-industry trade creation from the removal of the remaining EEC trade restrictions. As in the case of the three, however, the adjustment costs in the Community could be high, especially at a time of recession. Although, for this reason, the EEC has resisted making trade concessions likely to affect domestic producers adversely, political considerations (e.g. the need to encourage potential member countries, or to maintain balanced relations in the southern Mediterranean) have dictated that some form of trade agreement be negotiated with each of the Mediterranean countries. In these agreements the EEC has put increasing emphasis on cooperation, especially financial aid, and has structured trade concessions so as to avoid as far as possible inter-industry trade creation. In agriculture, this has meant, for example, giving stronger price guarantees to EEC producers, using tariff quotas and introducing import calendars. For textiles, voluntary export restraints and quotas have been employed. In this way the Mediterranean countries have derived some trade benefits at the expense of EEC taxpayers (reduced tariff revenues, increased surplus disposal costs) and through trade diversion against suppliers in the rest of the world, with the least possible damage to EEC producer interests and to short-term employment prospects.

10 EEC Trade Policies Towards Developing Countries

10.1 Introduction: trade and economic development

Trade policies towards developing countries are a central element in the EEC's attempt to construct a Community approach towards Third World development issues, especially over the last decade. The EEC Commission has suggested that a common development policy is a 'cornerstone of European integration' which should complement rather than displace national measures to assist Third World countries.[1] The national and Community approaches are distinct in that trade measures are, or should be, determined exclusively at Community level, whereas the bulk of the EEC countries' development aid is provided on a bilateral, member country basis rather than through the Community. Trade policy is then the key area in which the Community as such can bring its influence to bear on the immense task of generating a sustained improvement in the economic condition of the Third World.

That economic condition is most readily revealed by the low level of average *per capita* incomes in developing countries, signifying the meagre command over goods and services which their inhabitants possess. In 1980, it was estimated that some 2400 million people were living in the 48 countries whose annual incomes averaged below $500 per person (US average, $11,700). These average figures inevitably conceal a tremendous variety of individual circumstances, and it is important to bear in mind that Third World conditions range from utter destitution to near prosperity, from debilitating decline to rapid advancement. Nevertheless, through this diversity certain general characteristics emerge:

(i) The bulk of the population is engaged in subsistence or semi-subsistence agriculture, and there is relatively little industrial or service employment.

(ii)   There is much rural underemployment and, especially in the burgeoning urban conglomerations, heavy unemployment.

(iii)   Infrastructural provisions such as communications, power supplies and waste disposal systems are rudimentary and subject to frequent breakdowns.

(iv)   Standards of clothing, housing and education are low.

(v)   The margin of survival for the mass of the population is precarious and hinges on individual family efforts and vicissitudes; state welfare systems are minimal or non-existent.

(vi)   Malnutrition, hunger and even starvation are widespread.

(vii)   The provision of health care is sparse, disease is often endemic and mortality rates, especially among babies and small children, are high; but birth rates are even higher and most developing countries are experiencing rapid population growth, so that in the two decades to the end of this century it is estimated that the combined population of the Third World will rise from 3.5 to 5 billions.

In these circumstances it is not surprising that economic development is avidly espoused by the poor countries. The global experience shows, however, that there is no universal formula by which development can be achieved in a short space of time. In the best of circumstances, it is likely to take the least developed countries several generations to reach the levels of material prosperity currently enjoyed in the West, even if the world's resources were capable of supporting this. This reality contrasts harshly with Third World expectations.

The possible routes to development are several. One inward-looking approach, concentrating on self-help, is to reduce dependence on trade by developing home industries to produce substitutes for imports. This approach may only be effective in promoting growth in the larger countries whose markets are big enough to allow production to achieve the necessary economies of scale. It was widely discredited when attempted by a number of countries during the 1950s, but has renewed its appeal as a result of the recent stagnation in world trade.

The alternative to import-substitution is a more outward-looking system, based on the exploitation of comparative and absolute advantages through specialisation and trade. A country's consumption of some goods which could be produced only at relatively high cost is met by imports, and these are obtained in return for exports of goods which the country produces relatively efficiently. A possible drawback of this approach, especially if there are capital constraints, is that it may consign developing countries to exporting primary products and unsophisticated manufactures which in the past have been relatively undynamic areas of world trade. Further, it may not bring about the industrialisation to which the developing countries aspire.

For all except the large developing countries like India, it seems safe to say that economic development must have a substantial import content. The expansion of power supplies, for example, may require imported equipment whose production is technologically sophisticated, capital-intensive and uneconomic on a small scale. The import bill for development may be heavy even without the massive food purchases which some countries have been obliged to make in order to meet basic subsistence requirements. This bill has to be paid for with foreign exchange obtained from three main sources: export earnings, private capital flows and aid from foreign governments or multilateral agencies like the World Bank. Aid in the form of grants has the attraction to developing countries that there is no resource cost involved, but a combination of recession, political bias and western disillusion with past aid programmes has meant that the rich countries have not in general reached the aid targets set by the United Nations. Private capital flows are an important source of foreign exchange for developing countries but are fraught with difficulties, including the mutual suspicion of multinational companies and the governments of developing countries. Moreover, in the wake of the massive debt problems of Mexico, Brazil and Argentina in the early 1980s, it has become much more difficult for developing countries to borrow from the world banking system in order to fund their import bills, even for investment goods.

With aid and private capital flows in limited supply, developing countries must make their earnings from exports cover a large part of their import bills. However, the export experience of developing countries over the last three decades has, on the whole, been unfavourable. The reasons for this are an important element in any assessment of EEC trade policies since they influence the contribution which these policies could make towards Third World development.[2]

10.2 Trade problems of developing countries

The export problem of developing countries has been caused partly by inadequate supply: export production has not increased sufficiently fast because of various constraints, including the food demands resulting from rapid population growth and misguided government policies. Another part of the problem has been structural, in particular the concentration of exports on primary products for which the import demand in developed countries has grown slowly in volume terms during the post-war period, particularly in comparison with the dynamic growth of trade in manufactures during the 1950s and 1960s. The slow growth has a number of causes including: (a) the low income elasticity of demand for food in the rich countries; (b) increased competition from synthetic substitutes for products like natural rubber and cotton; (c) rapid productivity advances in agriculture in the rich countries enabling greater self-sufficiency in food; and (d) agricultural support policies in Europe, USA and Japan.

The effect of the slow growth in the volume of trade in primary products has been exacerbated at times for developing countries by falling prices for primary products relative to those of manufactured goods. It is however difficult to generalise about the developing countries' (net barter) terms of trade in the period from 1950 to 1973 because of periodic price booms—notably the Korean War boom of 1951–52, and the commodity price boom of 1973–74—making the result very sensitive to the precise time–period chosen; and the general problem of how to take proper account of improvements in the quality of manufactured goods. Since 1973, the developing countries have had to cope with a new and formidable terms-of-trade problem following the rapid escalation of oil prices.

Another concern of developing countries has been the year-to-year variability of their earnings from primary products due to short-term and cyclical shifts in demand and, especially, supply. These shifts have an amplified effect on world market prices because both demand and supply for primary products tend to be price inelastic. Developing countries are particularly vulnerable to unstable trading conditions because they have few foreign exchange reserves with which to cushion themselves against fluctuations in export earnings. Even though it has not been easy to demonstrate empirically that these fluctuations have a negative effect on economic growth in developing countries,[3] the instability of commodity markets remains a major policy concern of developing countries.

A few developing countries have been able to escape to some extent from the trade problems of primary products by building up their exports of manufactured goods to the rich countries. Starting from a low base, Third World exports of manufactures have grown rapidly in recent years, but most of the trade is concentrated in the hands of a few more advanced countries, the newly industrialising countries (NICs). The product range has tended to be narrow, focusing especially on areas like textiles and footwear, and this has prompted a growing protectionist reaction in the developed countries, resulting in the use of import quotas and the so-called voluntary export restraints. Protectionism has also handicapped developing countries seeking to add value to their raw material exports through processing. The rate of tariff applied in the rich countries tends to increase with the stage of processing (tariff escalation), giving a high rate of effective protection to their processing industries.[4]

10.3 Towards a New International Economic Order?

The number of independent developing countries increased markedly in the first two decades following the second world war, with the formal decolonisation of large parts of Africa and Asia. Political independence raised economic expectations, and led to a growing demand for fundamental changes in the economic relationship between rich and poor countries. In the view of many developing countries, a key impediment to their economic advancement was the existing system of world trade, based on the rules set out in the GATT. These rules were, it was claimed, fundamentally inappropriate to their needs. The kernel of their argument was that a system based on reciprocity left developing countries, whose markets were generally small and economically fragile, in a very weak bargaining position, and that the GATT's non-discrimination principle was not enough to ensure that developing countries benefited through trade with the rich countries. Instead, a system of positive discrimination in favour of developing countries was needed. The GATT was viewed as an organisation which served the interests of those countries which were already developed—a 'rich man's club'—and developing countries began to look elsewhere for a forum in which to advance their interests.

With the designation of the 1960s as the United Nation's first Development Decade, there was pressure from Third World countries for a special conference to discuss their trade and development problems. Despite opposition from some of the rich countries to a new trade forum outside the GATT, the first United Nations Conference on Trade and Development (UNCTAD) was held in 1964. The conference took the decision to establish UNCTAD as a permanent, global organisation with its own Secretariat. The first UNCTAD Secretary-General, Raúl Prebisch, played a key role in shaping and expounding a Third World view of trade and development issues which challenged western orthodoxy. In his Address to the 1964 conference he argued that the decline in the terms of trade of primary producers in the 1950s was not just a temporary aberration, but would become a persistent feature of the world economy. Its causes included, in Prebisch's view, the low income elasticity of demand for food in the rich countries, the substitution of synthetic materials for natural products and, much more contentiously, the monopolistic organisation of industry in the developed countries.[5] If unchecked, these factors would lead to an alarming growth in the trade imbalance and external indebtedness of the Third World. Accordingly, world trade policies needed to be revamped. In particular, Prebisch argued that the developed countries should assist the poor countries in relation to their terms of trade problems in two ways: (i) by setting up international commodity agreements (ICAs) which would ensure that developing countries received 'equitable' prices for their exports and would give them a guarantee of access to markets; and (ii) by establishing compensatory finance schemes which would transfer funds to developing countries in order to offset the balance of payments effects of falling commodity prices. Prebisch also recommended that the exports of manufactured goods from developing countries should be boosted by establishing regional groups of developing countries within which tariff preferences would be granted, and a system of non-reciprocal tariff preferences under which exports of manufactures from developing countries would be admitted tariff-free to the markets of the rich countries for a period of ten years.

The initial responses of the rich countries to the demands made in UNCTAD were disorganised, generally hostile and dominated by short-term considerations of self-interest, but, very slowly, some elements of Prebisch's programme have been implemented, including the introduction of non-reciprocal tariff preferences by a number of developed countries, including the EEC, in 1971–72.

These measures are the result of immense international efforts over two decades including an 'endless stream of conferences, charters and resolutions.'[6] UNCTAD itself has become an effective lobby on behalf of developing countries and has organised a series of rather unwieldy set-piece conferences (in 1964, 1968, 1972, 1976, 1979 and 1983).

In April 1974, the Sixth Special Session of the United Nations called for the establishment of a New International Economic Order (NIEO) and set out a programme which included many of Prebisch's earlier proposals such as ICAs (this time as the Integrated Programme for Commodities). Despite the efforts of the 1975–77 Paris Conference (on international economic cooperation), the Brandt Committee, and the informal Cancun Summit in 1981, little has been achieved, although a watered-down version of the Integrated Programme for Commodities has been agreed (see section 12.5, *The IPC*). The attempt to launch global North–South negotiations, proposed in 1979, remained grounded in 1984, the chief reason for this lack of progress over the last decade being the western economic slowdown: the US in particular has argued that little can be done to help the developing countries until the West's economic fortunes recover.[7]

10.4 The EEC's dual approach

The response of the EEC and its member countries to Third World demands for a NIEO has had two dimensions.[8] The Community considers that it has tried to play a constructive part in the dialogue between North (the rich countries of North America, Europe and Japan) and South (the developing countries), and claims that it has endeavoured at least to match the generosity of trade measures taken by other rich countries in favour of the South. Thus, the Community was the first to implement the UN's Generalised System of Preferences (GSP), has taken part in most ICAs, and supports the Common Fund for the Integrated Programme for Commodities. (These measures are discussed in Chapter 12.) Secondly, the EEC has taken particular actions to help the developing countries of Africa, where the member states see themselves as having a special responsibility. Under the Lomé Convention, the African countries are entitled to preferential tariff treatment, a compensatory finance scheme and EEC financial aid. (This Convention is the focus of Chapter 11.)

The two main trade instruments employed by the EEC and

other rich countries in favour of developing countries are non-reciprocal tariff preferences and international commodity agreements. The latter are examined in section 12.5; the trade implications of tariff preferences are considered in section 10.5.

10.5 Non-reciprocal tariff preferences

EEC trade policy is characterised by a complex layering of tariff preferences. The essence of these preferences is that they discriminate between imports according to their country of origin, so that the tariffs imposed on imports from one (more preferred) source are lower than the tariffs charged on similar goods from another (less preferred) source. The distinguishing feature of the EEC's use of tariff preferences in its trade relations with developing countries is that they are *non-reciprocal*. This means that developing countries are not expected in return to grant EEC exports any special tariff advantages, and are free to impose tariffs on goods from the EEC in order either to protect their own producers or to raise government revenue, as long as EEC products are not treated more harshly than imports from other developed countries.

The EEC operates two schemes of non-reciprocal tariff preferences in favour of developing countries: (a) the Community's version of the GSP, which is extended to all developing countries but is confined mainly to manufactured goods; and (b) the Lomé Convention, which covers all products but is confined mainly to African countries. In practice, most of the African exports which receive tariff-free treatment are primary products.

THE POTENTIAL BENEFITS OF TARIFF PREFERENCES TO THE RECIPIENT COUNTRIES

Non-reciprocal tariff preferences may involve the EEC in some losses to producers in protected industries as well as a decline in tariff revenue on imports from developing countries without offering the Community, in the short run at least, any offsetting commercial advantages on its exports. The EEC is prepared to accept this loss as a gesture of support to developing countries who have pleaded for 'trade not aid'. The hope is that non-reciprocal tariff preferences will help to stimulate economic development in the beneficiary countries through an increase in their export earnings, in two ways: (i) because developing countries are encouraged to increase the volume of their exports to the EEC, and (ii) because developing countries are able to charge a higher price for their existing exports.

Conceptually, an *increase in the volume of exports* could come about in two ways. The first is that preferences help developing countries' goods compete more vigorously against EEC production since they remove the price disadvantage of the tariff that previously handicapped exporters in the developing countries. This is the *trade-creation effect,* as low-cost Third World goods displace higher-cost, home-produced goods in the EEC market, and as consumption is increased through lower prices to EEC consumers. Trade creation will be more extensive if developing countries' exports consist mainly of competitive goods (i.e. goods similar to those produced in the EEC) than if they are mainly complementary goods (i.e. where there is no production in the EEC). However, in view of the very different economic structures of the Community and the developing countries, the scope for trade creation may be quite limited. Even where there is an overlap, as in agriculture or textiles, trade creation may be limited by the EEC's use of safeguard measures.

The second way is through *trade diversion.* The preferences give producers in the beneficiary countries a price advantage in relation to rival producers located in countries whose exports continue to face the full EEC tariff. Higher-cost production from the preference-receiving countries may then displace EEC imports from lower-cost, but less preferred, sources. Trade diversion will be potentially greater where the range of goods produced in the beneficiary countries is complementary to that produced in the EEC, but its extent will also depend crucially on how exclusive the preference system is. The more countries there are in the system, the fewer countries there are whose goods are discriminated against, and the less likelihood there is of trade diversion. From the developing countries' point of view, this is a particular weakness of the EEC's non-reciprocal tariff preferences: there are relatively few countries whose exports to the EEC face the full tariff.

In addition to the volume effect, non-reciprocal tariff preferences may enable the developing countries to *raise the prices of their existing exports,* without undermining the competitiveness of their goods in the EEC market. The beneficiary countries' terms of trade are thereby improved whilst there is, correspondingly, a deliberate worsening of the EEC's terms of trade. In effect the EEC transfers part of its tariff revenue to the exporters in the beneficiary country. Taken together, the volume and price effects described represent the static, once-for-all gain to the beneficiary developing country from tariff preferences. Perhaps more importantly, an initial increase in exports resulting from the gain in competitiveness may set in train lasting *dynamic effects*. The hope is that the initial increase in exports will stimulate investment in the export sector, absorbing under-used or unemployed resources, and generating a faster rate of economic growth.

THE CASE AGAINST NON-RECIPROCAL TARIFF PREFERENCES

The introduction of tariff preferences on manufactured goods in favour of developing countries was resisted in some industrial countries and especially in the United States.[9] There were four main arguments against preferences: (i) they would reduce the efficiency with which the world's resources are used; (ii) they would weaken the GATT; (iii) they would be ineffective in stimulating developing countries' exports; and (iv) as a form of aid their distributional impact would be inequitable.

The argument that tariff preferences lead to inefficiency is based on the belief that because developing and developed countries' economies tend to be complementary rather than competitive, trade diversion is likely to outweigh trade creation. However, there is some empirical evidence to suggest that in practice trade creation predominates. Furthermore, if there are divergences between private and social costs (e.g. where minimum wage rates are set in the presence of widespread unemployment) trade diversion may not reduce the efficiency with which resources are used. In any case, the static efficiency effects may be much less important than dynamic effects.

The institutional argument against preferences is that they undermine the GATT non-discrimination rule. But the GATT system may not survive unless most trading countries, including the developing countries, see it as beneficial. Nor is there convincing evidence that, as some have feared, tariff preferences create a vested interest which might slow down further multilateral reductions in tariffs: the power here remains firmly in the hands of the rich countries.

It has been argued that tariff preferences, whilst damaging the GATT, will have little effect on the export earnings of developing countries because tariffs are already generally low. But tariffs on some items of export interest to the Third World remain high, and the problem of tariff escalation is still important.

Finally, opponents of tariff preferences for developing countries have argued that if they are to be regarded as a form of aid, then the distribution between countries of that aid is inequitable. It would bear little relationship to criteria based on need, since the more successful, more advanced, developing countries would gain most. This argument cuts little ice with developing countries because, however imperfectly distributed, this form of aid would probably be additional to the aid they would otherwise receive. Furthermore, financial aid may not be as effective as tariff preferences in enabling developing countries to establish export-oriented infant industries.

Despite these misgivings, all the principal developed countries now accept that tariff preferences have a role to play in assisting the exports of developing countries, and each operates a version of the GSP giving manufactured goods from developing countries tariff-free entry to its market. The extent to which the beneficiary countries derive any advantage from these preferences depends on the detailed rules of each scheme and on the market situation for the products covered. This latter aspect is explored in the remaining part of this chapter.

THE EFFECTIVENESS OF TARIFF PREFERENCES

Whether or not a tariff preference will be effective in increasing the export earnings of the recipient country depends, amongst other things, on the relationship between export capacity in the recipient country (the African countries, in the example below) and import demand in the donor country (the EEC).[10] As the following example shows, if the export capacity is large relative to import demand for a standardised product, then the recipient country may derive no benefit from the tariff preference.

In Figure 10.1, it is assumed for simplicity that the supply of the focus good from non-African sources (S_w) to the EEC is completely elastic at the world price (Op_1) and that there is no EEC production. African export supply is given by S_A and EEC demand by D_{EEC}. With a revenue-raising non-preferential tariff of t ($=p_1p_2$),[11] the price of the good to EEC consumers is Op_2, imports are Oq_3 and EEC tariff revenue amounts to the area $(a+b+c+d)$. African exports to all destinations total Oq_1.

In these circumstances, the introduction by the EEC of a system of tariff preferences in favour of the African suppliers would have the following positive effects: (i) the African suppliers would now charge a higher price (Op_2) for their exports, without undermining their price competitiveness in relation to other suppliers; (ii) this would elicit an increase in African exports to Oq_2, all of which would be sold in the EEC since this is the only market in which they can obtain more than the world market price; (iii) EEC imports from other suppliers would fall to q_2q_3; and (iv) the EEC would lose tariff revenue on its imports from Africa, equal to area (a+b+c). The beneficial welfare consequences of these changes for the African suppliers would be twofold: a terms of trade gain on their initial export quantity of Oq_1, equal to area (a), and a producers' surplus gain on their additional exports equal to area (b), since their revenue from extra sales amounts to area (b+c+f) but against this have to be offset the extra production costs measured as area (c+f). Although the African countries have clearly benefited from their increased exports, these exports arise from trade diversion as q_1q_2 of lower-cost world supplies have been displaced by African supplies whose higher resource cost is measured by area (c).

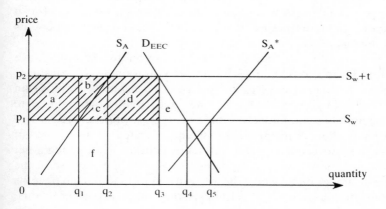

= initial tariff revenue.

Figure 10.1   The trade and welfare effects of tariff preferences

The same tariff preference system would have produced a very different result—from the African viewpoint, quite worthless—if African export supplies had been more abundant in relation to European demand. Suppose, for example, that in Figure 10.1 the African supply were shifted to the right, to S_A^*. With a non-preferential tariff (t) EEC consumption, imports and tariff revenue would remain as in the previous example, but total African exports at the world price would now amount to Oq_5. Under a system of tariff preferences, the African suppliers would be in a position to meet the whole of European demand and would have further supplies available which must be sold on the world market at the world market price. An attempt by any one of the African suppliers selling to the EEC to charge more than the world price would not succeed because it would cause other African suppliers to redirect their sales from the world to the EEC market, bringing the EEC price back to the world level.[12]

Tariff preferences in this example bring no advantages to the African producers but they tie them more closely to the EEC market. Before the preferences were introduced, African producers had no greater incentive to sell in the EEC market than elsewhere: the price they received was the same. With preferences, Africa is the sole source of supply for the EEC because only African supplies can reach EEC consumers at the world price; all other supplies are subject to tariffs and have a minimum price to EEC consumers of Op_2. It is then possible that an empirical investigation might reveal an increase in the volume of African exports going to the EEC market, but this has brought no benefits to the suppliers.

For the EEC, the introduction of tariff preferences would have the following consequences in this second example: (i) consumer prices would fall from Op_2 to Op_1 giving a consumers' surplus gain of area $(a+b+c+d+e)$; (ii) the price fall would stimulate consumption, and imports would rise to Oq_4; (iii) the EEC would lose the whole of its tariff revenue equal to area $(a+b+c+d)$; but (iv) this is exceeded by the consumers' surplus gain, giving a net welfare gain of area (e). Thus the revenue-raising purpose of the tariff is undermined whilst the African countries derive no benefits from the preferences,[13] although they may experience some redirection of trade.

This analysis also has relevance to EEC enlargement. An increase in EEC membership could expand EEC demand sufficiently to make the tariff preferences in the second example effective. But, equally, an effective arrangement could be undermined if the African supply were increased in consequence of EEC enlargement, as it was in 1975 when the Commonwealth African countries were brought into the Lomé Convention.

It has been implicit in the discussion thus far that the focus good is homogeneous, that is, that consumers regard supplies from all sources as identical and base their choice of supplier on price alone. This assumption seems broadly acceptable in relation to many of the primary products exported from Africa under the terms of the Lomé Convention. But in relation to the other EEC scheme of non-reciprocal tariff preferences (the GSP) it is more questionable. This scheme applies mainly to manufactured goods and there may be important qualitative differences between, for example, EEC and developing country goods in the same product category, so that they are not perfect substitutes.

Baldwin and Murray have examined the effect of tariff preferences for non-homogeneous goods, making the additional assumption that they are produced under conditions of constant cost.[14] Under these conditions, tariff preferences will have the potential to increase the export volume of developing countries through trade creation and trade diversion. But they will not affect the prices at which trade is conducted, unless quantitative restrictions such as voluntary export restraints are imposed. The magnitude of the trade creation and trade diversion effects will depend on how similar the beneficiary, non-beneficiary and EEC goods are in the eyes of EEC consumers—that is, on the elasticities of substitution.

11   The Lomé Convention

The Lomé Convention is the centrepiece of EEC policy towards the developing countries. At its inception in 1973 it was projected as a shining example of the innovative trade and aid arrangements demanded by the New International Economic Order. The Convention was seen as an attempt to move away from the neo-colonial exploitation of the poor by the rich to a situation of partnership and mutual respect: interdependence was to replace dependence. Much of the euphoria which greeted the signing of the Lomé Convention has now drained away as experience has shown that the partnership in practice has been elusive.

In this chapter, the origins of the Lomé Convention are reviewed briefly in section 11.1, the main economic provisions, particularly those relating to trade, are examined in section 11.2, and the effects on the trade of the participant countries are considered in section 11.3. The relationship between the Lomé Convention and the EEC's trade arrangements with other developing countries is discussed in Chapter 12.

11.1 Origins of the Lomé Convention

From a trade and aid perspective, a crucial feature of the Lomé Convention is that its membership is selective: it does not cover the EEC's relationship with developing countries in general. A subset—the associated countries—is selected for especially favourable treatment—the best trade conditions given to any countries short of full membership, plus more generous aid allocations from the EEC than for the Third World generally. The associated countries have not been chosen on the basis that they are, for example, the poorest and least developed countries in the world. Certainly, the Lomé Convention covers many countries, including those in sub-Saharan Africa, which are extremely impoverished but equally there are many very poor and populous countries which are excluded—Bangladesh, for instance. Instead, membership has been determined on the basis of historical-political factors, dressed up in a geographical cloak: the African, Caribbean and Pacific (ACP) countries.

To understand the reasons why the ACP countries receive special trade and aid conditions from the EEC, it is necessary to go back to the founding of the Community in 1958.[1] At that time, France and Belgium—two of the original EEC (6)—still had extensive colonial possessions in Africa and elsewhere. Their cultural and economic importance was considerable, especially to France which had investments in French-speaking Africa exceeding $1 billion.[2] Accordingly, France was adamant in its refusal to subject its imports from the colonies—built up as part of a free interchange of goods—to the EEC's common external tariff. Yet it was incompatible with the concept of a customs union to allow one member country alone to trade on a preferential basis with non-member countries. To add to the difficulties facing the EEC (6), Germany and the Netherlands were opposed in principle to discriminatory trade policies towards the developing countries and wanted the EEC instead to adopt a global approach to development issues.

In face of strong French pressure, the solution embodied in the Treaty of Rome was to continue the preferential trade links between France and her colonies, but to extend these to other EEC members. Thus Germany and Italy, for example, were required to give special treatment to goods imported from the French colonies (the 'Overseas Countries and Territories'), which were said to be 'associated' with the Community.[3] This arrangement was temporary in that the Implementing Convention was for five years only. Before it had expired, most of the African countries had become independent and their national governments pressed the EEC to extend the special relationship, probably more because of its political significance than for its economic success which was as yet unproven. The EEC acquiesced, and a new agreement, the Yaoundé Convention, was signed in 1963 which continued the membership and main provisions of the previous association. When this eventually expired in 1970, it was replaced by a second Yaoundé Convention, on similar lines to the first, which ran until 1975.

The next major step in the development of the association arrangements came with the British application for EEC membership. One of the key issues for negotiation was what to do about the Commonwealth countries which, under the system of Commonwealth Preference, had been able to export tariff-free to the British market. Many of these countries were extremely poor and some depended heavily on their sales to the UK. Britain accepted that EEC membership required that Commonwealth Preference as such would have to be phased out, but insisted on special arrangements for the developing countries in the Commonwealth.

A solution offering association to all of these countries was ruled out. However, in Article 58 of the Yaoundé Convention the EEC had stated that it would consider requests for association under the Convention from any state with an economic structure and production comparable to those of the existing associates, in consultation with the latter. On this basis, Nigeria (in 1966) and Kenya, Tanzania and Uganda (in 1968–69) did indeed negotiate associate status.

The EEC's definition of comparability in economic structure and production was stretched to include all the Commonwealth African countries plus the Commonwealth island states in the Caribbean and Pacific. The Asian Commonwealth countries— Bangladesh, India, Malaysia, Pakistan, Singapore, and Sri Lanka—plus Hong Kong were, however, considered non-associable. Ostensibly, the reason was that their economic situation was different from that of the African countries. The more likely reason was that their inclusion would have so diluted the association system as to make it of little value: of the main developing countries, only the Latin American countries and China would have remained outside.

After considering various alternative forms of relationship with the Community, twenty African, Caribbean and Pacific Commonwealth countries,[4] together with the existing Yaoundé Convention countries and four other African states,[5] negotiated an association agreement with the EEC in 1973. This was known as the Lomé Convention and was in effect from 1976 to 1980. A second Lomé Convention was negotiated for the period 1980 to 1985. The Conventions are the combined successors to the Yaoundé Conventions and the system of Commonwealth Preference, and represent the Community's continuing response to its colonial legacy.

11.2 The main provisions of the Lomé Convention

The Lomé Convention is a trade and aid agreement between the EEC countries collectively and 64 associated countries comprising sub-Saharan Africa (except Angola, Mozambique, Namibia and South Africa) and a number of island states in the Caribbean and Pacific. The emphasis of the Convention is on a partnership between the two groups of countries, which is reflected in the joint institutions that supervise and help to administer the agreement: the Council of Ministers, the Committee of Ambassadors and the Consultative Assembly.

The main provisions of the second Lomé Convention can be summarised as follows:

(a) Tariff preferences for practically all ACP exports: over 99 per cent of exports originating in the ACP countries have access to the EEC market free of tariffs and quotas.

(b) Special treatment for CAP products: although ACP exports of CAP products are still subject to levies, the reduced rate of the levies represents better treatment than is afforded to almost any other countries. Sugar and beef are covered by special quota arrangements.

(c) No reciprocal tariff preferences (reverse preferences) are demanded from the ACP countries.

(d) Stabilisation of export earnings: the STABEX system provides EEC funds to underwrite an export earnings stabilisation scheme covering most of the important non-minerals commodities supplied by the ACP countries.

(e) Stabilisation measures for the minerals industry: under SYSMIN, investment in the mining sectors of the ACP countries is supported with the aim of safeguarding future minerals supplies.

(f) Investment aid: through the European Development Fund and other schemes over 1000 million ECU are provided by the EEC each year to finance investment projects in the ACP countries. A Centre for Industrial Development has been established to channel assistance with industrialisation, including the transfer of technology, to the associated countries.

TARIFF PREFERENCES FOR THE ACP COUNTRIES

The general aim of the Lomé tariff preferences is to help the ACP countries increase their export earnings by liberalising access for their exports to the EEC market. Indeed, all except a tiny fraction of ACP exports can enter all parts of the EEC market free of tariffs and with no restrictions on quantity. As discussed in section

10.5, this preferential treatment could increase ACP exports through both trade creation and trade diversion. There are, however, a number of reasons why the Lomé preferences may, in practice, have little effect on ACP exports. First, it is obvious that if the EEC has a zero tariff for all suppliers there can be no tariff preference, and hence no trade-creation/trade-diversion effect. This is the case for the great bulk of ACP exports which are tropical foodstuffs and raw materials. Of the top fourteen ACP exports in the late 1970s, only two (coffee and groundnut oil) were subject to EEC tariffs in 1980.[6] A further product (sugar) was subject to variable import levies, but in any case ACP exports of sugar are limited by quota (see *Special treatment for CAP products,* below).

Secondly, where the EEC does use tariffs on products of export interest to the ACP, the general level of those tariffs is low (e.g. the CCT on coffee is 5 per cent and on cocoa 3 per cent),[7] and is being further reduced as a result of the Tokyo Round trade negotiations. Thus, in general, the margin of preference for ACP products is either zero or low and falling.

Thirdly, the scope for trade creation under the Lomé Convention is limited by the complementary rather than competitive nature of the EEC–ACP economies. Even where there does appear to be scope for trade creation (e.g. in sugar and textiles) the EEC has taken action to restrict ACP exports. Thus there are special rules for products covered by the Common Agricultural Policy (see *Special treatment for CAP products,* below), and on textiles—for example, the EEC in 1979 threatened to activate Article 12 of the Convention (a safeguard clause) to compel Mauritius to restrict its textile exports, even though the combined textile exports of all the ACP countries account for only a minute proportion of EEC textile consumption.

In the fourth place, there appears to be only modest scope for trade diversion. Mention has already been made of the EEC's limited use of tariffs in relation to primary products. For manufactured goods, it has to be borne in mind that not only do the exports of the ten member countries, the whole of EFTA and the Mediterranean countries have tariff-free access to the EEC market but so also do developing countries' exports under the GSP. The one advantage of Lomé, compared with the GSP, is that there are no formal *quantitative* restrictions. This remains a largely unexploited advantage, since the state of manufacturing industry in most ACP countries is embryonic.

Finally, the effectiveness of the Lomé Convention tariff

preference may be further compromised by the complex rules of origin (see section 6.3, *Rules of origin*). Tariff-free treatment is given only where, typically, more than 50–60 per cent of the value of the final product is added locally. This may be very difficult where there are no local components suppliers, for example, so the rules have been eased by allowing components and materials from the EEC or from other ACP countries to count as local. Moreover, the EEC is prepared to grant temporary derogations of the rules, in particular cases where this will help to establish *bona fide* manufacturing concerns.

SPECIAL TREATMENT FOR CAP PRODUCTS

The Lomé Convention gives unrestricted access to the EEC market for all products except those covered by the CAP.[8] For these products the general arrangement is that ACP exports get better treatment than products from all other non-member countries. Thus they are usually, but not invariably, exempt from tariffs, have relatively liberal quota controls, and face reduced rates of import levy. The EEC's approach has been cautious because of fears that unrestricted access for ACP products might undermine the price support given to European farmers or add unacceptably to the budget costs of CAP. In the second Lomé Convention there was some relaxation of the remaining restrictions.

Sugar is the CAP product of most vital concern to the ACP countries. It posed a particular problem in the negotiation of the first Lomé Convention because Britain had for some years been operating the Commonwealth Sugar Agreement under which sugar exports from Commonwealth countries were given a guaranteed market in the UK at fixed prices. A number of these countries were small and heavily dependent on their export earnings from sugar: Mauritius, Fiji, Guyana and Swaziland all derived more than a quarter of their export receipts from sugar from 1972 to 1974.[9]

Under the Lomé Convention, the EEC took over the Commonwealth sugar commitment from the UK, except for Australian supplies which received no special concessions. The EEC is obliged to purchase from specified ACP countries approximately 1.4 million tonnes of raw cane sugar a year for an indefinite period. (The Convention does provide for the possible termination of this commitment, after due notice has been given.) For each of the ACP states concerned, a national quota is fixed for sugar exports to the Community. If the country fails to supply the full quantity other than for reasons beyond its control *(force majeure)*, its quota for subsequent years may be reduced by the shortfall and this shortfall allocated to other countries. This threat is a real one: in 1979, the quotas for the Congo, Kenya, Surinam and Uganda were reduced following their failure to deliver the agreed quantities in 1977–78.

The innovative aspect of the Lomé sugar arrangements concerns the prices paid by the EEC for ACP exports: they are approximately the same as European sugar beet farmers receive, less freight costs, and are fixed annually in advance. Cosgrove Twitchett has described this as a 'revolutionary agreement' since it is 'one of the first working examples of indexing the price of developing countries' produce (sugar cane) to the level received by producers in developed countries (beet sugar).'[10] Between 1976 and 1978 this meant, for example, that the ACP countries received a price for their sugar exported to the EEC roughly double that on the world market. There is, however, a seamier aspect to the EEC's sugar arrangements. The Community currently has a large export surplus of sugar which is disposed of on the world market, generally with the aid of massive export subsidies. The effect of these disposals is to depress the price that ACP countries get for their sugar sales to non-EEC destinations. This is important because most ACP states have EEC sugar quotas amounting to less than 60 per cent of their production and they sell the remainder of their sugar on the world market. What the EEC gives with one hand may thus be taken away with the other.

The CAP is very restrictive in relation to beef imports which face a tariff, variable import levies, and strict animal health regulations. Some concessions have been made under the Lomé Convention since beef is an important source of foreign exchange for five ACP countries, Botswana, Kenya, Madagascar, Swaziland and Zimbabwe. Imports from these countries are exempt from tariffs and 90 per cent of the levies, provided that the quantities sold to the EEC are kept within 'traditional trade levels', as defined by quotas set annually by the Community, and the African countries impose an export tax of equivalent amount to the EEC tariff. The revenue forgone by the Community under this arrangement was estimated at about £3 millions in 1980.[11]

It may be added, although they are not CAP products, that the Lomé Convention contains special arrangements for bananas and rum in order to help Caribbean and, in the case of rum, West African producers to retain their traditional markets in the EEC.

THE NON-RECIPROCAL NATURE OF THE TARIFF PREFERENCES

Under the Yaoundé Conventions, the associated African countries were expected to offer the EEC reverse preferences, that is, EEC exports to Africa were to face lower tariffs than identical products from other suppliers. This helped to maintain the fiction that the EEC was creating a genuine free trade area with the African countries, and could thus be permitted to make discriminatory tariff reductions without infringing GATT rules. (A similar approach was used in relation to the Mediterranean countries; see section 9.2 *The reciprocity issue*.) The reverse preferences not only disadvantaged the African countries through trade diversion, but also generated conflict between the EEC and the US, which objected to the discriminatory treatment of its exports in Yaoundé Convention markets.

When the African Commonwealth countries negotiated association status, they firmly opposed the EEC's calls for reciprocity, and the Lomé Conventions make no demand for reverse preferences. The ACP countries must however grant EEC goods as favourable treatment as any non-developing country goods.

STABEX

Many of the ACP countries are heavily dependent on export earnings from a small number of commodities. These earnings can fluctuate sharply from year to year as a result both of rapid movements in world market prices and of alternations of good and bad national harvests. The Lomé Convention can help the ACP countries to tackle this instability problem in two ways: (i) by providing aid for investment projects (e.g. in irrigation) which may combat output fluctuations; and (ii) by providing loans which can offset the balance of payments consequences of sharp falls in export earnings in unfavourable years (a system of compensatory finance).

Although the Yaoundé Conventions had specified that EEC financial aid could be used to provide 'advances to alleviate the consequences of temporary fluctuations in price' (Article 17.4), the compensatory finance facility in the first Lomé Convention— STABEX—was a new departure for the Community. It was widely, though not universally, regarded as an innovative and progressive measure, consistent with the developing countries' view of a New International Economic Order.[12]

Under the second Lomé Convention the scheme works in the following way. If an ACP country experiences a downturn in its export earnings from a particular commodity, financial assistance from the STABEX fund can be given provided that certain conditions are met:

(i)   The commodity must be included in a list which covers mainly agricultural products in a raw or semi-processed state—e.g. coffee, tea, cocoa, bananas, groundnuts, coconut, palm oil, cotton, sisal, hides and leather, wood. Minerals are not included, though they account for a half of ACP export earnings. The EEC has stated its willingness to extend the list, and indeed the second Lomé Convention does cover more commodities than the first, though the additional ones are generally of minor importance (e.g. sesame seeds).

(ii)   The commodity must be of substantial importance to the export earnings of the applicant country: the basic rule is that the commodity must have accounted for 6½ per cent or more of the country's total export earnings in the previous year.[13] However, for the majority of ACP countries (least developed/landlocked/island states) the qualification rule is less stringent: the threshold is 2 per cent.

(iii) Export earnings from the commodity must be 6½ per cent or more below average earnings from that commodity in the previous four years. These earnings normally relate only to trade with the EEC, but exceptionally it may be permissible to include trade with other ACP countries and even total world exports. Again, the conditions are eased for the least developed/landlocked/island states; their trigger threshold is a decline of 2 per cent.

(iv)   The EEC must be satisfied that the decline in the country's export earnings in the EEC market has not been deliberately engineered through trade policy measures. Thus if earnings from *all* export destinations are above the average for the previous four years the application for assistance may be turned down.

(v)   The applicant country must certify that the items concerned were produced in its territory.

Assuming that these conditions can be met, assistance will be forthcoming. Its amount will depend on the shortfall in export earnings and the availability of STABEX funds in relation to requests for help. STABEX has been allocated 550 million ECU to cover its operation for the five years of the second Lomé Convention. In general, this is available in five equal, annual instalments with any unspent balance being carried forward. If these funds are insufficient to meet the claims made, then up to 20 per cent of the following year's allocation can be brought forward, and/or any claims may be met only in part.

One attraction of compensatory finance schemes is that they can be flexible according to the circumstances of the countries concerned. Thus for most ACP countries (the least developed/landlocked/island states) STABEX payments are non-repayable grants. For the twelve less badly-off countries, STABEX payments are, in principle, interest-free loans to be repaid over a seven-year period. The rules used to determine when a country is apparently in a strong enough position to repay are, however, complex: most payments from STABEX are grant-like transfers.

It should be emphasised that STABEX payments are made to the governments of the ACP countries concerned, and do not necessarily find their way back to the producers whose earnings have been cut: it is the recipient government which decides how the money is to be used. However, before the transfer is made the ACP state must indicate the probable use to which the funds will be put, and later is supposed to inform the EEC of the actual use. Article 23 of the Lomé Convention specifies that 'transfers must be devoted to maintaining financial flows in the sector in question or, for the purpose of promoting diversification, diverted towards other appropriate sectors and then used for economic and social development.'

It appears that much less than half of the total STABEX payments have gone to the sector whose export earnings fell.[14] This may be sensible where a sector is in structural decline and the need is for the development of new sources of foreign exchange. Research by Hewitt[15] shows that where STABEX aid was substantial and prompt it was helpful in stabilising an afflicted sector. However, part of the sector's problem not infrequently stemmed from the inefficiency of marketing boards and other agencies responsible for administering the sector, and these agencies frequently also handled the STABEX funds. Hewitt's general conclusion is that STABEX has provided significant budget support to recipient ACP countries and, since it is usually provided on an unconditional basis, has allowed increased flexibility in the government's development policy. Its balance of payments impact has invariably been helpful, though in many cases marginally so. However, it appears that STABEX has not been effective as a short-term stabilising measure, either internally or externally, because of lags in payment and limited coverage.

The ACP countries in general regard STABEX as a positive feature of the Lomé Convention and are anxious to see it developed and improved rather than discontinued. Certainly, the scheme has its stern critics—Wall, for example, in 1976 characterised STABEX as 'a technically cumbersome, bureaucracy-ridden, and politically sensitive scheme for making transfers, the concessionary element of which is variable, to a selected group of countries without regard to any sensible criteria covering overall need for aid.'[16] In the light of experience with STABEX during the two Lomé Conventions, the main criticisms levelled at the scheme are that:

- Most importantly, the funding is inadequate to deal with a general decline in commodity prices. During the 1970s, STABEX was called on mainly in situations where there was a persistent decline in the output of a particular export crop rather than where there were short-term fluctuations in prices and/or quantities. In 1980 and 1981, however, a fall in commodity prices, especially for coffee and cocoa,[17] led to claims against STABEX which the available funds were unable to meet in full; on average, only 53 per cent (*re* 1980) and 40 per cent (*re* 1981) of the amount claimed could be funded.[18]

- The coverage of commodities is incomplete, minerals and products subject to the CAP (notably, sugar, beef and tobacco) are excluded.[19] Thus the value of the scheme to individual ACP countries is very variable, depending upon their export crops. In the second Lomé Convention some action has been taken to help minerals producers (see SYSMIN below).

- Diversification of export products and markets is discouraged because only exports of agricultural products to the EEC are shielded by STABEX against earnings fluctuations.

- The establishment of processing activities, which are crucial to the development of the ACP countries, is inhibited, again because the scheme covers only unprocessed items (with the single exception of vegetable oils).

- The dependence and trigger thresholds are arbitrary. Thus a large percentage decline in the export earnings of a product of modest importance would be more likely to secure assistance than a small percentage decline in a product of greater importance, even though the absolute decline in the latter was larger. The thresholds cause the scheme to operate in an uneven and arbitrary way, but their elimination from the scheme would greatly increase the cost to the EEC.

- The product-by-product appoach ignores the overall position of a country's export earnings. For example, a country may receive a STABEX transfer for one commodity whose export earnings have declined even though its earnings from all export products have increased.
- No proper account is taken of inflation. Payment is only made when earnings in money terms decline, but in an inflationary period stable earnings in money terms—which would rule out a STABEX transfer—signify a fall in real terms, and a reduced ability to purchase manufactured goods.
- The stabilising impact is lost through delays in payments. The lag between establishing that earnings have declined and the payment under STABEX is estimated to be 6 to 18 months.[20] Apparently little of the delay is attributable to the Commission.
- The Commission, which operates STABEX on behalf of the Community, has considerable discretion within the rules to determine which requests for aid are to be granted. This could lead to inequitable treatment of some ACP countries.
- Viewed as an aid transfer mechanism, the distribution of assistance does not appear to correspond closely to need, in so far as this is revealed by *per capita* incomes: the poorest countries have received disproportionately little.[21] It should be added that this is always likely to be a feature of compensatory finance schemes, given that a country's participation in trade tends to increase with its level of economic development.
- The scheme duplicates the IMF compensatory finance scheme. However, there are important differences between the schemes—the IMF version is based on total export earnings and has a fixed repayment schedule, whereas STABEX is commodity-based, much more flexible regarding repayment, and has a large grant element.

In face of these criticisms, some modifications to STABEX may be incorporated into the third Lomé Convention, but the changes are not likely to be dramatic. The crucial test of EEC attitudes will be the extent to which the Community is prepared to increase its financial commitment to STABEX.

SYSMIN (OR MINEX)

The EEC is heavily dependent on imports for supplies of many important minerals and in recent years there has been growing concern over the long-term security of these supplies. Investment in exploration and the development of new sources of minerals appears to be lagging far behind what is needed if future shortages are to be avoided. The mining companies argue that investments in developing countries are inhibited by the political circumstances, in particular the risk that, once large investments have been made, the conditions under which a project operates may be radically altered by the host government. The EEC through the Lomé Convention has sought to get some kind of investment guarantee from the ACP countries, but this is a very sensitive area for developing countries and they have resisted any commitments which might erode their freedom of action. The parts of the Lomé Convention dealing with investment guarantees are thus characterised by 'vagueness, generality and self-contradition'.[22]

The ACP countries have approached the minerals issue from a different angle—they have requested export earnings stabilisation measures for minerals similar to those given to agricultural products under STABEX. Primarily because of the heavy costs that would be involved, the EEC has not been willing to undertake this. However a new scheme, SYSMIN, was introduced in the second Lomé Convention. This aims to help ACP states whose economies are heavily dependent on minerals exports to cope with the harmful effects on their income of serious *temporary* disruptions affecting their mining sectors. These disruptions may occur as a result of various factors beyond the control of the ACP states concerned, for example, 'accidents or serious technical mishaps, or grave political events, whether internal or external' (Article 52.2). The disruption may be actual or expected over the coming months, and may affect the capacity to produce or to export, and/or their export earnings. The disruptions must be serious, reducing capacity by 10 per cent or more if the ACP state is to qualify for EEC aid. Furthermore, the ACP state must derive more than 15 per cent (10 per cent if it is a least developed/landlocked/island state) of its exports from the product concerned. The list of eligible products comprises copper, phosphates, manganese, bauxite and alumina, tin and iron ore.

Under the second Lomé Convention, the EEC has set aside 282 million ECU for the use of SYSMIN. The Commission is responsible for administering the scheme, and payments to individual countries will depend on the seriousness of the problem affecting the minerals sector, the proposed use of funds, the possibility of joint finance with other bodies and the availability of SYSMIN funds. No single country may receive more than half of the funds available. SYSMIN payments are in the form of special low interest (1 per cent) loans made for a duration of 40 years, with a ten-year grace period. In addition to the SYSMIN facility, the Lomé Convention also makes special provision for assistance with mining and energy investment projects from the European Investment Bank. Loans may be made by the Bank on a case-by-case basis, up to a total of 200 million ECU.

The main concerns of the EEC regarding ACP minerals have been the disruption of supplies through political unrest, and the low level of investment caused by the risk of nationalisation or tight host government controls. SYSMIN goes some way to tackle the former—though a judgement of its significance can be made only as experience is accumulated[23]—but the Lomé Convention has made little headway on the latter.

FINANCIAL AID

Our focus in this book is on the EEC's trade relations, but it should be emphasised that the Lomé Convention is much more than a simple trade agreement between the Community and certain non-member countries. In the Convention the EEC hoped to create an integrated programme of assistance for the associated countries combining trade advantages—which, because of the structure of ACP exports, were of necessity limited—with a substantial Community commitment on financial aid and technical assistance.

The financial aid amounts to over 1000 million ECU a year and is provided by the EEC on a multilateral basis through a specially created agency, the European Development Fund (EDF).[24] The aid is spent in the ACP countries mainly on an individual project basis, but as part of an agreed overall development programme in each country. Projects supported include infrastructure provision, education and training, factory construction and equipment, integrated rural development and trade promotion. The aid is provided as outright grants or as 'soft' loans (over 40 years at a 1 per cent interest rate, and with no repayments in the first ten years). In addition, the EDF is authorised to lend certain sums to the ACP countries (see Table 11.1), and the interest payments may be subsidised by the EDF.

For some ACP countries, the Lomé Convention is the main source of foreign aid, and 17 ACP countries derive more than 40 per cent of their aid from this source. By contrast, for the EEC countries the Convention administers only a small part of their foreign aid programmes. Excluding Italy, about 85 per cent of EEC aid is bilateral and thus is controlled by the individual member states.

Table 11.1   *The second Lomé Convention: financial resources*

		(*million ECU*)
European Development Fund		4645
of which: grants		2998
soft loans		525
risk capital		284
STABEX		557
Sysmin		282
European Investment Bank		885
of which: loans		685
mineral projects		200
EEC Budget: Community delegates		180
	Total	5710

Sources:
EDF: Commission of EEC: COM (83) 296 of 31 May 1983,
with effect from 1 July 1983.
EIB and EEC Budget: Cosgrove Twitchett, *op. cit.*, p. 116.

The ACP countries have been critical of the Lomé Convention aid arrangements in several respects. The aid is insufficient; it is also not increasing in real terms per head of the population of the ACP countries and, most crucially, it does not appear to be additional: in effect, it has been funded from reductions in bilateral aid. The ACP countries have argued further that the attempt to administer the aid through a genuine partnership between the ACP and EEC countries has not been wholly successful. Although the ACP countries are fully involved in the development of projects, the purse strings are still firmly in the hands of the EEC: this does not constitute full equality in the ACP view.

There is also criticism from the ACP countries of the slowness with which the EEC disburses aid. The procedure is very bureaucratic, partly because the EEC has tried to involve the ACP countries in administration, and partly because the EEC countries are directly involved. The latter provide the finance for the EDF separately from the main EEC budget according to an agreed scale of national contributions, and they are anxious to secure the greatest possible payback via project contracts won by their home-based firms. EDF aid is in general tied to being spent in either the ACP countries or the EEC. According to the Commission, firms in the ACP countries have won less than 20 per cent of the international contracts, the most successful applicants being the French (29 per cent) and Italian (16 per cent), with UK firms trailing (7½ per cent).

Although the EEC aimed to integrate the trade and aid provisions in the Lomé Convention, there are many clashes between the two. For example, the development of processing industries in the ACP is said to be a priority of the aid programme but may be discouraged by certain provisions of STABEX. Similarly, the EEC has set up a Centre for Industrial Development in Brussels to promote industrial contracts between the EEC and the ACP, but has made no determined effort to promote a structural change in EEC industry which could create space for ACP manufactured exports.

11.3 The effects of the Lomé Convention on EEC trade with the ACP countries

The trade effects of the Lomé Convention are conditioned by the enormous diversity of the ACP countries. They range from oil-rich Nigeria with a population of 85 millions down to tiny island states, and are scattered geographically, though with a predominance of African countries. Another particularly relevant aspect of their diversity is in the range of their export-dependence on the EEC market: Togo, at one end of the spectrum sells 90 per cent of its exports to the EEC, whilst for the Bahamas, at the other end, the proportion is only 3 per cent. Clearly, with such diversity, the economic significance of the Lomé Convention must vary widely between the ACP countries. All, however, are developing countries and the commodity composition of their trade with the EEC reflects this. Their exports are dominated by agricultural and mining products which are exchanged for manufactures, and there is very little intra-industry trade.

The asymmetry of EEC–ACP trade also extends to the dependence of the two groups on each other's markets. In 1977, the EEC absorbed about 43 per cent of the total exports of the ACP countries, and supplied almost a half (48 per cent) of their imports. By contrast, the ACP countries were much less important trading partners for the EEC, accounting for only about 7 per cent of EEC trade with non-member countries. Again, however, there is a wide range of national experience, even between the member countries of the EEC.[25]

For France the ACP trade link is more vital than it is for other EEC members: more than one-eighth of French exports outside the Community are directed to the ACP countries compared, for example, with only 3.2 per cent for Germany and 6.4 per cent for the EEC as a whole (see Table 11.2). France and, to a lesser extent, the UK and Germany dominate EEC trade with the ACP countries: France accounts for a third of EEC exports and rather more than a quarter of imports, while the UK contributes a quarter of EEC exports and Germany receives more than a fifth of EEC imports. In the cases of France and the UK, this dominance reflects a long historical association with former African colonies. For Germany, the ACP countries are relatively minor trade partners but Germany's foreign trade sector is so large that the trade flows with the ACP countries are still an important part of the Community total. The pattern of relative importance in trade changed quite sharply during the 1970s, with the UK declining in importance both as an importer and as an exporter. The lost UK shares were taken up by Germany in relation to exports, and France in relation to imports.

Table 11.2   *The relative importance to the EEC countries of their trade with ACP countries, 1982*

	Each country's trade with ACP as percentage of total national trade with non-EEC countries		Each country's trade with ACP as percentage of EFC total	
	exports	imports	exports	imports
France	12.1	8.3	32.1	26.9
United Kingdom	7.6	4.3	25.2	15.1
Germany	3.2	4.8	16.5	21.9
Netherlands	8.3	5.9	8.0	9.8
Italy	4.5	4.8	9.8	13.8
Belgium–Luxembourg	6.7	7.9	5.6	10.2
Ireland	6.1	2.7	0.8	0.4
Denmark	3.9	2.4	1.7	1.2
Greece	3.4	2.0	0.4	0.6
EEC (10)	6.4	5.5	100.0	100.0

Source: Eurostat.

A principal aim of the Lomé Conventions was to improve the trade performance of the ACP countries as a contribution to their general economic development. On this basis, the ACP countries have a number of causes for disappointment at their trade experience under the first Lomé Convention. In particular (i) their trade balance with the EEC has moved into persistent deficit, (ii) their share of the EEC market has declined, and (iii) they have failed to make much headway in their attempt to diversify their exports.

The terms of trade of countries which export primary products in exchange for manufactured goods deteriorated substantially in the wake of the commodity price boom of 1973–74. This contributed to a shift in the trade balance of the ACP countries with the EEC from a position of surplus in the early 1970s to a deficit in 1978 (according to EEC data). The trade balance with the EEC tends to be regarded by the ACP countries as a barometer of the success of the Lomé Convention. From this perspectve, the results so far do not look encouraging. However, it should be borne in mind that the trade balance is only one component of the overall balance of payments. It is quite normal and desirable, within limits, for the ACP countries to balance a deficit on their trade account with a surplus on their capital account. In this way, aid and other capital flows may be used to finance the purchase abroad of investment goods.

A second area of ACP disappointment has been the decline in their share of EEC imports, which fell from 8 per cent in 1970–74 to 7 per cent in 1975–79, despite the ACP countries' various trade advantages under the first Lomé Convention. It is true that the ACP countries reduced a little the proportion of their exports going to the EEC during this period, but no more so than developing countries in general, and the latter managed to increase their share of EEC imports during the 1970s. The ACPs' loss of ground was not confined to the EEC market: the share of non-oil exporting ACPs in total world exports fell by a third, from 2.3 per cent in 1970 to 1.5 per cent in 1979.[26] Again, this compares unfavourably with the performance of developing countries in general since, excluding the oil exporters, the developing countries share of world trade increased during the 1970s, despite the adverse consequences of rising oil prices.

Given that developing countries as a group have an export commodity structure which is broadly similar to that of the ACP countries, the latters' poor export record does not appear to have a mainly structural explanation—that is, it is not attributable mainly to the ACP countries exporting the kind of goods for which the growth in the market was slow. It should be added however that ACP exports of manufactured goods are particularly limited. In general, the evidence seems to point to a general decline in the competitiveness of ACP exports, which the trade provisions of the

Lomé Conventions have been unable to reverse, at least not in the short term.

The ACP countries have also been disappointed that they were not able to reduce their export dependence on unprocessed primary products during the 1970s. Allowing for some inappropriateness in the tariff classification of goods, the share of manufactures in ACP exports appears to have been stable at about 2 per cent. As Moss has pointed out,[27] only for two manufactured products (ropes and cords) did the ACP countries manage to increase substantially their EEC market share in the 1970s, though there was a modest improvement for clothing, leather, textiles, essential oils and natural hormones. Even so, in absolute terms, the trade flows remained tiny, and for a number of products, like plywood, the ACP share of EEC imports fell.

MOSS'S STUDY ON THE EFFECT ON ACP EXPORTS TO THE EEC OF THE LOMÉ CONVENTION

Despite the generally disappointing trade performance of the ACP countries during the 1970s, there are some indications that the first Lomé Convention did have some beneficial effect on ACP exports, even if it was insufficient to offset other adverse factors. This beneficial effect applies to the non-oil exporting countries: the development of exports from oil-rich countries like Nigeria was dictated by events outside the Lomé Convention. For this reason, in this section attention will be confined to non-oil exporting countries, both amongst the ACP and amongst developing countries as a whole.

A recent study by Moss[28] has examined changes in the *share* of exports from the ACP and other developing countries which were directed to the EEC during the 1970s. In a comparison of the export performance of two countries, or groups of countries, the use of export market shares allows the researcher to abstract from differences in trade caused by different rates of growth of supply in the exporting countries. Attention can then be focused on differences in trade performance which are related to different *conditions of access* to import markets, such as the Lomé Convention arrangements for the ACP countries. General developments in import markets should show up in the export pattern of all exporting countries, whilst special arrangements for particular groups of countries should produce a differential export behaviour.

Moss's research showed that the proportion of (non-oil) ACP exports going to the EEC (9) remained unchanged between the early 1970s (1970–74) and the period of the first Lomé Convention (1975-79) (see Table 11.3). By contrast, all (non-oil) developing countries experienced a statistically significant decline of 10 per cent in the share of their exports going to the EEC during the same period.[29] Whilst there could be other explanations for this differential performance (e.g. differences in the commodity structure of exports) it seems likely that part of the explanation is attributable to the effects of the Lomé Convention. Disaggregation of the results by country groups adds credence to this argument.

The first Lomé Convention resulted in the amalgamation of two preference systems: the UK–Commonwealth, and the EEC (6)–Yaoundé Convention. The Commonwealth countries obtained preferential access to the EEC market for the first time, and the Yaoundé Convention countries gained new preferences in the UK market. Both the Commonwealth and Yaoundé Convention countries obtained new preferences in the Danish and Irish markets. The changing pattern of export market shares reflects these adjustments (see Table 11.3). Most notably, the share of Commonwealth ACP exports going to the EEC (6) increased by 14 per cent during the 1970s, whereas the comparable Yaoundé Convention share fell by 12 per cent, as these countries lost their exclusive preference in the EEC (6) market. Both Commonwealth ACP and former Yaoundé Convention countries increased their export shares directed to Ireland and Denmark, whereas the corresponding share for all developing countries was unchanged. The share of exports directed to the UK remained stable for both the Commonwealth ACP and former Yaoundé Convention countries, against a decline for developing countries as a whole. These results suggest that a reallocation of trade has taken place amongst the ACP and other developing countries in a manner which is broadly consistent with the changes in trade preferences caused by the implementation of the Lomé Convention.

It was remarked earlier that the tariff preferences given to the ACP countries are not very extensive. There may, however, be other reasons why the Lomé Conventions could encourage ACP exports to the Community, including the restriction of the STABEX payments to trade with the EEC; the special regimes for sugar, beef, bananas and rum; and the effect of aid arrangements on trade contacts. Moss found some evidence that those commodities which benefited from special arrangements under the first Lomé Convention fared better during the 1970s than those which did not.

Table 11.3 Changes in the share of ACP and other developing countries' exports directed to EEC countries, 1970–74 to 1975–79

Period	Developing countries	To EEC (9) from:			
		ACP total	Yaoundé C. countries	Commonwealth ACP countries	Previously non-assoc. countries
			% of total exports		
A 1970–74	27.08	46.41	63.27	37.85	41.33
B 1975–79	24.46	46.00	56.27	38.96	40.69
(B ÷ A) × 100	90	99	89	103	98
Stat. significance test[a]	—	*	ns	**	*

Period	To EEC (6) from:		To UK from:	
	Commonwealth ACP countries	Yaoundé C. countries	Commonwealth ACP countries	Yaoundé C. Countries
		% of total exports		
A 1970–74	17.10	58.70	20.07	4.38
B 1975–79	19.50	51.69	18.67	4.17
(B ÷ A) × 100	114	88	93	95
Stat. significance test[b]	—	**	—	ns

Source: Adapted from J. Moss, The Lomé Conventions and Their Implications for the United States (Boulder, Colorado: Westview Press, 1982), Tables 2–2, 2–8 and 2–10.

Notes: Table refers only to non-oil exporting countries.
[a] Compared with changes in the export shares of all developing countries.
[b] Compared with changes in the export shares of Commonwealth ACP countries.
** Significant at 99 per cent, * significant at 92.5 per cent level; ns not significant.

It should be pointed out, finally, that any beneficial trade effect that the first Lomé Convention had on the ACP countries was confined to the Commonwealth countries and to the four countries which were neither in the Commonwealth nor the Yaoundé Conventions. For the former Yaoundé Convention countries, the gains in the markets of the new EEC member countries (UK, Denmark and Ireland) no more than offset the effects of the loss of their exclusive preference in the EEC (6).

THE RETURN DIRECTION: EFFECTS ON EEC EXPORTS TO THE ACP COUNTRIES

The Lomé Conventions do not require the ACP countries to offer reverse preferences to the EEC; however the ACP countries are obliged to give similar conditions of access to their markets for all EEC countries. This might be expected to have led to some adjustments in the pattern of EEC exports to the ACP as, for example, exporters in the EEC (6) obtained similar terms of access to the Commonwealth ACP markets as those enjoyed by UK firms. Moss also found some indication of this from an examination of changes in the share of ACP imports supplied by the various EEC countries. In particular, Commonwealth ACP countries bought a higher proportion of their imports from the EEC (6), Denmark and Ireland, after the introduction of the first Lomé Convention, whilst the former Yaoundé Convention countries maintained their share of imports from the UK, Denmark and Ireland (but not the EEC (6)) against the trend for all (non-oil) developing countries (see Table 11.4).

There was some indication from Moss's study that the combined EEC exports to the ACP countries may have been assisted by the first Lomé Convention, even though it created no new trade preferences in favour of the EEC. Between the early and late 1970s, the EEC held on to its share of imports in the ACP market better than it did in developing countries as a whole. In the latter, the EEC's import share showed a statistically significant decline, whereas in the ACP countries the UK and EEC (6) import shares showed no significant change, and the combined Danish/Irish share increased (see Table 11.4).

The explanation for the relatively favourable performance of EEC exports in the ACP markets probably owes something to a number of factors outside the first Lomé Convention, such as the long-established trade, business and currency zone links between some EEC and ACP countries, and the tying of bilateral aid programmes which are oriented towards former colonies. But the

Table 11.4   Changes in EEC shares of ACP imports, 1970–74 to 1975–79

Imports of:	EEC (9)	Source of imports: EEC (6)	UK	D/I	US
All ACP countries					
Commonwealth	"	+	"	+	−
previously non-assoc	"	"	"	"	"
Yaoundé Convention	"	−	"	"	"
Total	"	"	"	+	−
Non-oil exporting					
ACP countries					
Commonwealth	"	"	"	+	"
previously non-assoc	"	"	"	"	"
Yaoundé Convention	"	"	"	"	"
Total	"	"	−	"	"
Non-oil exporting					
developing countries	−	n.a.	n.a.	n.a.	−

Source: J. Moss, *op. cit.*, Tables 2–6, 2–8, 2–10, 2–11 and 2–12.
Notes:
+   Statistically significant (at 95% level) increase in import shares 1970–74 to 1975–79.
−   Statistically significant decrease in import shares.
"   Change not statistically significant.
n.a. Data not available.
D/I Denmark and Ireland.

Lomé Convention may also have played a part, specifically:

- the rules of origin may have encouraged ACP producers to use components imported from the EEC rather than other developed countries;
- exports from Ireland and Denmark may have been helped by the rule that ACP countries must give most-favoured-nation treatment to all EEC countries;
- aid provided through the European Development Fund was tied to purchases in the EEC and ACP countries; and
- the Convention may have created a climate of opinion favourable to strong trade links with the EEC.

11.4 Conclusions

Looked at in terms of their contribution to the New International Economic Order, the results of the Lomé Conventions appear modest. The compensatory finance scheme—STABEX—which was introduced with so much acclaim has been short of funds for even its present restricted coverage. On sugar, the ACP countries benefit from a 'revolutionary' indexing of their export prices to EEC support prices, but there is no chance of a relaxation of the strict quota limits, and the EEC damages ACP earnings elsewhere by dumping its own surplus sugar on world markets. Over the otherwise fairly comprehensive, if minor, tariff preferences hangs the threat of EEC safeguard action, whilst on the issue of partnership between rich and poor countries the 'model' arrangements for administering the European Development Fund are seen by the ACP countries as giving legal parity but not real equality. In general, the contribution of the Lomé Conventions to the NIEO has lost its dynamism because the innovations of the first Lomé Convention have not been developed and extended in a powerful enough way. The EEC has felt constrained both by the web of its own conflicting trade policies and by the global recession (which has also prevented the Lomé Conventions from being more widely imitated by other countries).

The potential impact of the Lomé Conventions on ACP–EEC trade appeared likely to be small from the outset. As discussed in section 11.2, *Tariff preferences for ACP countries*, the scope for trade creation and trade diversion to boost ACP exports is intrinsically limited. However, the first Convention may have had some beneficial effect on ACP trade, since the ACP export performance in the EEC market was not as weak as the declining international competitiveness of ACP goods might have suggested. This effect was not strong enough to bring about any discernible change in the ACP's key trade problem areas of slow export growth, heavy dependence on unprocessed primary product exports, and trade imbalance.

The future development of the Lomé Convention is clouded both by the prospective enlargement of the EEC and by changes in the EEC's approach to its relations with developing countries as the colonial era recedes into history. Enlargement poses a considerable threat to some ACP trade interests, since Spain and Portugal, as well as Greece, will have unrestricted access to the Community market.[30] The ACP exports most likely to suffer are plywood, textiles, tobacco and furniture. In a broader context, Spain and Portugal have strong economic and cultural ties with the Latin American developing countries and their membership of the Community may in time alter the balance of EEC development policy. A more global approach would also be favoured by some of the existing EEC members including Germany, the UK and Denmark.

Although the ACP countries have been critical of certain aspects of the Convention, they wish it to be renewed since it gives them certain advantages, particularly in relation to aid, which they would otherwise not receive. Their demands for its improvement include: more aid, more finance and wider coverage for STABEX, an end to the safeguard clause on trade, and a more meaningful partnership in the operation of the Convention. The Commission also favours the retention of the African focus and has suggested that the Convention should be given an indefinite duration. France, with its strong cultural, trade and investment ties with Africa may be expected to endorse this view, but as mentioned at the beginning of this chapter, there are other EEC countries who favour a more global approach to EEC development policy. This issue will be taken up again at the end of the next chapter.

12 Trade Policies Towards Developing Countries in Latin America and Asia

More than a half of the world's population lives in the developing countries of Latin America and Asia. The physical environments and social and political structures of these countries are extremely diverse, but they share one overwhelming feature, the poverty of the mass of their inhabitants. This crucial feature colours the whole of their trade relationship with the Community. The actual strength of Asian and Latin American commercial links with the Community varies greatly—some Commonwealth countries, for example, trade extensively with western Europe, whilst others (e.g. the ASEAN group[1]) have a trade pattern which is increasingly oriented towards Japan; and the Latin American countries have traditionally strong trade links with the US. Excluding the oil exporters, the Latin American countries conduct about 25 per cent of their trade with the Community, and the Asian countries about 15 per cent. For developing countries as a group, the EEC is the single largest market. Trade with Asia and Latin America is also of substantial importance to the EEC, accounting for about 10 and 5 per cent, respectively, of the EEC's external trade. The trade flows are mainly inter-industry in character, the EEC exporting a range of engineering and other manufactured goods in exchange for tropical foodstuffs, raw materials and labour-intensive manufactures.

The EEC's trade and aid arrangements for Asian and Latin American countries compare unfavourably with the privileged treatment of the ACP countries under the Lomé Convention. In the hierarchy of EEC trade policies, the non-associated developing countries come near to the bottom, since exports from all of the countries in western Europe, the Mediterranean and Africa enter the Community on easier, usually tariff-free, terms. The starting-point of the EEC's trade policy towards the non-associated (Asian and Latin American) developing countries is the

195

most-favoured-nation tariff embodied in the CCT.[2] The tariff
barrier is, however, relaxed for many (mainly manufactured)
goods from the non-associated developing countries under the
EEC's version of the GSP (see sections 12.1 to 12.5).[3] In contrast,
as was described in section 7.3, many types of clothing and textiles
exported to the EEC are subject to quantitative restrictions under
the Multi-Fibre Arrangement. Trade in some agricultural products
is affected by International Commodity Agreements (section
12.6).

In addition to the trade arrangements with these non-associated
countries, the EEC also provides financial and food aid, though
the amounts involved are very modest when compared with the
number of people living in the Asian and Latin American
countries. The aid programme began in 1976 with an annual
commitment of 20 million u.a., and has been gradually expanded,
reaching 185 million ECU in 1982. About three-quarters of this aid
goes to the Asian countries and most of the remainder to Latin
America. The Community is a substantial donor of food aid to
developing countries, including 1 million tonnes a year of cereals,[4]
together with less regular contributions of dairy products and
sugar. In 1982, the value of this aid, at world prices and including
transport costs, was estimated at 700 million ECU. Non-associated
countries also benefit from other Community aid programmes: in
1982, 'exceptional' aid of 40 million ECU was provided for the
least developed countries, and there was also 75 million ECU of
emergency aid.[5]

12.1 The Generalised System of Preferences: origin and main features of the EEC's revised scheme

As was seen in section 10.3, it was argued at the first UNCTAD
Conference in 1964 that the industrial countries should suspend
their tariffs on manufactured goods imported from the developing
countries for a limited period. This met with strong opposition
from the US, which was concerned, amongst other things, with the
damage that might be done to the GATT system. The EEC was
less troubled by this aspect, but there were internal disagreements
over the form which the proposed GSP should take.

Germany and the Netherlands supported the idea of a single
scheme which all the industrial countries would apply, whereas

France and Belgium favoured a more selective arrangement, in the belief that it would enable them to maintain their special trade relationships with their former colonies. With each industrial country (or group of countries) free to draw up its own scheme, the EEC could omit from its version those products which were of particular interest to its African associates. The benefits which the African countries drew from their special trade preferences under the Yaoundé Convention, especially those deriving from trade diversion, would thus be protected from erosion. With this arrangement in mind, the African countries urged France and the European Commission to press the US to take part in a GSP in the hope that this would open up new markets for them in North America.[6]

Under strong pressure, particularly from the Latin American countries who looked enviously at the EEC's preferential trade ties with Africa, the US reluctantly dropped its opposition to the GSP in 1967. The US government had come to see the UNCTAD scheme of preferences as the lesser of two evils, the alternative being an escalation of regional trade preferences for developing countries along the lines of the Yaoundé Convention. In an attempt further to head off the regionalisation of trade, the US made it clear in 1968 that no country which gave preferential access to EEC exports would be allowed to benefit from the US application of the GSP.

Once US opposition in principle to taking part in a GSP had been overcome, events moved fairly rapidly. At the second UNCTAD Conference in 1968, there was unanimous agreement that a GSP should be established and intensive consultations began on the detailed provisions. The developed countries were unable to devise a single scheme acceptable to all the so-called donor countries, and instead each drew up its own version. In the end, there were eleven somewhat different schemes, but their general features were sufficiently acceptable to both developed and developing countries for the UNCTAD Special Committee on Preferences to give the go-ahead in October 1970 for the introduction of the GSP. One further hurdle remained — the contracting parties to the GATT had to exempt trade under the GSP from the non-discrimination rule. This was done in June 1971 when a ten-year waiver was granted.[7] The way was then open for the GSP to come into operation, and most European countries put their schemes into effect as from 1971 or 1972. The US scheme began in January 1976. In 1981, the EEC renewed its scheme for a second decade.

The main features of the EEC's revised GSP can be summarised as follows:[8]

(a) The scheme offers a *tariff preference for semi-manufactured and manufactured products* originating in the developing countries; these products are in general admitted to the EEC tariff-free, whereas similar products from countries outside the scheme face the full CCT.

(b) Tariff-free access is in principle *limited to certain quantities* of each type of manufactured good from the developing countries in any one year; beyond these limits the full CCT may be reimposed.

(c) The quantitative limits to tariff-free access are of practical importance only for a list of some *120 products regarded by the EEC as sensitive* in that unrestricted access for the developing countries' exports might cause serious problems for EEC producers; for these sensitive products a tariff quota system is in force which not only strictly limits the amount which each of the principal supplying countries can export tariff-free to the EEC as a whole, but also defines the amounts which can be shipped on this basis to individual member states.

(d) Some manufactured products, in particular *textiles, are substantially excluded* from the GSP; trade in textiles is regulated by voluntary export restraints under the Multi-Fibre Arrangement and various bilateral agreements.

(e) *Some agricultural products are included.* They enter the EEC at reduced tariff rates but the list of eligible products has been drawn up so as to minimise the effect on EEC farmers and on exports from the associated ACP countries.

(f) *Exports from the least developed countries receive especially favourable treatment:* they are exempted from the quota restrictions on sensitive products, even those on textiles and, up to certain limits, their agricultural products are not subject to tariffs.

(g) *The scheme is available in principle to all developing countries* on a non-discriminatory basis in the sense that each country can benefit in some way; however, in its detailed application it is increasingly selective in relation to the state of industrialisation of the beneficiary country.

(h) The GSP is not the outcome of negotiations with the beneficiary countries as is normal in matters of trade policy; *the preferences are non-reciprocal and are granted auton-*

omously by the Community; as such, they can be withdrawn at any time without breach of legal obligations.

(i) The scheme was renewed for a second term of ten years in 1980; the present rules cover the period 1981 to 1985.[9]

12.2 GSP: the beneficiaries, coverage and safeguards

The immediate objective of a scheme offering tariff preferences to developing countries is to boost their export earnings (see section 10.5). How successfully this objective is achieved in practice depends very much on the detailed rules governing the operation of the scheme, especially which countries are included, what the product coverage is, what kind of safeguard measures are employed, and how the scheme is administered.

SELECTING THE BENEFICIARY COUNTRIES
The GSP was supposed to be available to all developing countries but each donor country had to draw up its own list of beneficiary countries. Difficulties arose over those countries which were intermediate between developing and developed status and which naturally were keen to obtain the tariff advantages offered under the GSP. The problem for the EEC was threefold: (i) a number of EEC industries were coming under pressure from exports from the intermediate countries even without preferential tariff treatment. (ii) the intermediate countries were often the main trade rivals of the less developed countries, hence, if they were included in the GSP the advantage of the scheme to the less developed countries would be weakened, however, if they were excluded then the impact of the GSP on EEC trade might be very small. (iii) the choice of participants was politically sensitive since it is an expression of the relationship between the giver and the chosen.

The EEC tried to minimise the political problems of selecting the beneficiary countries by including in its GSP only those which were members of the UNCTAD 'Group of 77' and were thus self-styled developing countries. A number of countries outside this Group (in particular, Greece, Spain, Malta, Turkey, Israel, Bulgaria, Romania, Cuba and Taiwan) have tried to obtain GSP status from the various donor countries. Since 1971, when the EEC's version of the GSP began, Cuba and Romania have become beneficiaries under the Community's scheme. Taiwan remains outside—partly because the Community cannot afford to upset China which became a beneficiary in 1980. The Mediterranean countries mentioned above have not been included since they get a better deal under the EEC's Mediterranean trade policy.

At present the total number of beneficiary countries under the EEC's GSP scheme is nominally 126, plus 22 dependent territories (including Hong Kong). However, the actual use made of the scheme is much less than these numbers imply because about a half of the countries and territories have more favourable trade arrangements with the EEC under the Mediterranean policy and the Lomé Convention. The Community's GSP is thus mainly of interest to the Latin American and Asian countries whose exports would otherwise face the full CCT. The GSP played a role in softening the blow felt by the Asian Commonwealth countries after the UK joined the EEC and the UK's own relatively generous version of the GSP and the system of Commonwealth Preference were phased out in 1974 and 1978, respectively. The Asian Commonwealth countries were not admitted to the Lomé Convention (see section 11.1) but benefited from the revised version of the EEC's GSP which was introduced in 1975.

THE PRODUCT COVERAGE

A scheme of preferences designed to have maximum effect on developing countries' exports would give particular advantage to the simple, labour-intensive manufactured products like textiles and footwear in which many of the developing countries specialise. It would also include processed agricultural products and semi-processed products which are of special importance to the poorest countries. In contrast, the EEC's GSP has a product coverage which is the reverse of this: agricultural products and industrial raw materials are largely excluded or, at most, subject to token concessions. On manufactured goods, the scheme offers very liberal treatment to those products where the developing countries have no hope of competing (e.g. aircraft engines) but is very restrictive towards those products (especially textiles) where many developing countries have demonstrated a comparative advantage. Needless to say, this perverse product coverage seriously weakens the benefits which developing countries can draw from the scheme.

The shape of the GSP results from a conflict of interests for the EEC: by the time that account had been taken of possible adverse effects of the GSP on EEC producers as well as the likely erosion of benefits which countries with special trade preferences from the Community currently enjoyed, there was little scope for offering meaningful trade advantages to the non-associated developing countries in Asia and Latin America. This problem is well exemplified in the case of textiles. In order to protect EEC firms, most textile imports from developing countries have been subject for many years to strict quota control and generally face the full CCT. (The EEC's textile arrangements are described in more detail in section 7.3). Under the GSP, the EEC gives tariff-free treatment to about 10 per cent of the quota-controlled imports.[10] Thus, on this part of their trade the developing countries may benefit from higher prices, but the quota limits remain. Even this modest benefit is highly regulated. Detailed lists specify how much of each finely classified type of textile from each of the low-cost suppliers is to be exempt from tariffs in each year. The poorest and least competitive countries receive the largest shares.

Like textiles, agricultural products were also largely excluded from the EEC's GSP scheme, in this case to protect EEC farmers and to retain preferential treatment for African exports of tropical products. However, from a token representation in 1971, the list of eligible agricultural products has gradually increased: the maximum potential value of trade affected has risen from 450 million ECU in 1974 to 1700 million ECU in 1978 (the Community's 'offer'). For 1983, the Commission proposed reduced tariff entry for some 324 items, including for the first time such assorted gourmet delights as horseradish, ladies' fingers and snails![11] The main CAP products, subject to the levy system, remain firmly outside the GSP. In any case, the margin of preference given under the GSP is modest — it was 4 per cent initially (bringing the average rate of tariff down from 16 to 12 per cent)[12] but increased to 7.3 per cent by 1977.[13]

Some idea of the potential value of the GSP to developing countries can be gained by examining the product coverage of the scheme in relation to the pattern of exports of these countries. In the first place, the scheme obviously could not cover products which already entered the EEC tariff-free. These products — mainly raw materials destined for European processing industries — accounted for about 70 per cent of developing countries' exports to the EEC at the start of the scheme. Secondly, however, only about a quarter of the imports from the Third World which did face tariffs were included in the GSP, giving an overall coverage of about 8 per cent (i.e. 25 per cent of the dutiable 30 per cent). The low coverage of dutiable items indicates that the scope of the Community's scheme is much narrower than it could be, and reflects particularly the widespread exclusion of agricultural

202 The Political Economy of European Trade

products. Even for manufactured goods, the main focus of the GSP, it has been estimated that the EEC's original scheme covered only two-thirds of the developing countries' exports when account was taken of the textile regulations.[14] Currently, the main manufactured items completely omitted are 'certain semi-manufactures or products of first-stage processing ... notably raw hides and skins, certain textile primary products and certain metals up to the ingot stage.'[15] For industrial goods, the main problem facing developing countries is not so much the complete exclusion of some items as the complex and insidious system of safeguards which has grown up to restrict their most successful export products.

THE SAFEGUARD ARRANGEMENTS

Whilst the general aim of the donor countries is to help the developing countries to establish new industries, they are at the same time very sensitive to the damage which an upsurge of imports from developing countries could do to their own weaker industries. Hence, the GSP has to include safeguard arrangements which permit the donor countries to reimpose the most-favoured-nation tariff if problems arise. In fact, the EEC would like to go further than this in some cases by applying more penal restrictions, but it has not yet persuaded the majority of GATT countries of the wisdom of selective safeguards (see section 13.1, The failure of negotiations on safeguards).

The problems of the EEC and other donor countries in relation to imports of manufactured goods under the GSP centre on the more advanced of the developing countries, notably Mexico, Brazil, South Korea, Singapore, Hong Kong and Taiwan (though, as noted above, the latter is excluded from the EEC scheme). These countries achieved a rapid growth in the volume and range of their exports of manufactured goods during the 1970s and became known as the newly industrialising countries (NICs). Their exports are particularly competitive in certain areas where parts of the EEC industries have long suffered major problems (e.g. textiles and steel) or are running into increasing difficulties (e.g. electronics equipment and chemicals).

Under the various GSP schemes, donor countries have employed two main forms of safeguard instrument: escape clauses and tariff quotas. Under the escape clause, the donor country gives warning that it will reimpose the full most-favoured-nation tariff on all further arrivals in the event of a surge in imports which causes or threatens to cause serious damage to its home industry. A weakness of this arrangement is that by the time a problem has been identified and the necessary administrative procedures have been undertaken irreversible damage may have been done to the home industry. Furthermore, the escape clause also causes uncertainty for the developing countries since they do not have complete assurance that the goods which they are planning to produce for export will continue to receive tariff-free treatment. The EEC does not use escape clauses under its GSP scheme except for agricultural products, where the tariff concessions are in any case very limited.

Instead, the EEC's safeguard system for manufactured goods is based on *tariff quotas*, in the form of individual product ceilings or maximum country amounts. Under the tariff quota system, the EEC defines in advance the maximum quantity (usually expressed in value terms) of each product which it is prepared to admit tariff-free in a particular year. If imports reach this maximum quantity, then the CCT is reimposed on any subsequent imports until the end of the year. In practice, it would be impossible for the Community to keep up-to-the-minute records of all manufactured goods imported from some 120 countries into each of the ten EEC member countries. Hence, attention has been focused on a narrower range of goods where problems are most likely to arise, especially where they originate in the NICs.[16]

For the purposes of the safeguard system, three main groups of goods are recognised:

(i) *Non-sensitive products.* These comprise about 90 per cent of all the types of manufactured goods according to their tariff classification — many of them, of course, not produced in the developing countries — and they are allowed into the EEC tariff-free from all the beneficiary countries without any restrictions on quantity. There is, however, provision for the tariff to be reimposed where serious problems arise. This would apply to imports beyond a ceiling amount calculated according to a formula which adjusts the ceiling value over time to take account of inflation as well as allowing some increase in volume.

(ii) *Sensitive products subject to ceilings only.* These items are sensitive in the sense that European firms are struggling to compete against producers in the developing countries.[17] In 1983, there were 58 product groups (including 32 types of chemical) in this category.[18] They are subject to individual ceilings which set the maximum annual value of imports from any individual beneficiary country. If the ceiling were exceeded the tariff could be reimposed on imports from the country in question. Imports of all of these products are carefully monitored.

(iii) *Sensitive products subject to ceilings and maximum country amounts.*   In 1983 71 product groups were covered by this restriction. For each product, the most competitive supplying countries (usually one or two, but up to six) are allocated individual annual tariff-free quotas, beyond which imports would automatically be subject to tariff. The countries most frequently affected in 1983 were South Korea (28), Hong Kong (24), Romania (16), China (16), Brazil (14) and Singapore (5). In order to exercise a strict control over the entry of sensitive products from these countries to the Community, the quota on each product is subdivided between the EEC countries. To give the scheme some flexibility only 80 per cent[19] of the quota (the first tranche) is initially allocated between the Community members. This allocation is on a standard basis for most products so that the UK, for example, gets 21 per cent of the total, Ireland 0.5 per cent and Germany 27.5 per cent. As each country exhausts its quota it may apply for a further allotment from the 20 per cent held in reserve, and if towards the end of the year a country appears unlikely to use the whole of its quota then it may be required to return part of the remainder which can then be added to the reserve.

Beneficiary countries which are not subject to an individual country quota on a specific sensitive product are instead subject to ceilings as described for group (ii) products above. (See *The least developed countries* below, for exemptions from these restrictions.)

The designation of a product as sensitive clearly has important implications for the benefits which exporters of that product can derive under the GSP. There is, however, no automatic formula for choosing the sensitive products. The Commission argues that a variety of factors should be taken into account, including the state of development of the beneficiary country, its past record of exports of a product in relation to any quota restrictions, the share of imports in EEC consumption of the product, and the trade position of the beneficiary country. The danger in this approach is that it will be employed arbitrarily according to the power of pressure groups in the EEC and the political influence, or lack of it, of non-member countries.

It is very difficult to judge the restrictiveness of the GSP arrangements since this varies from country to country and product to product, and should be considered in relation to potential rather than to actual exports. For the non-sensitive products the pre–1981 scheme appears to have been generally liberal, since the notional quantities eligible for tariff-free treatment (the EEC's 'offer') greatly exceeded the actual value of GSP trade. The overall use of the GSP amounted to about 55–60 per cent of the tariff-free allocation. For sensitive products, where individual country limits were fixed, the number of cases in which tariffs were reimposed rose from 109 in 1974 to 172 in 1979.[20] Under the current GSP scheme, 92 cases were reported in the *Official Journal of the EC* of duties being reimposed in 1982, the countries most frequently affected being China, Brazil, Romania and India.[21] Whether or not this restrictive treatment of the more competitive developing countries will encourage other Third World suppliers to increase their exports to the EEC remains to be seen.

THE ADMINISTRATION OF QUOTAS

The way in which quotas are administered can have a decisive impact on how the benefits of tariff exemption on imports are distributed, and in particular whether these take the forms of a windfall profit to the firms which handle the import arrangements or of higher prices received by exporters in the developing countries.[22] In a number of EEC countries (Belgium, Luxembourg, Italy, and to some extent Germany) quotas have been administered under the 'greyhound system'. This means that as imports are cleared through customs so they are counted cumulatively against the import quota, and when the limit is reached the tariff is reimposed on all subsequent consignments. As the quota nears exhaustion, this can create uncertainty as to whether orders will receive tariff-free treatment, and may result in lower prices being paid to exporters; moreover, such a system tends to favour better organised, perhaps multinational, firms in the more advanced of the developing countries who can speed their product to the EEC in order to claim tariff exemption.

The alternative system which has been employed, for example, in the Netherlands, is to allocate the quotas in advance to importers, usually on the basis of their past imports. The danger for the GSP exporters under this arrangement is that where actual imports are likely to exceed the quota limit, the importing firms will be able to exercise monopsony power, holding down the price offered to the exporters in the developing country and enlarging their own profit margins. Also, if European producers have access to the import quotas, they may use their position to block GSP imports; this may have happened in France.

RULES OF ORIGIN

Imports under the GSP must comply with rules of origin, designed to deter trade deflection (see section 6.3, *Rules of origin*). The rules are similar to those used, for example, in the EEC–EFTA agreements, but they tend to bear more heavily on developing countries because they are less likely to have industries producing components which could be counted in as part of the local content. The EEC does not allow cumulation amongst GSP countries, except to a limited extent within certain regional groups (ASEAN, the Andean Group and the Central American Common Market). Thus components and materials imported from another GSP beneficiary cannot in general be counted as 'local content'.

THE LEAST DEVELOPED COUNTRIES

The EEC has aimed to make its GSP scheme more selective in recent years by tightening up the safeguard rules for the NICs and by progressively relaxing the conditions applying to the least developed countries.[23] From 1978, all industrial products from the latter countries, including textiles, have been exempted from EEC tariffs and face no quantitative restrictions. Furthermore, from 1979, their agricultural exports have also been freed from tariffs, and are exempt from the quota provisions on cocoa butter and soluble coffee.

12.3 The effects of the GSP on trade

From the outset, researchers pointed out that the impact of the GSP on trade was likely to be small because of its limited product coverage, the safeguard restrictions on products where the developing countries might be competitive and the limited margin of preference.[24] These predictions have been broadly borne out in practice: there is a consensus view that the trade effects of the GSP have been modest.[25] An extensive study by the Overseas Development Institute[26] 'found it very difficult to find any evidence that it had any significance, except in one or two categories such as engineering goods which are non-sensitive.'[27] Certainly, developing countries in Asia and Latin America did increase their share of the EEC market for manufactured goods after 1971, but the role of the GSP in this appears to have been slight.

There are considerable difficulties in estimating the effects which the GSP may have had, in particular in finding a 'normal' pattern of exports with which to compare the GSP experience. One possibility is to compare the growth of developing countries' exports to the EEC and to the USA during the period 1971–75 after the EEC had introduced its version of the GSP, but before the US scheme began operation. A faster growth of the developing countries' share of the EEC market might indicate that the GSP was having a positive effect. Langhammer has used this approach, relating the exports of the developing countries to the EEC and the US to apparent consumption in those countries.[28] His findings, however, suggest that developing countries' exports fared worse in the EEC market than in the US, except for food, textiles and wood — ironically, these are the products which are either not covered by the EEC's GSP, or are subject to strict quota controls. Langhammer concluded that the attractions of the large, homogeneous US market may have outweighed the benefits of the EEC's GSP.

It is a striking feature of the EEC's scheme that only a minority of the imports which are supposed to be included in the GSP actually receive tariff-free (or tariff-reduced) treatment. In 1978, the proportion was 27 per cent for all developing countries, and 35 per cent for ASEAN.[29] There are several explanations for this. One is that on sensitive goods the tariff-free quotas are usually set well below the actual import levels. Thus, for example, the ceilings on sensitive industrial goods (excluding textiles) imported from ASEAN countries were equivalent to only about 18 per cent of the actual trade flow; hence four-fifths of the trade would in any case be subject to tariffs.[30] But even these restrictive ceilings tend not to be fully used up — in 1976–78, the utilisation of quotas for sensitive products averaged about 71 per cent.[31] There were some products, for example steel, where the quotas exceeded the trade flow and hence were not fully used; also, because of supply difficulties, some exporting countries may not have been able to take up their full quota allocation while other countries had come up against their individual limits. There may further have been some mismatch between trade flows and the allocation of quotas between the EEC countries.

Even where there are no effective quantitative limits to tariff-free treatment, as for non-sensitive goods, a high proportion of the EEC's imports of GSP products from developing countries have failed to get tariff exemption. Taking the ASEAN example again, the proportion of their exports of non-sensitive GSP goods to the EEC which did not receive tariff concessions under the GSP scheme in 1978 were 80 per cent for industrial goods (excluding textiles) and 30 per cent for agricultural products.[32] Some of these goods may not have met the origin requirements, having received only a limited amount of processing in the country which despatched them to the EEC. On other goods, the margin of preference may have been considered too low by the exporter to warrant the additional complications of applying for tariff-free entry. In 1976, the tariffs on non-sensitive products averaged 7.8 per cent, compared with 8.9 per cent for semi-sensitive and 12.1 per cent for sensitive products.[33]

National protectionist policies within the EEC are also responsible for an under-utilisation of the GSP. This is suggested by the wide variation in the proportion of non-sensitive GSP imports which receive GSP treatment in the various member countries. On industrial imports from ASEAN countries in 1978, the proportion was only 10 per cent for France, Italy and Benelux, compared with 26 per cent in the UK and 33 per cent in Germany.[34] For agricultural goods, the utilisation of the GSP was higher, perhaps because the importers were frequently EEC processing firms who might be organised to claim the tariff exemption better than distributors. Again however, Italy (43 per cent) and France (61 per cent) together with Ireland (25 per cent) had low rates of utilisation compared with other countries whose GSP shares were in the range 72–83 per cent.[35] In France and Italy, but also in the UK and Belgium, domestic producers have strong links with the importing agencies and may be able to obstruct the usage of the GSP. National protectionist pressures are also evident in the applications made under Article 115 of the Treaty of Rome to restrict the indirect importation of developing countries goods via another EEC country when the national import quota has been used up. Langhammer has observed that whereas France, Ireland and the UK have made extensive use of Article 115 to block indirect imports from ASEAN countries, Germany never did even though it was ASEAN's biggest EEC customer.[36]

In general, it appears that part of the reason for the apparent ineffectiveness of the GSP is that the tariff quotas on sensitive goods are too small. Hence, the GSP may provide some aid to developing countries by permitting them to charge a higher price on some of their existing exports, but does not give them a price incentive at the margin for them to export more to the EEC.[37] Even this aid benefit is in doubt since, with most senstive goods not receiving tariff-free treatment, importing firms will often be in a strong position to hold their purchase price down and to secure for themselves a windfall profit from the tariff exemption. On the non-sensitive goods, there is no quota restriction problem but the GSP may often not be attractive because of the low margin of preference.

This margin has been undermined since the GSP began in 1971 by a considerable expansion in the number of countries whose exports get tariff-free treatment in the EEC—notably the new member countries of the Community, the EFTA countries, some Mediterranean countries and the Commonwealth ACP countries. Furthermore, the preference has been eroded by the tariff reductions negotiated during the Tokyo Round. This could reverse some of the gains made by developing countries under the GSP, especially where these have been made through trade diversion. Even trade-creation gains could be lost if there are other lower cost non-EEC suppliers. Estimates of the relative importance of trade creation and trade diversion under the GSP vary widely, though there is agreement that the overall effect is small.[38] Against possible trade losses through erosion of the GSP have to be set both the trade creation gains from lower most-favoured-nation tariffs and the greater certainty that attaches to tariffs that are bound under the GATT, rather than reduced autonomously under the GSP. Baldwin and Murray concluded that the developing countries had more to gain from across-the-board, most-favoured-nation tariff reductions than through a continuation of existing preferences.[39] This view is contested by other researchers: an UNCTAD study suggested that the Tokyo Round tariff cuts would result in a substantial net loss for developing countries.[40]

12.4 Conclusions on the GSP

Despite the EEC Council's claim that 'experience in the initial period has shown that the Community scheme has to a large extent achieved its intended objective',[41] the general view is that the

EEC's version of the GSP has been a flop. Criticism has focused on three issues:

(i)   As discussed in the previous section, the trade impact of the scheme has been very small; in particular, the EEC has minimised the trade creation impact either by excluding products or by fixing strict quantitative limits to tariff-free treatment.

(ii) A very high share of the benefits of the scheme, as measured by the volume of imports admitted to the EEC under the GSP has gone to a limited number of more advanced developing countries (the NICs)—in 1977, for example, seven countries (Yugoslavia, Malaysia, Hong Kong, India, South Korea, Brazil and Romania) accounted for over 60 per cent of the the EEC's GSP imports, and 15 countries for 85 per cent.[42] The least developed countries appear to have made little use of the scheme.

(iii) The complexity of the scheme, particularly in relation to the safeguard measures—'the way in which quotas and ceilings are decided and announced results in an inequitable and inefficient scramble for licences on a first come, first served basis. It can mean that for a considerable part of the year importers are holding unnecessarily large stocks, only part of which may have benefited from preference.'[43]

The changes made to the EEC's GSP scheme when it was renewed in 1981 represent the EEC's response to these criticisms. The most severe reaction would have been to abandon the GSP approach entirely and to look for other ways of helping the developing countries to industrialise. This was never a serious option because it would have been very damaging to the North–South dialogue: developing countries are strongly committed to the GSP even if it brings them only very limited gains. It would also have been seen as yet more evidence of growing EEC protectionism. Nor was it politically acceptable to deal with the problem of the NICs simply by removing some of them from the scheme, even though this could have been dressed up as an attempt to concentrate help on the least developed countries. Instead, a way of restricting EEC imports from the NICs had to be found within the GSP scheme. Administratively, a relatively simple expedient would have been to exclude from GSP treatment certain broad categories of goods from particular developing countries which would be strongly competitive in those categories even without preferential treatment. The EEC, however, was anxious to avoid any selective exclusion of NICs, and preferred instead to resort to the complex system of tariff quotas described earlier, even bowing to national protectionist pressures by retaining the subdivision of the tariff quotas between the member countries. The product coverage of the scheme was not substantially widened.

The current, revised version of the GSP is perhaps simpler than its predessor but is unlikely to have much more impact on trade. From a protectionist viewpoint, it retains tight safeguards for sensitive European industries whilst not unnecessarily provoking the wrath of the NICs by excluding them from any part of the scheme. For many developing countries, 'the GSP remains of disappointing value to their export efforts; it is inadequate, insecure and complicated.'[44] As a contribution to the NIEO, the EEC's GSP is decidedly lightweight, even though the GSP itself stands as UNCTAD's main achievement in the field of trade.

12.5 International Commodity Agreements for primary products

The Multi-Fibre Arrangement (see section 7.3) is one of a number of formalised attempts by governments to influence or regulate world trade in particular product areas through international commodity agreements (ICAs). Most ICAs deal with unprocessed primary products, and since 1945 agreements have been operated for wheat (beginning in 1949), tin (1953), sugar (1953), olive oil (1956), coffee (1962), cocoa (1972) and rubber (1979).[45] Their principal concerns are world prices, internationally-held stocks, and the volume and direction of trade. The GATT has played only a minor role in relation to ICAs, though its provisions were modified in 1966 to accomodate trade restricting ICAs which promoted the interests of developing countries. The negotiating framework for commodity agreements has been provided by the United Nations which requires the participation of both importing and exporting countries. Since 1964, UNCTAD has been a forceful advocate of ICAs to organise world trade in favour of developing countries.

The post-war ICAs have been established with two principal objectives in mind: to stabilise world commodity markets by reducing price fluctuations over a period of years, and to bring about a sustained increase in the average market price of a commodity, particularly where this is of major export interest to developing countries. In addition, ICAs aim to create a forum for the discussion of trade problems and an exchange of information. Some less ambitious ICAs confine themselves to these latter aspects.

The main instruments used by the fully-fledged ICAs are buffer stocks and export restrictions. A *buffer stock scheme* operates through the establishment of an agency acting on behalf of the member governments.[46] The agency purchases supplies of a commodity in a period when prices are low, storing them and then releasing them back on to the market when prices are high. In this way, the peaks and troughs of commodity prices are smoothed out.

The aim of an *export restriction scheme* is to prevent commodity prices from falling to a low level by cutting back the volume of exports. If the demand for the commodity is inelastic, exporters as a group should increase their export revenues since the beneficial effect on prices should more than offset the reduced volume of trade. A big problem with these schemes, however, is to persuade all of the exporting countries to cut back their sales; in principle, this is done by allocating each country a maximum quantity (quota) for exports over say three months or a year. There is however a strong incentive for individual countries to stay outside the scheme and benefit from the higher prices without having to restrict their sales.

THE INTEGRATED PROGRAMME FOR COMMODITIES (IPC)

At the beginning of the 1970s, world commodity prices, which in general had been stable or declining in real terms over the previous two decades, increased sharply. The most dramatic rise occurred in oil (petroleum) prices which trebled at the end of 1973, but most of the leading primary products also recorded large price increases. These developments aroused considerable concern in the western countries about the future cost and security of food supplies and raw materials and, in particular, about the danger of OPEC-style restrictions on exports spreading to other commodities. Governments in the developed countries became more amenable to international action aimed at stabilising commodity markets. This found expression in the call for a New International Economic Order at the UN in 1974 and, more specifically, in UNCTAD proposals for an Integrated Programme for Commodities (IPC).

The plan for the IPC centred on the establishment of international agreements for 18 commodities, based on buffer stock schemes which would be financed by a common fund. It was estimated that the fund would need resources of $6 billion in order to deal with all 18 commodities.[47] The main incentive for the developed countries to take part was the possiblity that stabilised commodity prices might reduce the rate of inflation[48] and might make future supplies more secure.

When commodity prices fell back to pre-boom levels and even lower in the late 1970s, western governments began to get cold feet over the IPC. There were concerns that a standard instrument—buffer stocks—was being proposed for commodities with widely differing market characteristics—there was doubt that buffer stocks would be effective at stabilising prices and worry that the IPC would raise commodity prices to the detriment of western consumers. Most particularly, there was a reluctance to provide the massive funds said to be needed. Eventually, in 1980, it was agreed that the IPC should have no more than $750 million, but only $400 million were to be available to assist buffer-stock operations. This was far too small for the IPC to be able to play an important role in financing buffer stocks directly (e.g. under the ICA for cocoa, only one of the 18 commodities in the IPC, $230 million were spent on buffer stocks in the autumn of 1981 alone). The remaining $350 million is earmarked for market promotion and research and development projects in commodity-producing countries. Even the more modest IPC was slow to gain endorsement by the western countries, and the deadline for ratification has had to be repeatedly extended.

Meantime, progress in negotiating further ICAs has been slow, though a rubber agreement was concluded in 1979 and an agreement on jute was open for signature in 1983. The existing ICAs have run into difficulties in the face of a widespread depression of commodity prices. Several have no market intervention functions (e.g. wheat, sugar and olive oil) and those which do have insufficient financial resources to support market prices at the agreed levels (e.g. cocoa). Looking back over the post-war experiences of ICAs it is difficult to find convincing evidence that they have had much impact on commodity markets, except for short periods, and then only to a limited extent.[49]

INTERNATIONAL COMMODITY AGREEMENTS AND THE CAP

The governments of the member countries of the EEC hold differing views about the desirability of ICAs, according to their general attitudes towards market intervention, their national dependence on imports and their countries' political and economic ties with the Third World. This diversity of views has given the EEC less influence in international commodity negotiations than its importance in world trade might suggest. In an attempt to improve on this, the member countries agreed in 1981 to change their arrangements for negotiating ICAs. Even for non-CAP products they would endeavour to establish an agreed Community position so that they could be represented by a joint delegation with the Commission acting as spokesman. The individual member states would still be required to sign the ICAs, along with the Community. In practice, the agreed Community position on non-CAP products has tended to be intermediate between the advocacy of commodity controls by the developing countries and the sceptical opposition to this from the US. The EEC is a party to all of the existing ICAs on tropical agricultural products and raw materials.

For CAP products, the EEC favours the organisation of world markets through a series of comprehensive ICAs covering minimum world prices, stocks, food aid and production policies. However, these have failed to materialise, except for an International Sugar Agreement (ISA), of which the EEC is not a member. The absence of the EEC has undermined the effectiveness of the ISA, since the agreement aims to prevent the collapse of world market prices by restricting exports through quotas. The EEC, without this constraint, has continued to dispose of its surplus on the world market, depressing prices by its use of massive export subsidies and thereby damaging the export earnings of a number of developing countries. The sugar market is of vital importance to these countries, and agricultural protectionism in the rich countries has deprived them of a substantial part of their export market, as well as depressing their export prices.

The crucial factor in the EEC's absence from the ISA and in the general failure to make progress with ICAs for temperate agricultural products is the Community's unwillingness to put the CAP on the international negotiating table.[50] It is true that there may be some limited scope for market-stabilising buffer-stock agreements which do not call domestic policies into question. However, a more comprehensive, market-regulating ICA would inevitably involve some linked adjustment of national agricultural support policies. The priority given to domestic farm interests in the EEC implies that the prospects for international agreement on the CAP products included in the IPC are not bright.

12.6 Conclusions: EEC trade policies towards developing countries

THE COMMUNITY AND THE NEW INTERNATIONAL ECONOMIC ORDER

For two decades, Third World countries have been pressing through UNCTAD for major changes in international trade arrangements. The EEC's record in responding to the calls for a New International Economic Order is mixed, but compares favourably in some respects with that of other developed countries. In particular:

- The EEC was the first to introduce the GSP, and its scheme is probably more generous than, for example, that of the US.
- The EEC has taken part in all of the international commodity agreements, except for sugar.
- It has introduced an innovative scheme of compensatory finance (STABEX).
- It has indexed the price received by developing countries for a primary product to the European support price (sugar, under the Lomé Convention).
- It has dismantled EEC protection against imports of some products from the Third World (but often only for selected countries), and has even lowered some barriers against imports of competing agricultural products (again only selectively, and very cautiously).
- It has given support to regional trade arrangements between developing countries (e.g. the cumulative origin rules for ACP countries, and the non-preferential trade agreement with the ASEAN countries).

On the debit side, in relation to the NIEO, the Community's most serious failings concern its treatment of the NICs, particularly over selective safeguards and graduated reciprocity (see below), its parsimonious attitude towards the Common Fund for the IPC and its non-participation in the ISA.

CRITICISMS OF THE EEC'S TRADE POLICIES TOWARDS DEVELOPING COUNTRIES

Assuming that the chief purpose of having special arrangements for trade with Third World countries is to assist their development efforts, a number of criticisms can be directed at current EEC policies.

The EEC places emphasis in its policies on the use of tariff preferences in favour of developing countries. It is, however, doubtful if the various tariff preferences have had more than a very modest impact on the relevant trade flows, though individual developing countries attach substantial importance to retaining and if possible enhancing the preferences which they enjoy. The scope for trade creation under the preference schemes has been limited by the generally complementary nature of the EEC and Third World economies. Even where there is some potential, the EEC has deliberately restricted its exploitation through excluding certain products (especially those covered by the CAP), and through narrowing and qualifying the concessions for the more advanced of the developing countries who may have the capacity to displace EEC production. The trade-diversion effect of the EEC's trade policies towards developing countries may also be small in that: (i) the export competitiveness of the more-preferred, ACP countries has been generally weak; (ii) there is relatively little production overlap between developing and non-EEC developed countries; and (iii) EEC tariffs are now generally low (although on some products of export interest to developing countries, such as footwear, the effective rate of protection may be high).

It is arguable that the developing countries will be more likely to obtain improvements in their trade arrangements if they can act together. A second criticism then of EEC policy is that by granting special preferences to certain countries such as the ACP group, the Community has weakened the unity and hence the bargaining power of developing countries (see *Selective versus general preferences*, below).

A third criticism concerns the effects of the CAP on agricultural trade. The EEC has encouraged developing countries to step up food production through its financial and technical aid programmes. At the same time, however, the CAP hampers Third World agricultural exports by denying them markets in the EEC if they compete with EEC production and by depressing world agricultural prices through the use of export subsidies. The EEC's agricultural trade policies also help to destabilise world markets, to the particular disadvantage of developing countries who have few foreign exchange reserves to cushion them against fluctuating export earnings. The primacy given to the maintenance of the CAP is illustrated by the failure of the EEC to take part in the ISA, despite the Community's general support for commodity agreements.

Although the EEC's trade policies towards developing countries have the declared aim of assisting Third World development, they have done little to cushion poor countries against the damaging effects of economic retrenchment in the Community. On the contrary, EEC policies have tended to become more restrictive in recent years, especially towards the NICs. This is unfortunate because the rise of the NICs is one of the most encouraging features of the world economy in recent years. Their example shows that developing countries can succeed in hauling themselves out of poverty by an outward-looking development strategy.

The NICs export a growing range of mainly labour-intensive manufactures, thus helping to break the neo-colonial mould of trade relations in which poor countries export raw materials and other primary products to the rich countries in exchange for manufactures. The EEC's policy reaction to this change has been largely defensive — for example, tight restrictions have been imposed on clothing and textile imports, and the tariff-free quotas under the GSP have been deliberately ungenerous. In some respects, developing countries have received less favourable trade treatment from the EEC than have the rich countries; for example, developed country exports of clothing and textiles have not been subject to quota restrictions: similarly, the Community has placed limits on imports of cereals substitutes (manioc) from Thailand but not on imports (of corn gluten) from the US. The explanation for such discrimination is straightforward: developing countries have less bargaining power and fewer opportunities for retaliation than countries like the US.

EEC restrictions on imports from the NICs are to some extent understandable in view of the adjustment difficulties facing European industry at a time of high unemployment. However, fundamental changes in the structure of the world economy are occurring, and a reorganisation of European industry is inevitable. This change may be hastened by the Second Enlargement of the Community. Trade restrictions, besides damaging the NICs, may rebound on the Community if the NICs are unable to meet their debt repayments because of a shortfall in export earnings. Rich and poor countries alike stand to lose from a crisis in the world's banking system. Furthermore, there is a danger that if EEC protectionism continues to intensify it will act as a brake on European, and world, economic recovery.

THE COMMISSION'S 1982 MEMORANDUM ON THE COMMUNITY'S DEVELOPMENT POLICY

In 1982, the Commission published a Memorandum setting out its views on the future direction of the Community's trade and aid policies for the Third World.[51] The Memorandum broadly endorses the present approach, including a continued commitment to the use of selective tariff preferences. In relation to the Lomé Convention it is suggested that the arrangement should have an indefinite duration instead of a limited timespan of five years. The main trade provisions would continue as at present, but there would be improved consultations between the EEC and the ACP countries to deal with any problems at an early stage. The membership of the Convention would continue to be geographically restricted, though Angola, Mozambique and Namibia would be encouraged to take part. The Commission also envisaged the possible creation of regional groups among the ACP countries.

As to the Mediterranean countries, the Commission recognises the crucial importance of their trade relations with the Community in the context of the Second Enlargement. Comprehensive cooperation agreements are recommended which cover trade, aid and collaboration in various fields like energy and research. Also, whilst appreciating the political difficulties involved, the Commission would welcome any possibility (at present, remote) of putting trade relations with the Mediterranean countries onto a regional basis similar to that under the Lomé Convention.

For the non-associated countries, the Commission favours: (i) the further development of the GSP; (ii) the establishment of cooperation agreements with individual countries and regional groups, including provision for financial aid; (iii) the encouragement of regional groups of developing countries; (iv) continued Community support for the North–South dialogue; (v) EEC participation in international commodity agreements; and (vi) in association with other developed countries, the extension of STABEX to all of the least developed countries.

Recession has made its mark on the Commission's Memorandum. There is very little mention of trade liberalisation for the benefit of developing countries. Instead, there is emphasis on 'predictability' and 'security' in trade relations. The implication is that, as in textiles policy, the EEC will continue to give access to present levels of exports from the developing countries but makes no commitment to increase these in any substantial way.

SELECTIVE VERSUS GENERAL PREFERENCES FOR DEVELOPING COUNTRIES

Within the EEC there is a range of views on the desirability of geographical concentration in the Community's development policy. France favours giving priority to relations with the Mediterranean countries and Africa, whilst the Netherlands, Germany, Denmark and the UK would probably prefer a more global approach. The Commission's 1982 Memorandum comes down firmly in favour of the Afro-Mediterranean emphasis and for a variety of reasons, none of which seems wholly convincing from a non-French perspective.

If, for example, the justification for concentrating aid under the Lomé Convention on certain African countries is that they are very poor, why should not the Community's aid programme address itself to all of the most impoverished nations, regardless of geographical location? Similarly, if the bias towards Africa is to respect the obligations derived from Europe's colonial past, claims could likewise be made for the Indian subcontinent in relation to the UK, Indonesia in relation to the Netherlands and soon much of Latin America in relation to Spain and Portugal.

What of European economic interests? Special relations with the African countries may be cultivated because of their importance as a source of raw materials supply: in 1979, these countries supplied France with 27.8 per cent of its non-EEC primary industrial supplies but for none of the remaining EEC countries was the proportion more than 10.6 per cent. In any case, for future security of supplies the EEC might be better advised to cultivate global sources of supply rather than putting all its eggs into an African basket. There is a similar geographical divergence of interests between France and the other EEC countries in relation to export markets. In 1979, the African countries purchased 24.4 per cent of French non-EEC exports, compared with 9.9 per cent for the other EEC countries. Indeed, for these countries, Asia was a more important export market than sub-Saharan Africa.

Any discriminatory trade policy runs the risk of diverting trade away from a low-cost to a higher-cost source of supply. In view of the different production patterns of developed and developing countries, any trade diversion resulting from Third World preferences is likely to mean that one group of developing countries gains at the expense of another. This will have a divisive effect on developing countries, as well as making the countries selected for special treatment more dependent on the preference-givers than if the latter pursued a more global policy.

These arguments suggest that the EEC ought not merely to perpetuate its existing preferential arrangements by automatically renewing them, but should give careful thought to the desirability of a more global approach to trade relations with developing countries.

13   Trade Relations with the United States and Japan

As previous chapters have shown, the EEC has accumulated an impressive network of trade agreements covering the whole of western Europe, most of the Mediterranean countries and, in one form or another, many parts of the Third World. Non-preferential tariff treatment (the so-called most-favoured-nation treatment) is reserved principally for two groups of countries: the state-trading countries of Eastern Europe (for whom tariffs in particular are a minor influence on trade flows) and the non-European industrialised countries—the United States, Japan, Canada, South Africa, Australia and New Zealand. The EEC's trade relations with this second group are supposed to be conducted on a multilateral basis through the GATT, though there are a good many bilateral contacts and arrangements; Canada has a non-preferential trade agreement with the Community.

The importance of the GATT arrangement is that it provides a set of agreed rules for the orderly conduct of world trade. Without this legal framework trade would be inhibited by the uncertainties created by arbitrary government actions. Indeed, this is the reason why there is—and should be—growing concern over the current tendency for governments to bypass the established GATT rules through discriminatory trade agreements and under the cover protectionism. During the 1970s, much of the trade policy effort of the industrialised countries focused on a major round of trade negotiations in the GATT (the Tokyo Round). These negotiations are reviewed in section 13.1 in order to identify the issues on which the EEC and its major trading partners are at odds. Since the conclusion of the Tokyo Round negotiations in 1979 there have been a series of transatlantic trade disputes between the US and the EEC, even at times talk of a 'trade war'; these disputes are examined in section 13.2. Tension has also mounted in EEC trade relations with Japan, particularly in view of the very large Japanese trade surplus with the Community, and this has led to an important change of emphasis in the EEC's trade relations with

Japan (section 13.3). In section 13.4, the attempt by the GATT members to reaffirm their support for an open trading system at a special Ministerial Conference in 1982 is reviewed.

13.1 The Tokyo Round negotiations 1973–79

A major function of the GATT is to organise negotiations aimed at reducing barriers to trade and, since 1947, seven major negotiating rounds have been held. The early rounds were successful in re-establishing a more orderly system of trade; tariffs on about a half of world trade were bound by international agreement, and the level of protection was significantly reduced.[1] But during the 1950s relatively little further headway was made in cutting tariffs. The momentum was regained in the Kennedy Round of 1964–67 (see section 6.2). These negotiations were prompted by US concern over the potential economic division of the western world following the formation of the EEC, and the possibility of its enlargement to include the UK. The linear approach to tariff-cutting was employed for the first time, and large reductions were agreed in tariffs on industrial goods. Little progress, however, was achieved in reducing restrictions on agricultural trade, in making changes helpful to developing countries' exports, or in tackling non-tariff barriers, apart from a new code on anti-dumping duties.

Those areas where the Kennedy Round negotiations had largely failed became the primary target of the next set of negotiations, launched in Tokyo in November 1973. In return for devaluing the dollar in terms of gold in December 1971, the US had obtained the agreement of the EEC and Japan to the holding of comprehensive multilateral talks on fundamental trade issues within the GATT.[2] The negotiations could scarcely have been launched at a less opportune time—the world monetary system was in a state of crisis following the break-up of the Bretton Woods system of pegged exchange rates, and the trebling of oil prices in the autumn of 1973 had dealt a massive shock to the world economy. Expectations about what could be achieved in the Tokyo Round were low. As Casadio wrote at the time, 'the emphasis will be not so much on expanding world trade as on finding some agreement to avoid adverse effects on trade. In fact, if a certain amount of protectionism has to be accommodated as it seems it must be, the sensible thing to do is to consider all possible ways of limiting its more harmful effects.'[3]

Opinion in the EEC about the desirability of substantial trade liberalisation under the GATT was divided. In France, enthusiasm for the Tokyo Round was described as 'approximately zero', and there was a similar apprehension about reducing barriers to trade in the UK. By contrast, in Germany, the prospect of freer trade was welcomed, and the European Commissioner Haferkamp stressed the EEC's support for the GATT system. He argued that the EEC's priority in the Tokyo Round was to modify the GATT rules to permit more flexibility in the use of selective safeguards (i.e. restrictions on rapid increases in low-cost imports from particular sources including Japan and the NICs). In addition, the EEC wished to negotiate substantial cuts in US tariffs, with the minimum number of exceptions to the across-the-board cuts, and to see both a new international agreement on cereals and an international arrangement for trade in dairy products.[4]

With opinions in the EEC divided, the Commission was in no real position to take the lead in getting the Tokyo Round talks moving. It was not until after the election of US President Carter and the appointment of Mr Robert Strauss as his Special Trade Adviser that any urgency was injected into the negotiations. Strauss broke the deadlock that had arisen between the US and the EEC by bowing to EEC pressure for separate negotiations on agriculture, by being more receptive to EEC views on international commodity agreements and on selective safeguards, and by proposing that tariff cuts should be phased in slowly over a long period. The final phase of the Tokyo Round negotiations, which focused very much on the EEC, the US and Japan, but involved a total of 99 countries, began in January 1978; a final agreement was signed in November 1979.

The length of the Tokyo Round negotiations is not surprising in view of the difficult world economic conditions during the 1970s and the complexity of the issues discussed. In addition to tackling the old protectionism of tariffs, the negotiations grappled with the new protectionism in its various non-tariff guises, as well as the related issues of selective safeguards, agricultural trade arrangements and trade measures in favour of developing countries. The outcome of the negotiations is reviewed below.

THE RESULTS OF THE TARIFF NEGOTIATIONS
Before any real progress could be made in the tariff negotiations, agreement had to be reached on the formula by which across-the-board tariff cuts were to be made. The two main protagonists, the US and the EEC, each favoured a formula which would result in a

larger cut in the other party's tariff than in its own. Thus the EEC, which had fairly uniform rates of tariff for most products, favoured a tariff-harmonisation approach which would cut high tariffs proportionately more than low tariffs. By contrast the US, whose tariff rates were more dispersed and included many which were high, favoured something closer to a straight percentage cut in all tariffs. Behind the EEC support for tariff harmonisation there was also a desire in some quarters to prevent the CCT from losing its significance as a trade barrier in relation to products where EEC tariff rates were already low; the CCT was valued as a symbol of European political unity and as the basis for politically advantageous preferential trade agreements. A compromise was reached between the EEC and the US in which the EEC accepted a somewhat higher average tariff cut than some member countries wanted in return for a measure of tariff harmonisation (the 'Swiss formula'). In general, the size of the tariff cuts which were eventually agreed increased with the size of the initial tariff, except for the highest tariffs (over 25 per cent) where the percentage reductions were mostly small.

Expressed in percentage terms, the Tokyo Round tariff cuts appear impressive enough: on average, tariffs were reduced by about 33–8 per cent of their post-Kennedy Round (1971) levels. However, these cuts relate to tariffs which, in nominal terms, were already low, so that the absolute reductions were small: for example, the weighted average of EEC tariffs on industrial goods is due to fall by less than two percentage points, (from 6.6 to 4.8 per cent—see Table 13.1). The impact on trade is likely to be modest, especially as the tariff changes are to be phased in over a ten-year period, in eight equal instalments for most goods. The EEC stated that, after five years, it would reconsider the implementation of the final tariff cuts; as a gesture towards checking the spread of protectionism the Community announced in December 1983 that it would accelerate the planned tariff cuts, provided that other countries followed suit.

NEGOTIATIONS ON NON-TARIFF BARRIERS

For the first time in the series of major trade negotiations under the GATT, the main emphasis in the Tokyo Round was on tackling non-tariff barriers (NTBs) to trade. This reflected the view that, whilst the level of tariffs had in general been reduced to modest proportions, world trade was being increasingly restricted by *non*-tariff measures. These NTBs assume a wide variety of forms (see section 5.2) and just identifying them presents major

Table 13.1   Tariff reductions on industrial goods[1]
agreed in the Tokyo Round (TR)

		EEC	US	Japan[2]	Ten[3]
Simple	pre–TR	8.1	12.1	10.2	10.6
Average	post–TR	5.6	7.0	6.0	6.5
% reduction		31.0	42.0	41.0	38.0
Weighted[4]	pre–TR	6.6	6.2	5.2	7.2
Average	post–TR	4.8	4.4	2.6	4.9
% reduction		27.0	30.0	49.0	33.0

Source: Adapted from Corbet, H., 'Importance of being earnest about further GATT negotiations', *World Economy* vol. 2 (1979), Table 1, p. 328.
Notes:
[1] Excluding petroleum products.
[2] After implementing the Kenedy Round agreement Japan reduced its tariffs by 20% across the board.
[3] EEC, US, Japan, Canada, Sweden, Norway, Switzerland, New Zealand, Austria and Finland; the averages are weighted by the trade of each country.
[4] The simple average on each tariff line is weighted by each market's MFN imports on that line.

difficulties. Nevertheless, there is evidence that their incidence has increased considerably in the last decade. For example, Page's work suggests that the proportion of world trade which is subject to import and/or export controls rose from 40 per cent in 1974 to 48 per cent in 1980.[5] For the EEC, the corresponding proportions were 36 and 45 per cent; the US figures were remarkably similar.

The goods most frequently controlled by importers have been food, clothing and textiles, and steel, but machinery and transport goods, including cars and television equipment, have also been affected by NTBs.[6] Controls on manufactured goods are more frequently directed against developing countries' exports than products from other industrial countries. (For the EEC, Page suggests that the proportions affected in 1979 were 34 and 11 per cent, respectively.[7]) Moreover, it is on trade in manufactured goods that the controls appear to be growing fastest: in the EEC, the share of manufactured imports which were controlled rose from 0 to 16 per cent between 1974 and 1980.[8] These data on the incidence of NTBs do not of course reveal how restrictive the controls are. There is some evidence, however, that their impact is substantial and possibly much greater than that of tariffs.[9]

NTBs cannot, in general, be liberalised by across-the-board measures as with tariffs; instead they require individual negotiation, which is often a very slow process. The approach used in the Tokyo Round was to identify the key areas where government (non-tariff) practices restrict trade, and to negotiate codes of conduct for each of these areas. The rationale for these codes is that individual countries have little incentive to reform their practices unilaterally since in the short term this would appear mainly to benefit foreign exporters and might cause some job losses at home. If, however, other countries undertake similar reforms in return, then all can benefit from increased trade and specialisation. In order to enforce reciprocity, commitments under the Tokyo Round codes are not automatically extended to all GATT members, as are tariff concessions. They apply only on trade between countries which are signatories to a particular code, and this therefore could lead to discriminatory treatment between contracting parties. However, the major industrial countries generally accepted all of the codes; some of the more advanced developing countries and some East European countries have accepted certain of the codes.

The Tokyo Round codes of conduct were concerned with the following areas: technical regulations and standards, customs valuation, import licensing procedures, government procurement, subsidies and countervailing duties, and anti-dumping duties.[10] Since EEC practice, incorporating the rules under the new codes, has already been discussed in earlier chapters, the codes will be considered only briefly here.

Agreement on technical regulations and standards.   This code is a potentially important innovation, for the first time, GATT members are committed not to allow the specification of standards to create unnecessary obstacles to trade, not to discriminate between nationally-produced goods and imports in the application of standards, and, wherever possible, to use agreed international standards. Aggrieved governments now have legally-binding rules under which they can complain about, and seek redress for, infringements of the code by signatory countries. The effect of the code for the EEC is to extend the rules which apply between the member countries (see section 5.3, *Harmonisation of technical standards*) to trade with most other industrial countries.

Agreement on customs valuation.   This code replaces an earlier code under which the customs valuation of a good was based on the theoretical concept of the 'normal price', a concept which was prone to abuse. The general criterion now is the actual transaction value (see section 6.3, *Customs valuation*). EEC exports should benefit in particular from the termination by the

US of its 'American Selling Price' system whereby the customs valuation of certain benzenoid chemicals was determined by the level of US market prices rather than the offer prices of the imports.

Agreement on import licensing procedures. The aim of this code is to ensure that the licensing system does not become an additional source of trade restriction. Government practice must conform to a set of rules dealing with licences which are supposed to be issued automatically for all intended imports (as in cases where a government is simply seeking to monitor imports), and with those issued on a restricted basis (where the licences are used to implement a system of quotas). EEC practice was already consistent with this code (see section 6.4, *Safeguard measures.*).

Agreement on government procurement. This code seeks to open up large government contracts to competitive foreign suppliers by setting out detailed rules for tendering and for the award of contracts. Although, for example, some EEC countries have not been prepared to open up telecommunications, energy and transport purchasing, the Agreement could affect some $35 billion of contracts a year. Too much should not be expected of the Agreement, however, since similar rules in the Community have been largely ineffective (see section 5.3, *Opening up government purchases to foreign suppliers*).

Agreement on subsidies and countervailing duties. Although Articles VI and XVI of the GATT already contained rules regarding countervailing duties and subsidies, there were problems in applying them. The EEC, for example, complained that in the US countervailing duties were applied on imports even where it had not been demonstrated that the imports had in any way damaged US industry. For its part, the US strenuously attacked the EEC's increasing use of subsidies. The new code requires proof both that a subsidy has been bestowed on the manufacture, export or transport of a product and that there is a link between imports and injury to a domestic industry, before countervailing duties may be applied (see section 6.4, *Anti-dumping duties*). The code recognises that there are legitimate social and economic reasons for the use of government subsidies, but requires that signatories using subsidies must seek to avoid both injury to the domestic industries of other signatories and the erosion of trade benefits to which these other countries are entitled under the

GATT. Except for primary products (see *Negotiations on agriculture* below), export subsidies are banned, and the code contains an illustrative list of types of export subsidy.

Agreement on anti-dumping duties. This is a revision of the 1967 code. The main changes include a distinction between subsidised and dumped imports, and the abandonment of the rule that dumping must be the principal cause of injury to a domestic industry. Now, it is sufficient that material injury is caused by dumped imports.

The Tokyo Round codes on NTBs entered force in January 1980, except for those on standards and government procurement which took effect a year later. It will be some time before their operational significance can be clearly judged. In this respect, a crucial feature of the codes is their procedure for conciliation and dispute settlement. A standing committee drawn from the participant countries is charged with overseeing each code. Where there is disagreement between countries on a particular issue, the committee may seek advice from technical experts and/or a panel may be established to examine the problem and make rulings. The committee has the sanction of authorising the withdrawal of benefits under a code from offending countries.

THE FAILURE OF NEGOTIATIONS ON SAFEGUARDS

On the vital issue of safeguards, the Tokyo Round negotiations failed to make progress. Article XIX of the GATT already permitted emergency action (e.g. an increase in tariffs) to be taken on a temporary basis where a country experienced a sudden increase in imports of a particular product which caused, or threatened to cause, serious injury to domestic producers. With the rapid increase in exports of some manufactured products from the NICs over the last decade, there has been no shortage of problems of this kind in the developed countries. Little use has been made of Article XIX however, mainly because under the GATT rules emergency action must be non-discriminatory. Thus restrictions would have to be taken against imports from other developed countries, as well as from the low-cost producer whose exports are having a disruptive effect: these countries might respond by taking strong retaliatory action. For this principal reason, emergency action in the developed countries has increasingly taken the form of illegal (e.g. quotas) or extra-legal (e.g. voluntary export restraints) controls on imports from particular low-cost sources.

In order to bring emergency actions back into the framework of the GATT rules, revisions to the GATT safeguard arrangements were discussed in the Tokyo Round. Under pressure from the UK and France, the EEC sought to modify the rules so that safeguards could be employed under certain conditions against selected countries.[11] This was resisted by the NICs and Japan, who saw themselves as the principal targets for selective action. At the same time, the NICs had to bear in mind that in the absence of a reform of the rules their exports would still be subject to discriminatory control measures, but without the benefit of effective international surveillance. Other developed countries, such as the US, also had reservations about selective safeguards because they feared that this might be the thin end of the wedge, leading to a complete undermining of the GATT non-discrimination principle. Although the search for a compromise solution continued into 1980 after the Tokyo Round agreements had been signed, it eventually ended in failure. What Commissioner Haferkamp had described in 1977 as the EEC's key objective in the Tokyo Round proved beyond reach.

NEGOTIATIONS ON AGRICULTURE: THE US AND THE CAP

Agricultural trade has been a perennial source of friction between the EEC and the US. The villain of the piece, in US eyes, is the highly protectionist CAP. The US argues that whereas European exporters have liberal access to the US market for the manufactures in which they specialise, the CAP denies the US the opportunity of fully exploiting its comparative advantage as a low-cost food exporter. Specifically, the US complains that the CAP restricts US exports to the Community, destabilises world markets, and squeezes US exports out of their traditional non-EEC markets through the use of export subsidies. During the Kennedy Round negotiations, the US made a determined (but unsuccessful) attempt to alter the shape of the CAP before it was fully established. The US objectives in the Tokyo Round were more limited, focusing on better access for US farm exports to the EEC and curbs on the EEC's use of export subsidies.

The EEC's attitude to negotiations on agriculture was, not surprisingly, mainly defensive: it would not take part in any negotiation which might call into question either the principles of the CAP or the methods employed, especially the variable import levies and export subsidies. It pointed out that the US already had a huge agricultural export surplus with the EEC averaging 6 billion ECU in 1982–4. Critics were reminded that the Community had an inescapable commitment to support the incomes of its farmers, the bulk of whom were far worse-off than their US counterparts. This commitment was already very costly to European taxpayers as well as to consumers, and the EEC would resist demands for better access to the European market which would add to this burden. Instead, the Community would press its case for greater coopera-tion between exporters in international market management. It would also be prepared to negotiate some liberalisation of tariffs and quotas on agricultural products which were not produced on any scale in the EEC. The conflict with the EEC over agricultural trade was one of the main problems facing the US in its attempt to get the Tokyo Round negotiations moving in 1977. As a compromise, a twofold approach was agreed involving negotiation of tariff reductions on the usual request and offer basis (which the US preferred), and discussion of international market manage-ment for selected commodities (which the EEC preferred). Although other countries participated in both of these approaches, the key agricultural issue in the Tokyo Round negotiations was the need to find an arrangement acceptable to both the US and the EEC.

The tariff negotiations led eventually to reductions being agreed which were widespread but probably of limited significance for the development of world agricultural trade because the tariffs concerned were already low and the demand for the products was highly price-inelastic in the developed countries. In the EEC, the concessions affected mainly non-competing products, but the Community also granted levy-free quotas on imports of certain items produced within the EEC such as citrus fruit and tobacco. In return, the EEC obtained similar concessions for its own exports.

Despite US reluctance to organise world markets in collabora-tion with the EEC, two steps in this direction were made in the Tokyo Round. First, under the code on subsidies and countervail-ing duties it was agreed that export subsidies for primary products should not be used to gain more than an equitable share of markets in those products, account being taken of shares in the last three years. It is evident that this is a very vague agreement, capable of divergent interpretations. Even so, it represents a step-down for both the EEC and the US: for the EEC, because it marks the beginning of an acceptance by the Community of some external discipline in relation to its agricultural export subsidies, and for the US, because it involves an acceptance of the use of export subsidies as part of the CAP.

The second step towards market organisation concerns the negotiations on particular commodities.[12] Negotiations on dairy products led to an agreement between the EEC and New Zealand on minimum prices in international trade for butter, milk powder and some types of cheese. There is some evidence that this has helped to raise world prices for butter substantially, and curtailed the cost of EEC export subsidies.[13] An agreement on beef, signed by Australia and the EEC, was more modest in scope, confining itself mainly to better information and consultation. A third set of negotiations on an international wheat agreement was carried on outside the Tokyo Round proper but was reckoned to be part of the overall trade package. The aim was to set up an internationally coordinated stockpile of grain which would give some security against a poor global harvest and which would also help to stabilise world wheat prices. The negotiations eventually foundered because although the US and the EEC reached an accommodation over the operation and funding of the stockpile, developing countries were dissatisfied with certain aspects of the deal, including the price that they would have to pay for wheat imports.[14]

The failure of the wheat talks left the Tokyo Round results for agriculture looking very thin. There were just enough concessions for the US not to reject the deal but no real movement towards freer trade. For the EEC the most important outcome was that the CAP emerged unscathed.

THE TOKYO ROUND AND DEVELOPING COUNTRIES

The Tokyo Round produced some benefits for developing countries—notably tariff cuts by the industrialised countries on tropical products, specially favourable terms for the developing countries to participate in the codes of conduct on NTBs, and a formal agreement that preferential tariff treatment for developing countries should be a permanent feature of world trade arrangements.[15] The developing countries also benefited from the tariff cuts on industrial products agreed between the developed countries, although the average cuts on products of export interest to developing countries were only 25 per cent, compared with 39 per cent for goods predominantly traded between developed countries. Even these cuts are a mixed blessing since they reduce the value of preferences for developing countries under the GSP. Overall, the advantages for developing countries from the Tokyo

Round package are small in relation to the enormity of their trade problems. However, they did not attempt to block the final deal because this would have provoked a major crisis in the GATT. For all its deficiencies, the GATT system is seen to be better for the Third World than the alternative of anarchy in which the weak countries would be even more disadvantaged.

CONCLUSIONS

Victoria Curzon Price has described the Tokyo Round negotiations as 'extraordinarily unproductive and disappointing',[16] a vast labour over six years for little result. This assessment seems to be borne out by Deardorff and Stern's *ex ante* analysis of the effects of the Tokyo Round on world trade and welfare.[17] Using a general equilibrium model embracing 34 major trading countries and 29 industries, it was concluded that the tariff changes, the agricultural concessions and the public procurement code[18] would boost world trade by 1.8 per cent, and the economic welfare of the industrial countries by 0.01 per cent. Another major study, by Cline *et al.*[19] shared the view that the static welfare gain would be very small in relative terms (e.g. 0.03 per cent for the EEC) but argued that with the associated dynamic effects the gain would be five times greater. Moreover, these gains were not once-for-all but would continue over future years. Taking these future effects into consideration, Cline *et al.* suggested that the gain to the EEC was about 1.4 per cent of its 1974 GNP, or $19 billion. Even apart from the many heroic assumptions that the studies mentioned were obliged to make (e.g. over elasticities of substitution between alternative suppliers), the results are bound to be very tentative since the main achievement of the Tokyo Round is the set of codes of conduct on NTBs. The significance of the codes will depend on the way governments choose to implement them, and that only time will reveal.

From an EEC perspective, the results of the Tokyo Round were mixed. The GATT system remained intact and the agreed tariff changes may produce some useful gains on intra-industry trade with other industrialised countries, through trade creation and a reversal of former EEC trade diversion. For EEC trade relations with the United States the key Tokyo Round issues were US demands for better access to the Community market for their agricultural products and high technology goods.[20] The problem was that the EEC preferred the *status quo* on transatlantic trade to any bargain which included a significant liberalisation of EEC trade in these two areas. Consequently, the CAP emerged from the Tokyo Round largely unscathed and the position in the European market of agricultural exporting countries like the US, Canada, Australia and New Zealand will continue to deteriorate unless and until there is a major reform of the CAP.

For high-technology goods, the hopes of the US for an improvement in trade arrangements with the EEC rest on the government procurement and subsidies codes. Again, however, there is no sign of a fundamental change in European industrial policies: support for national firms in the advanced technology area continues unabated. It is difficult, therefore, to believe that the new codes will have much impact. It is true that for aircraft it has been agreed to abolish all tariffs, but the conditions are rather special: the US already has an overwhelming dominance in the market for larger passenger aircraft, but EEC producers have some hopes of expanding sales to the US, and there is as yet no significant Japanese challenge.

For EEC trade relations with Japan, the most significant aspect of the Tokyo Round was the failure to agree on a revised safeguard clause. Hence the EEC regarded the outcome of the Tokyo Round as unsatisfactory, and afterwards continued to pursue new trade arrangements with Japan in a bilateral framework (see section 13.3).

13.2 Current issues in transatlantic trade

The USA and the EEC are each other's largest trading partners, and it is hardly surprising that in the deteriorating international trade situation of the last decade serious friction between them has developed on a number of trade issues, mostly involving products where inter-industry trade predominates. While the Tokyo Round negotiations were in progress, the resolve of governments in the industrial countries to resist protectionist pressures was stiffened by the desire not to torpedo an eventual agreement. But disputes which had been bottled up to some extent during this period later on became more open. Friction has surrounded in particular the impact of the CAP on US agricultural exports, subsidised EEC steel exports, US embargoes on East–West trade, and the volatile exchange rate of the dollar.

CONFRONTATION ON AGRICULTURE
About a third of US exports to the EEC are primary products, mainly agricultural (see Table 13.2). Annual US agricultural

Table 13.2   *US–EEC trade 1970–83*

Year	Exchange rate $1	EEC exports (fob)	EEC imports (cif)	Exports– imports
	ECU		billion ECU	
1970–2 average	0.95	10.46	12.04	−1.58
1977	0.88	20.61	26.04	−5.43
1978	0.78	23.26	28.59	−5.33
1979	0.73	25.21	34.20	−8.99
1980	0.72	26.78	44.60	−17.82
1981	0.90	37.17	49.59	−12.42
1982	1.02	42.91	53.83	−10.92
1983	1.12	50.28	53.48	−3.20

Sources: Eurostat, *Monthly External Trade Bulletin*, Special Number 1958–81, and no. 6, 1984.

exports to the EEC were valued at 9.5 billion ECU in 1982–4 and were particularly concentrated on animal feeding-stuffs, including their cereals and oilseed (e.g. soya beans) constituents. The principal US concern is the periodic threat of the EEC to introduce new restrictions on imports such as corn gluten, soya beans and vegetable oils in order to make room for increased EEC production. Thus far, the US has warded off these threats by warning that it would take retaliatory action against EEC exports.

The US is also concerned about the EEC's growing use of agricultural export subsidies. It claims that, contrary to the Tokyo Round agreement, they are being used to enlarge the EEC's share of world markets to the detriment of the US. The US has threatened to deploy its own export subsidies to preserve its market share and to increase the cost to EEC taxpayers of surplus disposal. A number of warning shots have been fired, including a large-scale subsidised sale of flour to Egypt in January 1983 which recaptured for the US a market that had been dominated for some years by subsidised EEC exports. The US seems to want to reach an informal world market sharing agreement with the EEC on cereals. But the EEC cannot undertake this without a radical reform of the CAP which would firmly control production; without this, the EEC could find itself caught between rising production and restricted export outlets, leading to an unsustainable increase in stocks and budget costs.

TRADE IN MANUFACTURED GOODS
Transatlantic trade is more evenly balanced for manufactured

goods than for agricultural products, and there is a substantial intra-industry component. EEC exporters have been particularly successful in selling instruments, non-electrical machinery and a wide range of products from the chemical and pharmaceutical industries in the US market. They hold about a 40 per cent share of US imports of these products, against a 20 per cent share for other manufactured goods where competition from Japan and the NICs is more intense. The EEC is very dependent on its motor vehicle exports to the US; in 1981, they contributed 15 per cent of earnings from manufactured exports, but face intense competition from Japanese products. For cars, the EEC's surplus of bilateral exports over imports was 3.5 billion ECU in 1981; other areas of bilateral export surplus were steel (3 billion ECU) and footwear (500,000 ECU).

The US steel industry, like the EEC industry (see section 7.2), has had a very difficult time over the last decade, with low capacity utilisation, out-of-date plant and severe import competition, especially from Japan. Imports from the EEC have come under attack on the grounds that they are heavily subsidised. In 1977, the US introduced a trigger price system which fixed a minimum import price based on low Japanese production costs, but in the depressed state of the steel market these controls were circumvented. The system was suspended, and in January 1982 US steel companies launched a series of anti-dumping and countervailing duty suits against EEC steel.

Following US official investigations which suggested that steel exports from the UK were being subsidised by up to 40 per cent, and from France and Belgium by 20–30 per cent, the US announced swingeing duties on EEC steel. The EEC Commission complained that a proper distinction had not been drawn in the investigations between operating subsidies and funds granted for the restructuring of the European industry; furthermore, EEC exports—amounting to about 6 per cent of US consumption— were being made scapegoats for the failure of the US industry to modernise and rationalise. In October 1982, agreement was reached on the voluntary restraint of Community exports until the end of 1985. Renewed conflict broke out in the steel sector in 1983 when the US announced restrictions on its imports of special steels. The EEC responded by seeking compensation under the GATT rules.

As to US exports of manufactured goods to the EEC, their strength lies mainly in research and development intensive products, especially machinery and aircraft. US exports of computers and office machinery to the EEC were valued at 4 billion ECU in 1981, and the US accounted for two-thirds of EEC imports. For aircraft, the US is an even more dominant supplier with sales of possibly 3 billion ECU in 1980. The principal US concerns in the advanced technology sector are competition from Japanese manufacturers on certain products and subsidies from European governments to national firms. US exports may have suffered as a result of the establishment of manufacturing plants in the EEC by many US-based multinational companies. They have been attracted to Europe by various investment bribes and by the desire to overcome non-tariff barriers such as the general preference of government agencies for buying locally-produced goods.

EAST–WEST TRADE[21]
Following the Soviet invasion of Afghanistan and the declaration of martial law in Poland, the US tried to bring pressure to bear on the USSR by tightening up trade controls. On both occasions, the US felt that it received only grudging support from its European allies. This is partly because the European countries tend to take a more positive view of the benefits of trade for stabilising East–West political relations, and partly because the European stake in this trade is much greater than that of the US, despite large-scale US grain sales to the USSR.

In response to the Polish crisis, President Reagan announced restrictions on US exports of sophisticated machinery for the Siberia–western Europe gas pipeline. This choice of sanction reflected concern over the transfer of advanced technology to the USSR and the future dependence of western Europe on Soviet energy supplies. In June 1982, the US administration infuriated its European allies by announcing the prohibition of exports under pre-existing contracts of oil and gas equipment by foreign firms which are subsidiaries of US firms. The EEC governments took strong exception to this attempt to interfere with economic activity in Europe and, with problems over the transatlantic steel trade unresolved, US–EEC relations reached a low point.

The EEC responded by raising again the issue of DISCs (Domestic International Sales Corporations), through which US exporters could defer a large part of their tax liabilities almost indefinitely. A GATT panel had ruled in 1981 that some aspects of DISCs amounted to an export subsidy and should be withdrawn. The US had accepted the ruling, but had made no promises to reform an arrangement which has given a large boost to US exports. The pipeline equipment embargo was, however, dropped in October 1982 and, along with a settlement of the steel dispute, transatlantic trade relations improved in time for the 1982 GATT Ministerial Conference. However, the US's attempt to extend its law and trade regulations to overseas companies is a major source of current conflict between the EEC and the US. The US sees measures such as the renewal of the Export Administration Act as essential to prevent 'a virtual haemorrhage of strategic technology to the Soviet bloc'. In the EEC, US actions are seen as infringing the sovereignty of European countries.

TRADE AND EXCHANGE RATES

The US 'benign neglect' of the dollar during the late 1970s aroused European discontent because of the large swings in the dollar exchange rate and the consequences of these for trade and inflation. Between 1976–7 and 1979–80 the dollar depreciated against most of the European currencies, for example by 25 per cent against the German mark. Whilst this helped to curb the cost to Europe of fuel and raw materials the prices of which are fixed in dollars, it caused problems for transatlantic trade because it did not reflect relative changes in costs. The price competitiveness of US exports increased causing particular difficulties in the chemicals sector, especially when combined with chronic over-capacity worldwide, and controlled oil prices in the US. There was a series of anti-dumping suits against US exports of chemicals, synthetic fibres and textiles, but the problem abated with the strengthening of the dollar after 1980. Indeed, the strength of the US dollar in the early 1980s has played an important part in the escalating US trade deficit, the job losses in many American import-competing industries, and the consequent spate of protectionist demands in the US Congress.

CONCLUSIONS

In recent years, transatlantic trade relations have been acrimonious, with warnings issued of an impending trade war. In general, however, trade has held up quite well given the difficult economic conditions and both the US and the EEC have refrained from a full-scale confrontation. Each side is acutely aware that the transatlantic trade relationship is crucial to the maintenance of the whole GATT system. It is, however, symptomatic of the malaise of the system that disputes between the two major GATT members have been dealt with by bilateral negotiations resulting in trade restrictions not sanctioned by the GATT nor subject to formal international surveillance (e.g. steel). Even where resort is made to the GATT procedures, neither side seems prepared to accept a panel finding as conclusive, but merely part of the propaganda campaign.

13.3 The EEC's trade relations with Japan[22]

The western economic system now rests on three main pillars: the United States, the EEC and Japan; between them they account for over half of the total GDP of the non-Communist world, and 60 per cent of its trade. Japan is the smallest of the pillars, though gaining relatively on the others, its GDP is only about a half that of the EEC countries combined, and the Community's share of world trade, at 22 per cent in 1980, was almost three times as large as Japan's. Much of the Community's trade is between the member countries, however, and if this is excluded then the degree of dependence on international trade is about the same for Japan and the EEC: the average of imports and exports expressed as a percentage of GDP was about 12 per cent for the EEC (9) and 11 per cent for Japan in 1979. Another point of similarity is in the broad commodity structure of trade: both economies have a heavy dependence on imported fuels and raw materials which are paid for largely with export earnings from manufactured goods.

The Japanese economy has, however, proved to be much more adaptable than that of the US or EEC in recent years. The pattern of production has been shifted towards technologically-advanced growth industries and this has helped to maintain a fast rate of productivity improvement despite the unfavourable world econo-mic environment. In trade, labour-intensive products like textiles, which used to be the mainstay of Japanese exports, have been displaced by research and development intensive goods like advanced consumer electronics and numerically-controlled machine tools. Japan's dynamic trade performance, in which its share of world trade in manufactures has risen from 10 per cent in 1973 to 13 per cent in 1981, cannot be ascribed to dumping, low wage rates or a conspiracy between Japanese businessmen and government ('Japan Incorporated'). The industrial policy behind Japan's success is unremarkable—as Abegglen has observed, it is the context rather than the content of Japanese industrial policy that is exceptional, and this includes a highly educated labour force, a growing abundance of non-human capital, and a highly competitive and entrepreneurial private sector.[23]

TRADE PROBLEMS FOR THE EEC

Trade relations with Japan have been a source of tension for the Community for some years. The main concerns have been the huge deficit on the bilateral balance of trade, Japanese dominance of the markets for a number of advanced technology products, pressure on EEC exporters in non-EEC markets, and the relatively low level of EEC exports to Japan.

In a multilateral trading world, there is no particular reason why trade between any pair of countries should be in balance; it is the overall balance, taking into account capital flows too, which matters. Nevertheless, the bilateral trade imbalance with Japan has been of acute concern to Europe because of its size and the speed with which it has grown (see Table 13.3), and especially because of the background of massive unemployment and economic stagnation in Europe. In the Community, imports from Japan, unmatched by a similar flow of exports in return, are widely regarded as contributing directly to the unemployment crisis.

Table 13.3   EEC–Japan trade 1970–83

Year	EEC exports (fob)	EEC imports (cif)	Exports– imports
		billion ECU	
1970–2 average	1.42	2.34	−0.92
1977	3.11	8.58	−5.47
1978	3.75	9.53	−5.78
1979	4.66	10.35	−5.69
1980	4.59	13.31	−8.72
1981	5.60	16.20	−10.60
1982	6.31	17.95	−11.64
1983	7.31	20.58	−13.27

Sources: Eurostat, *Monthly External Trade Bulletin*, Special Number 1958–81, and no. 6, 1984.

The second source of concern to the EEC is the so-called 'laser approach' of Japanese exporters in concentrating on exports of particular products. Some of these products have been developed behind protection in the Japanese market and then have been launched on European markets in such volumes as to overwhelm the rival European products. This process is particularly alarming to European governments because it appears to be leading to Japanese domination of the key research and development-intensive industries to which Europe is looking for a revival of industrial employment. The Japanese share of the EEC market for manufactured goods is at present small—about 0.72 per cent of apparent consumption compared with almost double that level in the US—but it is rising fast.

Perhaps more ominous is the competitive pressure on European exporters in non-EEC markets. EEC exports have been losing ground to Japanese goods in recent years in all regions except the fast expanding OPEC market. As Sautter has remarked, the EEC faces a 'global industrial challenge' from Japan.[24] In view of the importance of European export earnings from sales to third country markets, this is a challenge which Europe cannot avoid by protectionism at home, though it may be a factor behind the view, especially in France, that the EEC should concentrate on cultivating its trade relationship with the Lomé Convention countries whilst Japan focuses its exports on the Asian Pacific region.

In the view of many European firms, the Japanese market for manufactures is hard to penetrate. This cannot be attributed in the main to quota or tariff restrictions since in that sense the Japanese market is a good deal more accessible than the EEC's. European complaints focus on technical barriers to trade—for example, testing procedures and safety standards—and on the nature of the distributive system which makes it difficult for imports to gain a toehold in the market. Japanese spokesmen argue that European exporters should try harder, but as Meynell has pointed out, Europe already holds a 20–5 per cent share of the Japanese imports of manufactures and the real problem is the low propensity of the Japanese to import manufactures.[25] European exports thus benefit little from faster Japanese economic growth and indeed these benefits may be outweighed by the adverse terms-of-trade effects of Japanese growth on raw materials costs for EEC industry.

In focusing on the EEC's trade problems, it would be a serious mistake to conclude that the economic development of Japan has had entirely negative consequences for Europe. Amongst the benefits to Europe have been the creation of a zone of stability and prosperity in the Far East, the advent of low-cost, innovative and quality products for European consumers, and a competitive stimulus to the European economy.

THE COMMON COMMERCIAL POLICY AND JAPAN

As Japan was not a founder member of the GATT, the contracting parties were able to place conditions on her accession to the

Agreement in 1955. As they were entitled to under Article XXXV of the GATT, a number of countries (including the UK, France, Belgium and the Netherlands) agreed to Japanese admission only subject to discriminatory treatment. This discrimination was eventually eliminated following the negotiation of bilateral agreements with the countries concerned (UK 1963, France 1964, Benelux 1964) in exchange for the inclusion of safeguard arrangements of a selective nature.[26] When the EEC attempted to put its trade relations with Japan onto a Community footing through a bilateral trade agreement in 1969, the hope was that the remaining quotas on Japanese exports to certain EEC countries could be ended in return for a safeguard agreement along the lines of the existing ones for France and the Benelux countries. Japan, however, could not accept such a safeguard arrangement, not least because it implied that Japan was still not recognised as an equal partner with the other industrialised countries. The negotiations were abandoned.

A greater success attended EEC and Japanese participation in two GATT initiatives during the 1970s. Under the Multi-Fibre Agreement, a bilateral Japan–EEC agreement was signed which abolished the remaining quotas on Japanese textiles exports, but included a selective safeguard clause (never used) of the kind that the EEC had been pressing for in the 1969 approach.[27] The GATT Tokyo Round negotiations succeeded in further reducing the tariff barriers on trade between the EEC and Japan but, as described in section 13.1, there was still no agreement on a revision of the GATT Article on safeguards.

The failure to secure a general EEC–Japan trade agreement has meant that a collection of national quotas on Japanese exports has lingered on (see section 4.2) and several member countries continue to operate national safeguard clauses on imports from Japan. EEC countries have sought their own trade deals with Japan, especially in securing voluntary export restraints. Thus on cars, Japanese exports to the EEC are restricted by a variety of national measures (see Table 13.4).

It has been very difficult to establish a Community approach to trade relations with Japan because national government attitudes towards Japanese competition diverge sharply.[28] France has espoused a policy of promoting national champions such as Renault, operating at the European level with protection against non-EEC imports. Britain, by contrast, has encouraged the import of Japanese technology and investment to sharpen up its industrial performance. In Germany, the general approach has been to avoid

Table 13.4   *National restrictions on Japanese car exports*

	Type of control	Japanese share of market
Italy	pre–EEC quota	minimal
France	imposed market share limit (1977)	3%
UK	market share agreement	11%
Germany	export restraint agreement	11%
Benelux	export restraint agreement	
Denmark	no control	32%

Source: *Financial Times*, 6 October 1982, 9 December 1983 and 23 January 1984; G. Shepherd, p. 142, in Tsoukalis, *op. cit.*

protectionism as far as possible—though German resolution has been weakening in face of rising imports from Japan—in order to ensure that German goods maintain their competitiveness in international markets. It is not surprising, therefore, that the common positions of the Council of Ministers often appear to be attempts to paper over internal disagreements. Consequently, the Japanese 'are not entirely convinced that the EC functions fully as the representative of the Member Countries on external policy' and often find it more 'appropriate' to deal individually with the member countries.[29]

COMMUNITY ACTIONS TO RESOLVE THE TRADE IMBALANCE WITH JAPAN

During the 1970s, with the exception of arrangements for textiles and steel, EEC policy concentrated mainly on pressing Japan to open up its market to European goods. In response, the Japanese government made occasional gestures of liberalisation, which were carefully timed to defuse tension at critical periods but had little impact on trade flows. As the bilateral trade imbalance increased, the emphasis in EEC policy shifted and in November 1980 the EEC Council called on Japan to restrain its exports to the Community. In its common strategy of March 1982, the Council continued to regard Japan's low import propensity as the 'root cause of economic friction', but issued 'an invitation to Japan to provide tangible assurances that in future years it would pursue a policy of effective moderation [Eurospeak for selling less] to the Community as a whole, particularly of cars, colour television sets and tubes, and certain machine tools.'[30]

In order to reinforce its demands, the EEC announced at the same time the initiation of procedures under GATT Article

XXIII, claiming that the EEC's reasonable expectations regarding the trade benefits arising from the GATT negotiations had not been fulfilled in relation to Japan, because of that country's low propensity to import manufactured goods. Following the statutory consultations with Japan, in December 1982 the EEC asked for the setting-up of a GATT working party to investigate its complaint. If the complaint were to be upheld, the EEC might be able to suspend its GATT tariff obligations on imports from Japan and then to introduce emergency restrictions.

As EEC pressures mounted, the Japanese government announced a series of measures from 1982 on aimed at making their market more accessible to foreign manufacturers. These included tariff cuts, increases in quotas, improved customs procedures, changes in the distribution system, and less restrictive product testing arrangements. The key step came, however, in February 1983 when Japan eventually agreed to restrict its exports to the EEC of ten sensitive products (cars, vans, fork-lift trucks, motor cycles, quartz watches, hi-fi equipment, colour TVs, colour TV tubes, video recorders and numerically-controlled machine tools). Japanese export cartels will limit supplies to the EEC, no doubt at higher prices than before, and their arrival in the EEC will be monitored under the Community's surveillance system. Figures for the first eleven months of 1983 show that although sales of machine tools and video recorders declined compared with 1982, exports of the other products continued to increase substantially (e.g. quartz watches + 27 per cent) and the EEC's bilateral deficit with Japan rose to 13 billion ECU in 1983. Japan's global trade balance reached a record surplus of 36 billion ECU, and the current account surplus a record 24 billion ECU.

The export restraint agreement was negotiated by the Commission, underpinned by threats of national action by France and Britain, and for the first time sets limits for Japanese exports to the EEC market as a whole. The Commission regarded the agreement as evidence of a turning-point in the Community's relations with Japan, and described the deal as the 'final stage' in the protracted negotiations between the two sides. The Commission looked forward to cooperation with Japan in various areas including research in science and technology, joint investment projects, technological transfer, joint development aid projects and informal cooperation to secure a 'more realistic and stable exchange rate' for the yen.[31] For its part, the Japanese government clearly felt that enough had been done in 1982 and 1983 for the EEC's complaint in GATT to be dropped. However, in April 1983 the

Commission took the complaint a step further by referring it to the GATT Council.

CONCLUSIONS

A principal feature of the EEC–Japanese trade relationship is the failure—in contrast to relations with the EFTA countries or the USA—to develop a substantial two-way exchange of manufactured goods from which both parties might benefit in terms of product specialisation and the exploitation of economies of scale.[32] This means that there is no real shared interest in the development of EEC–Japan trade, nor is this offset by other strong shared interests—for example in defence—as there is in the case of US–Japanese relations. Against this unhelpful background, the EEC has not been able to reach a comprehensive trade agreement with Japan and important trade measures in Europe remain in national hands. However, in general, Japanese goods are eligible for most-favoured-nation treatment under the GATT, though this is increasingly compromised by voluntary export restraints.

The aim of the export restraints is to give European producers a breathing space in which to reorganise to meet the Japanese challenge. The restraints may also help to contain the growing trade imbalance between Europe and Japan, as well as encouraging Japanese firms to establish manufacturing facilities in the EEC. In general, this should be a welcome development since it brings new jobs and advanced technology to Europe, and helps to create a shared interest which is important for the harmonious development of trade relations.

The danger of export restraints is that, in the absence of a clearly defined policy for reorganising European industries, the pressure to turn temporary trade controls into permanent protection may prove irresistible. As previously observed, the EEC members are widely divided over the appropriate industrial policy response to the Japanese challenge. Unless agreement can be reached in this area, including a commitment to the creation of a more unified European market, the prospects for European firms in many areas of advanced technology are poor.

As with transatlantic trade, trade problems between the EEC and Japan have been exacerbated by exchange rate developments. In particular, Europeans have often argued that the Japanese yen has been undervalued in relation to European currencies for long periods.[33] European interest rates have been held at a high level in an attempt to prevent EEC currencies from weakening against the dollar because of the fear that this would increase the cost of oil imports. However, with relatively low interest rates in Japan, this has given European currencies an unwanted strength against the yen, which has further strengthened the competitive position of Japanese goods. US and EEC pressures on Japan to allow the yen to develop as an international currency resulted in 1984 in an undertaking by Japan to expand the Euroyen market by allowing more Japanese currency to be held outside the country.

Despite the 1983 agreements on voluntary export restraints, the prospects are that tension in trade relations between the EEC and Japan will continue to be acute. Problems arise from (i) the Japanese challenge in advanced technology goods; (ii) competition in non-European markets for exports of manufactured goods; and (iii) competition for supplies of oil and raw materials. The danger is not particularly that Europe will step up its restrictions on Japanese goods and that this will escalate into a bilateral trade war, because Japan's ability to retaliate given the unbalanced bilateral trade is limited. Rather, there is a danger that protectionism will spread to other countries, since European restrictions would deflect Japanese goods elsewhere.

13.4 The GATT Ministerial Conference, November 1982

Alarmed by the rising tide of protectionism in world trade, GATT members agreed to hold a special Ministerial Conference in November 1982. The aims of the conference were twofold: to get governments to reaffirm publicly their commitment to an open trading system, and to establish priorities for future work on trade liberalisation within the GATT. As the date of the conference approached, amidst bitter trade disputes between the leading GATT members, the Secretary-General, Mr Dunkel, tried to win support for a 'ceasefire' on protectionism—that is, a formal agreement by the member countries not to introduce any new trade restrictions for a specified period. The EEC, however, was opposed to this on the grounds that there was little point in signing agreements which would not be honoured.

The conference itself narrowly avoided deadlock after 'frenzied and often incoherent negotiating sessions' in an atmosphere of bitter and frequently embarrassing conflict.[34] Disputes occurred between (i) the US and developing countries over US calls for trade concessions from the NICs and a liberalisation of trade in services; (ii) the EEC and developing countries over the EEC's demand for selective safeguards; (iii) the US/Australia and the EEC over the protectionist nature of the CAP, and especially over the EEC's use of agricultural export subsidies; and (iv) in a more muted fashion, the US, EEC and Japan over the latter's limited imports of manufactures. There were wide divisions between the EEC members (the French Minister Jobert, for example, regarded the conference as useless and inopportune) so that the EEC Council had to remain in almost permanent session in order to construct a 'Community view'.

At the end of the five-day, 88-nation meeting, a declaration was adopted by the contracting parties which reaffirmed 'their commitment to abide by their GATT obligations'. However, this was dismissed by the Australian delegation as merely papering over the cracks: 'In most, if not all, of the important issues the words are vague, ambiguous and shrink from firm commitment.'[35] Even so, the EEC insisted on issuing a parallel text watering down still further its undertakings.[36] In the declaration, the GATT Ministers agreed:

- To establish a committee to examine measures affecting trade in agricultural products with the aim of making recommendations, in 1984, concerning the liberalisation of this trade. (The EEC, however, does not consider itself under any obligation to engage in new negotiations on agriculture.)
- To construct within a year a comprehensive understanding on safeguards dealing with transparency, coverage, injury criteria, duration, compensation and disputes procedure.
- To adopt revised arrangements for dispute settlement and to avoid obstructing rulings which go against them.
- To review, with the aim of liberalising, quantitative restrictions and other non-tariff measures.
- Not to use trade sanctions for non-economic reasons.
- To invite GATT members to exchange information on trade in services and to review this issue in 1984.
- To undertake various actions in favour of developing countries including better GSP or MFN tariff treatment, liberalisation of trade in tropical products, and a review of the MFA.

The declaration which was finally wrung out of the GATT Ministerial Conference marked a recognition by the participants of how much they would stand to lose from a complete breakdown in the world trade order. Without an agreement, the restraints on protectionism would be even looser. Furthermore, the agreement does commit the GATT members to work together on key problem areas such as agricultural trade measures. At the Williamsburg Summit meeting in June 1983, the commitments to the open trading system and to the GATT programme were ritually reaffirmed. Japan took the lead in November 1983 in pressing for a new round of GATT negotiations, regarding these as the best defence against bilateral pressure on exports and imports. The move also helped to establish Japan as a fully-fledged trading country, and might create a better domestic climate for the Japanese government's trade liberalisation measures. Key negotiating issues would be trade in agricultural products, services and high technology goods. The US, with its strong export interest in these areas, supported the proposed negotiations and suggested a starting date of 1986. The EEC reaction was more cautious, arguing that the present GATT work programme should be completed first. Developing countries' reactions were generally hostile.

The future of the GATT trade system hinges on the relationship between the three trade blocs whose trade policies have been the subject of this chapter—the US, Japan and the EEC. The turbulent and troubled events of the last decade—the oil price rises, the recession and volatile exchange rates, for example—have put a massive strain on this relationship, and the GATT system is dangerously close to collapse. If there are now signs of some economic recovery in Europe as well as the US, it is important that multilateral cooperation in the GATT should be intensified so that recovery is not snuffed out by rising protectionism.

14   Trade Relations with the East European Countries and the OPEC Group

14.1   Trade relations with the East European countries

Trade relations with the East European (COMECON) countries[1] constitute a major gap in the EEC's Common Commercial Policy since most of these countries are not members of the GATT nor, with one exception, do they have trade agreements with the Community. The EEC therefore administers its trade arrangements with the COMECON countries on a largely autonomous basis. COMECON (the Council for Mutual Economic Assistance) was founded in 1949 and its European membership comprises the USSR and its Warsaw Pact allies (Bulgaria, Czechoslovakia, the German Democratic Republic (GDR), Hungary, Poland and Romania). The USSR was hostile to the creation of the EEC, regarding it as the economic arm of NATO, and has refused to recognise the Community by negotiating a trade agreement with it. This created an impasse because from 1970 the Treaty of Rome requires that all trade agreements involving the member countries should be handled at the Community level. In an attempt to overcome the recognition problem, the deadline was postponed until the end of 1974 for the COMECON countries, after which date all bilateral trade agreements involving individual EEC member countries had to be discontinued.

Only Romania so far has signed a trade agreement with the Community, though Hungary has been having informal talks with the EEC about a trade deal since 1982. For COMECON countries other than Romania, exports to the EEC are regulated by quotas fixed by the EEC on a year-to-year basis. In addition, there is a network of cooperation agreements between individual EEC countries and individual COMECON members. The agreements list the sectors in which the countries wish to promote cooperation and give details of the administrative arrangements and specific cooperation projects. There is supposed to be consultation between the EEC member countries and the Commission over the nature of the cooperation agreements, but it appears that the rules are often circumvented and that the 'concertation' of the cooperation arrangements is not very effective. However, it is estimated that only about 10 per cent of trade with the COMECON countries is based directly on such arrangements. Credit policies also play a major role in East–West trade and again there is no common EEC policy. Harmonisation of credit arrangements on trade with the COMECON countries has made little progress and the measures are still conducted on a national basis.

COMECON representatives approached the EEC in 1973 with a view to negotiating an agreement which would regulate trade between the two organisations. This, however, was unacceptable to the Community because COMECON as such has no commercial policy and no competence to conclude trade agreements on behalf of the member countries. Furthermore, an EEC–COMECON agreement would seem to tighten the Soviet Union's grip on the East European countries. The EEC is therefore holding out for agreements with individual countries in the bloc.

The agreement with Romania—often the most independent of the COMECON countries in relation to foreign policy—took effect in January 1981. Romania had already obtained tariff concessions on its exports to the EEC under the GSP, and no further tariff advantages were offered in the bilateral agreements. However, quota restrictions on Romanian products were abolished or suspended according to the products concerned; in return, Romania agreed to increase and diversify its purchases of Community products. In fact, trade between the EEC and Romania declined during the first two years of the agreement and consideration is being given to a Romanian suggestion that a new, more far-reaching economic cooperation agreement should be negotiated.[2]

Although there are no overall trade agreements between the EEC and other COMECON countries, some sectoral agreements dealing with EEC imports of steel and textiles have been concluded since 1975 between the EEC and individual COMECON members, but these were unilaterally imposed by the EEC without proper negotiations. Czechoslovakia, Hungary, Bulgaria, Romania and Poland have agreements fixing market shares and minimum prices for steel exports to the EEC, and these countries (excluding Czechoslovakia) also have agreements with the EEC on textiles.

Apart from the general problem of trade arrangements between countries with different economic systems, trade relations between the EEC and the COMECON countries have raised a number of particular difficulties concerning barter agreements, internal German trade and western trade embargoes.[3] The East European economies are based on a rigid central planning system, and foreign trade is carried out through state import and export monopolies. Trade tends to be regarded as of subordinate importance—a means of obtaining certain supplies required for the fulfilment of the central plan rather than an opportunity to participate in a worldwide system of specialisation and exchange.

Within COMECON, trade is conducted by barter, that is goods are exchanged for other goods rather than for money, and this system has been spreading increasingly to trade with western countries. The reasons for this development are particularly the serious shortage of hard currency in most of the East European countries and the often poor quality of the goods offered for export, which might otherwise be difficult to dispose of. Various forms of compensation agreement are used: about 10–15 per cent of transactions are full or part barter, but most take the form of reciprocal purchasing arrangements under which the western exporter undertakes to buy East European goods equal to the value of a given percentage of his supplies. Buy-back deals are increasing in importance under which western factories or industrial plant are purchased and paid for with products manufactured by the plant. The danger with these various forms of compensation agreements, where they involve products which compete with those manufactured in the EEC, is that they will undermine and disrupt EEC markets. They represent a form of concealed dumping—indeed, a high proportion of EEC anti-dumping cases have been concerned with products from COMECON.

Under a special provision of the Treaty of Rome, imports from East Germany (GDR) to West Germany are not subject to EEC tariffs or quotas.[4] Instead, West Germany regulates the trade by strict controls and special licensing procedures. This arrangement has given firms there the opportunity to transfer some of the more labour-intensive parts of their production to the GDR where labour costs are lower (outward processing), and this has been further assisted in the past by an interest-free 'swing' credit granted by Germany to the GDR to facilitate trade between the two countries. There was some concern in the 1970s amongst other

EEC countries that the special internal German trade arrangements were being abused to provide a back door to the Community market which avoided the payment of customs duties. However, only a very small proportion of GDR goods are re-exported from Germany to other EEC countries, amounting to about 0.02 per cent of German exports to its EEC partners.[5]

Since 1947, the western countries have cooperated in COCOM (the Coordinating Committee, which comprises the NATO countries plus Iceland and Japan) with the aim of stopping the export of strategic goods to the USSR.[6] COCOM is responsible for determining which goods are to be embargoed. However, there is a belief amongst US firms that COCOM embargoes are often circumvented by European firms. Furthermore, in recent years the US has tried to use more severe trade restrictions in order to bring pressure to bear on the Soviet Union—thus, following the invasion of Afghanistan, the US government imposed an embargo on wheat sales to the USSR beyond those which had previously been set out in the 1976 US–USSR Grain Agreement. For its part, the Community undertook not to undermine the effectiveness of the US embargo by increasing its food sales to the USSR. However, the EEC reacted angrily to US attempts to restrict the supply of gas pipeline equipment to the USSR by European firms in the wake of the declaration of martial law in Poland.[7]

Despite the many problems encountered, trade between the EEC and the COMECON countries is substantial. The USSR is the fifth largest export market for Germany and the sixth for France, and ranks in the top four for imports to Germany, Italy and the Benelux countries. Poland is also a major source of imports for the Community. Altogether, the COMECON countries account for 8 per cent of EEC imports (raw materials and fuels from the USSR, farm products from Bulgaria, Hungary and Poland, and a variety of manufactured goods from the GDR and Czechoslovakia). The return flow of EEC exports includes modern technological processes and equipment (subject to COCOM controls) and foodstuffs, and takes about 6 per cent of EEC exports.

The future prospects for EEC–COMECON trade are uncertain, and a number of factors suggest that the growth of trade in the 1980s will be less rapid than in the past. These factors include the slowdown in economic growth in both East and West, increased political tension, growing EEC protectionism in areas in which COMECON countries have an export interest (e.g. agriculture, textiles and steel), EEC tariff preferences for rival developing country suppliers, and the need for East European countries to increase their exports to the USSR in order to meet the increased cost of their oil supplies.

14.2 Trade relations with the OPEC countries

Trade relations with the members of OPEC (the Organisation of Petroleum Exporting Countries) occupy an important position for the EEC countries, not only because of the magnitude of the trade flows involved (some 20 per cent of the EEC's external trade) but also because of the heavy dependence of the EEC on imported energy supplies, chiefly oil from the OPEC countries. After the second world war, abundant supplies of oil at low prices encouraged a shift in energy use in Europe away from indigenous supplies of coal to imported oil. By 1973, when the Arab–Israeli conflict precipitated a quadrupling of oil prices and an embargo on oil supplies to the US and the Netherlands, the EEC was reliant on imports for about two-thirds of its energy supplies. Partly because of a deliberate attempt to make a more efficient use of energy and to develop alternative energy sources, but mainly because of the coming onstream of North Sea oil and gas supplies and the slowdown in energy usage during the recession, EEC self-sufficiency in energy has increased, but the Community still relies on imports for more than half of its needs.

The sharp rise in oil prices in 1973 led to a massive increase in the EEC's trade deficit with the OPEC countries (see Table 14.1). However, the EEC succeeded in maintaining a fairly stable 40 per cent share of OPEC imports, and as the much higher oil revenues of the OPEC countries were spent on imports during the 1970s so the EEC's bilateral trade deficit with these countries subsided. In the wake of the Iranian revolution in 1979 a further escalation of oil prices led to a second cycle of huge trade deficits for the EEC countries, followed by a rapid movement back towards more balanced trade (see Table 14.1).

Although the EEC countries have taken some joint measures in relation to energy supplies, as the Commission has observed, 'The diversity of situations in the Community countries and the prerogatives guarded by the Community Member States have so far prevented the once for all implementation of a common energy policy.'[8] The absence of a common policy contributed to the disarray in which the Community found itself at the time of the

Table 14.1   EEC–OPEC trade, 1971–83

Year	EEC exports	EEC imports	Exports– imports	$\dfrac{Exports}{imports} \times 100$
	billion ECU			%
1971	4.6	11.7	−7.1	39
1972	5.2	11.9	−6.7	44
1973	6.7	15.5	−8.8	43
1974	11.6	39.2	−27.6	29
1975	18.7	33.8	−15.1	55
1976	23.9	42.6	−18.7	56
1977	30.0	43.0	−13.0	70
1978	31.5	38.8	−7.3	81
1979	30.7	52.8	−22.1	58
1980	37.2	68.1	−30.9	55
1981	53.5	75.4	−21.9	71
1982	55.6	71.9	−16.3	77
1983	52.1	61.2	−9.1	85

Sources: Eurostat, *Monthly External Trade Bulletin*, Special Number 1958–81, and no. 6, 1984.

first oil shock in 1973. Some EEC countries favoured a united front towards the oil-exporting countries so that the EEC could use its bargaining power as a major consumer of oil to influence oil prices and to prevent discrimination between EEC countries over the supply of oil. In the event, divisions of view led to national deals with the oil exporting countries, as favoured by France.

In 1974, the Euro-Arab Dialogue was initiated 'to establish a high degree of cooperation between Europe and the Arab world.'[9] From the EEC point of view, such cooperation would reduce the danger of an interruption of vital oil supplies, whilst the Arab countries sought to obtain at least a more sympathetic understanding of their position in the Middle East conflict. The Dialogue was suspended at the request of the Arab countries in April 1979 following the Camp David peace agreement between Israel and Eygpt, but has since been resumed. The Dialogue provides a channel of communication between the Community and some of its most vital trade partners, but its impact on trade arrangements appears so far to have been slight. The EEC, however, signed bilateral trade agreements with several OPEC countries including Algeria (under the EEC's Mediterranean policy), Nigeria (under the Lomé Convention) and Iran (a non-preferential agreement in 1963).

15 Protectionism and the Common Commercial

It is not over-dramatic to suggest that the Common Commercial Policy has now reached a critical juncture. The Community is embroiled in trade disputes with many of its major trading partners, especially the United States and Japan; at the same time, there is increasing resort to national measures by the EEC countries. Against a background of rising protection in international trade and Europe's failure—at least initially—to share in the West's economic recovery, the Community must make some fundamental decisions, if only by default, about the future direction of its trade policies. If nothing is done to strengthen the CCP, it may become of only minor significance for the conduct of EEC trade—a reflection of the Community's failure to find, and to give expression to, a shared interest in trade sufficient to outweigh for each of the member countries the perceived advantages of national freedom of action.

Reaching a new Community consensus on trade policy has been made more difficult by (i) the disputes over the EEC Budgetary arrangements; (ii) the prospective increase in EEC membership which would add to the problems of the declining industries in the existing member countries and dislocate the EEC's Mediterranean trade arrangements; and (iii) the unsatisfactory international exchange rate regime which in recent years has permitted large swings in real exchange rates between the European currencies, the US dollar and the yen.

At the heart of the EEC's current trade policy problem is the Community's attitude towards protectionism in intra- and extra-EEC trade. The protectionist issue is explored in this chapter in relation to the EEC's hierarchy of trade preferences (section 15.2) and to the growth of trade restrictions on the products of both old (section 15.3) and new (section 15.4) industries. First, however, it is important to take stock of the current state of EEC trade policies. This is the purpose of section 15.1.

The current state of EEC trade policies: a summary

The main findings of this book on the current state of EEC trade policies are summarised here in relation to four key questions:

1. To what extent has the EEC succeeded in replacing national trade policies with a truly Common Commercial Policy? The EEC countries set out in 1958 to merge their national trade policies into a single CCP, based on a customs union. In this, the six original member countries together with the four new members have had considerable success. In particular, they have:

- abolished tariffs and quotas on intra-EEC trade (see section 5.1),
- abandoned national tariffs in favour of a common customs tariff which each of the member countries applies (sections 6.1 and 6.3),
- taken action to harmonise certain trade practices, such as anti-dumping measures, (section 6.4),
- implemented common trade measures as part of Community sectoral policies for agriculture and steel (Chapter 7),
- established EEC trade agreements with many outside countries (sections 6.5 and 6.6), and
- negotiated as a group in the GATT, notably in the Kennedy and Tokyo Rounds (sections 6.2 and 13.1).

On the debit side, however, the EEC countries have:

- failed to eliminate many of the non-tariff barriers to trade within the Community, so that intra-EEC transactions are still regarded by EEC firms as foreign trade, major price differences persist between the national markets in the EEC, and restrictions on agricultural trade within the Community (e.g. monetary compensatory amounts) continue despite the common sectoral policy (section 5.2),
- been obliged to prevent the free circulation of some goods within the EEC because of the failure to establish a uniform approach to the use of quotas on trade with non-member countries (section 6.4, *Import quotas*),
- failed to put safeguard measures fully on to an EEC basis,
- not yet negotiated EEC trade agreements with the COMECON countries (except Romania) and Japan, so that national

measures remain important (sections 14.1 and 13.3), and
- most importantly, lost ground in recent years in the pursuit of a common approach to trade because of a proliferation of national trade restrictions (section 5.3).

Thus the present situation is mixed: whilst there has been a substantial movement towards a unified EEC approach in the more visible areas of trade policy, it is clear that the member states still retain considerable independence of action, especially in protecting import-competing industries.

2. What contribution has the EEC made through the CCP to the GATT world trade order?   As, collectively, the world's largest trading entity, the EEC bears a major responsibility for the maintenance of an orderly trade system. On the positive side, it can be argued that the EEC has helped to sustain the GATT system by:

- trying to frame its trade regulations and agreements at least arguably within the letter of the GATT, even if not always within the spirit, (e.g. by avoiding the imposition of import restrictions against selected suppliers but negotiating instead voluntary export restraints), and
- taking a leading role in various rounds of multilateral tariff negotiations, and generally cooperating with other countries in the framework of the GATT (sections 6.2 and 13.1).

However, EEC actions have frequently clashed with GATT principles; in particular:

- whereas the GATT calls for non-discrimination in trade, the EEC has created a hierarchy of trade preferences—a 'pyramid of privilege' (sections 6.6 and 15.2),
- whereas the GATT seeks to foster a multilateral approach to trade issues, the EEC's approach is increasingly bilateral (see e.g. section 13.2), and
- whereas the GATT sanctions protection by means of tariffs only, the EEC is increasingly resorting to non-tariff measures (sections 7.1–7.3 and 13.1, *Negotiations on non-tariff barriers*); the EEC is actively contributing to the retreat to a system of managed trade, especially through the use of voluntary export restraints (sections 7.3, 13.2, and 13.3).

It may be added also that, although the EEC has taken part in the GATT negotiations, it has done so somewhat reluctantly, and further that the Community has helped to devalue the GATT disputes settlement procedures by rejecting unfavourable findings.

3. What contribution has the EEC made through the CCP to more open world trade?   Several important contributions may be suggested; thus the EEC has:

- helped to reduce tariffs through multilateral tariff disarmament as noted above,
- established a series of industrial free trade areas which allow manufactured goods to move free of tariffs and quotas throughout the whole of western Europe (Chapter 8), and
- granted tariff preferences to selected groups of developing countries, for example, in the Mediterranean region (Chapters 9, 11 and 12). How beneficial these have been depends partly on the extent to which they have been trade-creating rather than trade-diverting.

Conversely, the EEC has contributed to the rising tide of protectionism through its growing use of non-tariff trade restrictions (Chapter 7). In mitigation, the EEC claims that these restrictions give a breathing space for the reorganisation of industries whose structural difficulties have been exacerbated by an upsurge of imports. Experience suggests however that, once granted, protection tends to become entrenched. Protectionism in the EEC may be strengthened by the system of decision-taking, which allows the possiblity of national vetoes. The issue of protectionism and the CCP will be returned to in the final sections of this chapter.

4. What contribution has the EEC made through the CCP towards a resolution of the trade problems facing developing countries?   In section 12.6, it was concluded that the EEC's response to developing countries' calls for a New International Economic Order compared favourably with that of other industrial countries in some respects—notably with regard to the GSP, ICAs, STABEX, sugar imports, selective reductions in import barriers, and support for regional trade arrangements between developing countries. However, a number of important criticisms were made. In particular:

- EEC tariff preferences have been of limited value to developing countries,
- EEC policies have weakened the unity, and hence the

bargaining power, of developing countries,
- the CAP hampers Third World agricultural exports, and
- the Community has done little to cushion poor countries against the damaging effects of economic retrenchment in the Community; EEC trade policies in relation to the NICs have been defensive and unconstructive.

15.2 Protection and preferences

For various reasons, the EEC has evolved a highly discriminatory and complicated set of preferential trade agreements which have left the GATT most-favoured-nation relationships as often the treatment given to the least favoured countries. There are some indications that the tariff preferences have affected trade patterns though—not surprisingly in view of the generally low level of the CCT—the impact is probably modest. Nevertheless, those countries which occupy the more favoured positions in the hierarchy of preferences are anxious to retain their special treatment for political as well as economic reasons.

To the extent that this special treatment leads to trade diversion rather than trade creation, the benefits to one group of countries (e.g. signatories of the Lomé Convention) may be obtained at the expense of another group: this is a potential source of conflict which could be damaging for the Community; for example, it was one reason behind the EEC's attempt to standardise its trade arrangements with the Mediterranean countries during the 1970s.

Pressure from the US has been instrumental in persuading the EEC to modify some aspects of its trade preferences which might have harmed US exports. Thus, the EEC has abandoned its demand for reciprocal tariff concessions from developing countries which benefit from EEC preferences. However, there are some indications that US attitudes towards trade discrimination may be shifting—in the Caribbean Basin Initiative, for example, the US has granted special trade concessions to a regional group of developing countries. Moreover, powerful domestic interests in the US have been lobbying for some time for greater reciprocity, sector by sector, in US commercial relations, and US trade officials were reported in 1983 to have floated the idea of a two-tier trading structure in the GATT in which a group of countries (a 'super-GATT', 'GATT plus' or 'GATT of the likeminded') engage in freer trade between themselves than with 'ordinary' GATT members.[1]

With a general weakening of support for the GATT non-discrimination principle, the EEC emphasis on preferential trade relations with selected countries might become one element in a move towards the division of the world into regional trading blocs embracing rich and poor countries (e.g. the EEC/Africa/the Mediterranean, the US/Latin America, and Japan/East Asia). In an uncertain world, such blocs may seem to offer a greater security of supplies and of markets, as well as reinforcing political allegiances. However, in view of the dissimilar economies which they draw together, they could lead to damaging inter-bloc diversion, and to greater economic and political dependency, especially for the poor countries. Most importantly, the emergence of regional trade blocs threatens the survival of the GATT open trading system upon which much of the post-war economic prosperity of the western world has been based. This can be seen as the main danger in the EEC's preferential approach to its external trade relations.

EEC producer interests have played an important role in shaping the Community's hierarchy of trade preferences. In particular, the EEC's trade agreements appear to have been designed to minimise *inter*-industry trade creation, at least in relation to sensitive sectors like agriculture, clothing and textiles. By contrast, trade creation of an intra-industry nature, which is more likely to occur in trade with other advanced countries, has not been similarly resisted—indeed, it appears to be an important element in the success of the EEC–EFTA agreements, and accounts for a substantial proportion of the transatlantic trade generated by multilateral tariff reductions under the GATT. The general failure of intra-industry trade to develop between the EEC and Japan is, in the Community's view, an important source of trade friction.

As suggested in section 2.4, where the EEC has, for politico-strategic or other reasons, negotiated trade agreements with countries which have dissimilar economic structures it has used various devices to restrict inter-industry trade creation in sensitive industries. This is particularly well exemplified in agricultural trade arrangements with the Mediterranean countries where the EEC uses tariff quotas, off-season concessions, levy reductions tied to observance of minimum import prices, etc. These devices enable the Community to offer some advantages to the Mediterranean countries with minimum damage to EEC farmers, but at the expense of Community taxpayers and/or exporters in the rest of the world.

In view of their adjustment problems, some form of temporary protection for EEC producers in sensitive industries may be inescapable. What is more open to criticism is that with few exceptions (e.g. the paper industry in the EEC–EFTA agreements) the special treatment of sensitive industries under the EEC's preferential arrangements appears to be permanent. Thus EEC consumers will continue to be denied access to cheaper sources of supply, and the Community will forgo some of the gains from increased specialisation and trade.

15.3 The New Protectionism and old industries[2]

Not only has the Community avoided the dismantling of protectionism in certain sectors, but in recent years—and in contrast to the initially liberal stance of EEC trade policies—there has been a clear tendency towards increased protectionism. This has not generally taken the form of increased tariffs; indeed, the CCT is still being reduced under the Tokyo Round accords. Instead, there is a New Protectionism ('the measures in the grey areas between legality and open breach of GATT rules'[3]) often taking the form of voluntary export restraints. The growth of protectionism in EEC policies is seen in the tougher controls under the latest Multi-Fibre Arrangement, the bilateral agreements restricting EEC steel imports, the tightening-up on the NICs in the GSP, and voluntary restraints on Japanese exports. Also, when world food prices fall, as they have tended to since the boom of the early 1970s, the CAP system provides for an automatic increase in the margin of protection under the variable import levy mechanism. In addition to Community action, individual EEC countries have increasingly restricted trade through non-tariff measures.

A number of reasons can be suggested for the rise in New Protectionist measures, including (i) the recession and the high level of unemployment in the western countries; (ii) the large swings in exchange rates since the break-up of the Bretton Woods pegged exchange rate system, which may have fuelled protectionist pressures at times; (iii) the negotiated reduction of tariffs under the GATT Kennedy and Tokyo Rounds leading to demands for alternative forms of protection; (iv) the increased intervention of governments in their national economies, especially through industrial policies which discriminate in favour of home-based firms; and (v) in the EEC, a tendency for trade policies to be determined in response to the demands of the most protectionist members of the Community.

The explanation for the last point seems to be that the more liberally-inclined countries are obliged to agree to tight Community control on imports in order to persuade countries like France and the UK not to resort to national trade restrictions. In principle, such national measures ought to be prevented by the member countries' commitment under the Treaty of Rome to the CCP, and by the powers of the Commission to curb state aids. However, in practice, the member countries are inclined to put sectional interests before Community obligations. Thus, in order to avoid a break-up of the single market, the Commission has developed sectoral policies in certain areas which involve EEC restraints on imports. In this way, the EEC has tried to externalise its problems in some sectors (e.g. steel) by throwing part of the burden of adjustment on to non-EEC countries.

The rise of EEC protectionism must be seen in the context of the slowdown in the rates of world economic growth and trade expansion, both of which halved in volume terms between 1963–73 and 1974–80 (from 6 and 8 per cent respectively, to 3 and 4 per cent). This slowdown has been accompanied by heavy unemployment in most western countries, whose governments have been under domestic pressure to restrain imports in order to prevent futher job losses. In turn, the increased resort to trade restrictions may have deepened and prolonged the recession, especially by increasing the uncertainty facing new investment projects.[4]

During the recession, the EEC's older industries have been forced to make major changes. In the clothing and textile industries, for example, more than a million jobs were lost between 1971 and 1981; similarly, during the 1960s and 1970s more than 10 million farmers and farmworkers left the land as employment in agriculture fell from 19 millions in 1960 to 9 millions in 1980. Most of the job losses in the older industries are attributable to technical change, reinforced by a slackening of demand during the recession, rather than to inroads made by foreign suppliers; indeed, in the case of agriculture the degree of self-sufficiency has risen.

The decline of employment in these older industries, although massive, has not been fast enough in the sense that large parts of the industries concerned would still not survive without continued protection. But governments have recognised that the costs of adjustment may be high for those directly involved and for some of those indirectly involved (e.g. retailers in the steel towns). These costs are particularly high during the recession when there are fewer incentives for investment in new industries which could create jobs to replace those that have been lost. Over and above the privately borne costs, there may be social costs to the loss of jobs in an industry if the transfer of employees to new areas of the country means the under-utilisation of social overhead capital (e.g. hospitals) in the depressed areas, and over-utilisation of schools, roads, and so on, in the booming areas. Slowing down the pace of change until it can be more easily accommodated may then bring important social benefits.

In drawing up government policies towards declining industries, there are good reasons for preferring measures which deal directly with those adversely affected by change and which help them to adjust to changing economic conditions, rather than measures offering blanket protection. Compensation to those who have suffered losses may be desirable on equity grounds as well as being politically necessary in order to overcome resistance to change. In the long run, compensation (e.g. for scrapping plant, redundancy payments, technical assistance to small firms) may be less costly to society than measures of protection which may:

(a) lock in skills to low-productivity uses in older industries, and indeed draw in new resources, thereby harming growth industries;

(b) be very costly to consumers in terms of lower prices forgone;

(c) damage the interests of other industries which use the products of the protected industry;

(d) lead to lost export sales as other countries retaliate or are simply forced to cut back imports because of reduced export earnings;

(e) prevent some developing countries from earning sufficient from their exports to meet their international debt repayment obligations, thereby weakening the world banking system in whose proper functioning the EEC has an important interest;

(f) be very difficult to end, because they inflate asset values in the protected sector (e.g. land prices under the CAP) and thus create a vested interest opposed to liberalisation—in short, temporary measures have a habit of becoming permanent;

(g) tend to spread within countries, because each concession made weakens the ability of a government to resist further claims, and between countries, for 'if governments lose confidence in each others' commitment to respect the rules they cannot maintain their own resistance to the demands of the protectionist lobbies';[5] and

(h) damage and eventually destroy the GATT open trading system.

Western governments are fully aware of the harmful effects of a general spread of protectionism. At international meetings such as the GATT Ministerial Conference in 1982 and the Williamsburg Summit in 1983 they regularly reaffirm their belief in the GATT open trading system as being in their own, and the world's, best interests. They do not appear to believe that the benefits achievable through the liberal post-war trading arrangements have been exhausted.

So why have trade restrictions increased? The explanation may be that the increased uncertainty of the recession years has pushed governments to adopt a more short-term view of events. In the short term, protection can undoubtedly bring benefits to (or avoid losses in) the sector concerned, even though it may be eventually counter-productive. Powerful industry lobbies can bring strong pressure to bear on the government to introduce protectionist measures and once these are conceded for one industry a bandwagon effect may ensue as other industries also demand restrictions on imports.

Warnings about the danger of escalating protection and the need for a more liberal approach to trade policy have been made by academics, by part of the media and by international organisations like the GATT. It is accepted that dismantling protection would lead to a further decline in Europe's older industries though probably not to their elimination. At the same time, the export opportunities for the low-wage countries, especially the NICs, would increase and they in turn would be able to import more products from the West's growth industries. Doubts about the EEC's ability to take full advantage of this are discussed in the next section.

15.4 The New Protectionism and new industries

There are fears in Europe that the EEC is being squeezed between the NICs on the one hand and the US and Japan on the other, in the sense that the NICs are capturing an increased share of world trade in labour-intensive products, whilst the US and Japan dominate trade in the research-intensive products. This could worsen an already very serious unemployment problem in Europe.

A sustainable increase in employment can come about only if economic growth rates can outpace rising labour productivity. An important constraint on growth rates for most countries is the balance of payments position which is strongly influenced by the propensity to export, relative to the propensity to import. That is, growth rates will tend to be higher where the income elasticity of demand for a country's exports is high, and the income elasticity of demand for its imports is low.[6] To the extent that the income elasticity of demand in world trade for advanced technology products is high, it will be advantageous for countries to have a concentration of such goods in their export structures.

This gives a strong incentive for governments to try, through the use of industrial policies, to redirect their economies towards the production of technologically sophisticated goods. They are aided in this by the recognition that in 'certain (broad) sectors national resource, factor, and technology endowments are sufficiently similar that comparative advantage may be relatively arbitrary and subject to manipulation.'[7] If then the government in one major trading country, say Japan, intervenes successfully to shift the national export product mix towards growth industries, governments elsewhere may feel that unless they follow suit they will be left with a mix of low-growth industries. Various forms of non-tariff protection are widely used to support the development of new industries (e.g. discrimination in public procurement policies for telecommunications or computers).

In these circumstances, it seems unlikely that governments in Europe will respond positively to calls for a genuine liberalisation of trade in advanced technology products, since this will give an advantage to the early starters especially the United States and recently, Japan. Bearing in mind the importance of modern industries for growth and employment, all of the larger industrial countries are likely to insist on a national presence in a range of advanced technology industries. An alternative to liberalisation might then be negotiation sector by sector of a *modus vivendi* in the GATT, recognising that it may not be universally acceptable for trade in the growth industries to be dominated by one or two suppliers, and that each country may insist on a share in modern, footloose industries. For this purpose new, more comprehensive rules might be required dealing with non-tariff barriers and temporary tariff increases might be permitted for infant industries tied to national trade performance (i.e. tariffs would be reduced as the sectoral trade moves from deficit towards balance).

Some observers doubt that negotiations to liberalise or to manage trade could be successfully negotiated on a global basis and instead have suggested that an attempt should be made to manage trade at the European level—the 'Fortress Europe' approach. Hager,[8] for example, has argued that:

(a) in post-war western Europe, emphasis has been placed on improving the pay, conditions and job security of workers, with incomes and savings channelled to 'non-productive' social infrastructure and services; oligopolistic collusion has allowed European firms to sell on a 'social cost plus' basis to the rest of the world.

(b) Increased competition from Japan and the NICs has undermined this arrangement; the socio-economic conditions in these countries are quite different from those in Europe (e.g. Europe has controlled labour markets but has free capital markets, whereas the NICs have free labour markets but capital allocated by central plans or strategic consensus by a handful of entrepreneurs and bureaucrats). Without managed trade, Europe must either change its life-style or accept low growth and high unemployment—the option of moving up-market to advanced technology and specialised products is too limited.

(c) To leave the management of trade to national governments risks 'Balkanising' Europe and hence the break-up of the free trade area.

(d) Alternatively, 'we must face up to the paradox that free markets within Europe requires managed trade with outsiders.'

Hager has been vigorously criticised by Hindley,[9] in particular for failing to explain—or even to consider—the crucial issue of why protection across the board might bring advantages to the EEC. Also, the argument that there are two distinct socio-economic worlds seems to be based on a very arbitrary division of the non-communist countries. Wolf[10] has pointed out that protection at the EEC level implies income transfers not only from consumers to producers within countries but also between countries (as with the CAP). Such transfers would penalise the more efficient countries to the advantage of the less efficient, and would almost certainly involve bitter intra-Community arguments.

Thus several options confront the Community: to take part in an attempt to liberalise trade through the GATT; to seek instead to achieve a global consensus on the management of trade; to retreat into a 'Fortress Europe' strategy; or to pursue national protection policies. Which route is chosen will have profound consequences for the future of Europe and for the world trading system.

Notes

Chapter 1

1. M. Palmer *et al.*, *European Unity: A Survey of the European Organisations* (London: Allen & Unwin, 1968) p. 258.
2. *Financial Times*, 26 January 1984.

Chapter 2

1. P. Mishalani *et al.*, 'The pyramid of privilege', in C. Stevens (ed.), *EEC and the Third World: a Survey 1* (London: Hodder & Stoughton in association with ODI and IDS, 1981).
2. More strictly, taking into account the 'small country' case, 'because it is to the advantage of one and not to the disadvantage of the other'.
3. K. Lancaster 'A new approach to consumer theory', *Journal of Political Economy*, vol. 74 (1966), pp. 132-57.
4. H.G. Grubel and P.J. Lloyd, *Intra-Industry Trade* (London: Macmillan, 1975) Ch. 3.
5. W.M. Corden, *Trade Policy and Economic Welfare* (Oxford: Oxford University Press, 1974), pp. 104–9.
6. J. Viner, *The Customs Union Issue* (New York: Carnegie Endowment for International Peace, 1950).
7. Except in the special case of pure trade diversion where the price level is unaffected.
8. R.G. Lipsey, 'The theory of customs unions: trade diversion and welfare', *Economica* vol. 24 (1957), pp. 40–6.
9. In Figure 2.1, if the home country's tariff had initially been p_1p_2 instead of p_1p_3, then the country's price level would have been unaffected by customs union formation; hence, there would be no trade creation, only trade diversion. Similarly, if at the initial price level of Op_3 home demand and home supply had been equal, so that there were no imports, then trade diversion would be ruled out and the formation of a customs union would be purely trade creating.

10. More formally, the welfare effects caused by the formation of the customs union shown in Figure 2.1 are as follows:

increase in consumers' surplus = (+ d + a + e + b   )
reduction in producers' surplus = (− d   )
loss to taxpayers of tariff
revenue   = (− e   −c)
_____
            net effect = (+ a   + b   − c)

where the consumers' surplus represents the difference between what consumers would be willing to pay and what they actually pay, and the producers' surplus represents the difference between variable costs of production and gross revenue, i.e. the return to the fixed factors of production.

11. But the larger the union is with respect to the rest of the world, the less tenable is the simplifying assumption made in this section of a constant import price.

12. J.E. Meade, *The Theory of Customs Unions* (Amsterdam: North-Holland, 1955), Ch. VIII.

13. C.A. Cooper and B.F. Massell, 'A new look at customs union theory', *Economic Journal,* vol. 75 (1965), pp. 742–7.

14. Since trade diversion brings no benefits to non-member countries—indeed, it reduces their exports to the union—it must also be concluded that trade diversion is damaging from a global perspective.

15. R.J. Wonnacott and P. Wonnacott, *Is Unilateral Tariff Reduction Preferable to a Customs Union? The Curious Case of the Missing Foreign Tariffs—or, Beware of the Large Country Assumption* University of Maryland, Working Papers 80–37, 1980; and *American Economic Review*, vol. 71 (1981), pp. 704–14.

16. Assuming that compensation to owners of specialised resources in the protected sector is possible.

17. A.J. Jones, 'The theory of economic integration', in A.M. El-Agraa (ed.), *The Economics of the European Community* (Oxford: Philip Allan, 1980).

18. see section 3.2.

19. H. Petith, 'European integration and the terms of trade', *Economic Journal*, vol. 87 (1977), pp. 262–73.

20. H.G. Johnson, 'An economic theory of protectionism, tariff bargaining, and the formation of customs unions', *Journal of Political Economy*, vol. 73 (1965), pp. 256–83.

21. W.M. Corden, 'Economies of scale and customs union

theory', *Journal of Political Economy*, vol. 80 (1972), pp. 465–75.

22. J. Waelbroeck, 'Measuring the degree of progress of economic integration', in F. Machlup (ed.), *Economic Integration Worldwide, Regional, Sectoral* (London: Macmillan, 1976).
23. P.B. Dixon, 'Economies of scale, commodity disaggregation and costs of protection', *Australian Economic Papers*, vol. 17 (1978), pp. 63–81.
24. S.J. Prais, *Productivity and Industrial Structure*, NIESR Economic and Social Studies XXXIII (London: Cambridge University Press, 1981).
25. J. Müller, 'Competitive performance and trade within the EEC', *Journal of Institutional and Theoretical Economics*, vol. 137 (1981), pp. 638–63.
26. F.V. Meyer, *International Trade Policy* (London: Croom Helm, 1978), pp. 47–51. See also section 5.2.
27. Corden, (1974) *op.cit.*, pp. 224–31.
28. M.E. Kreinin, *Trade Relations of the EEC: an Empirical Investigation* (New York: Praeger, 1974), p. 19.
29. A study of the effects of multilateral tariff cuts in industrial countries suggested that a conservative estimate of the dynamic effects would put them at five times the static effects. (W.R. Cline *et al.*, *Trade Negotiations in the Tokyo Round: A Quantitative Assessment* (Washington, The Brookings Institution, 1978).)
30. Grubel and Lloyd, *op.cit.*, p. 130.
31. Corden, (1974) *op.cit.*, p. 107.
32. W.A. Brock and S.P. Magee, 'Tariff formation in a democracy', in J. Black and B. Hindley (eds), *Current Issues in Commercial Policy and Diplomacy* (London: Macmillan for TPRC, 1980).
33. R.E. Caves, 'Economic models of political choice: Canada's tariff structure', *Canadian Journal of Economics*, vol. 9 (1976), pp. 278–300.
34. H.H. Glismann and F.D. Weiss, *On the Political Economy of Protection in Germany*, World Bank Staff Working Paper (WBSWP) no. 427, 1980. Other publications in this series include: E. Grilli, *Italian Commercial Policies in the 1970s*, WBSWP no. 428, 1980: P.M.K. Tharakan, *The Political Economy of Protection in Belgium*, WBSWP no. 431, 1980; E. Verreydt and J. Waelbroeck, *European Community Protection against Manufactured Imports From Developing Countries: A Case Study in The Political Economy of Protection*,

WBSWP no. 432, 1980; K. Anderson and R.E. Baldwin, *The Political Market For Protection in Industrial Countries: Empirical Evidence*, WBSWP no. 492, 1981; and K.A. Koekkoek, J. Col and L.B.M. Mennes, *On Protectionism in the Netherlands*, WBSWP no. 493, 1981.
35. V. Cable, *Protectionism and Industrial Decline* (London: Hodder & Stoughton, 1983).
36. See, for example, C. Farrands, 'The political economy of the Multi-Fibre Arrangement', in C. Stevens (ed.), *EEC and the Third World: A Survey 2* (London: Hodder & Stoughton in association with ODI and IDS, 1982).

Chapter 3

1. For comprehensive reviews of the development and principles of the GATT, see K. Kock, *International Trade Policy and the GATT 1947–1967* (Stockholm: Almquist & Wicksell, 1969); and K.W. Dam, *The GATT, Law and International Economic Organisation* (Chicago and London: University of Chicago Press, 1970).
2. A.I. MacBean and N. Snowden, *International Institutions in Trade and Finance* (London: Allen & Unwin, 1981), p. 64.
3. *Ibid*; see also R.G. Lipsey and K. Lancaster, 'The general theory of second-best', *Review of Economic Studies*, vol. 24 (1956–57), pp. 11–32.
4. H.G. Johnson, *The World Economy at the Crossroads* (Oxford: Oxford University Press, 1965), pp. 43–7.
5. The OEEC became the Organisation for Economic Co-operation and Development, with a membership extended to the United States and other non-European industrialised market economy countries in 1961.
6. R.E. Baldwin, *Non-tariff Distortions of International Trade* (Washington: Brookings Institution. London: Allen & Unwin, 1970), p. 2.
7. General Agreement on Tariffs and Trade, *International Trade 1957–58* (Geneva: GATT, 1958), p. 295.

Chapter 4

1. For a review of measurement techniques and empirical estimates, see D.G. Mayes, 'The effects of economic integra-

tion on trade', *Journal of Common Market Studies*, vol. 17 (September 1978), pp. 1–25.

2. J. Williamson and A. Bottrill, 'The impact of customs unions on trade in manufactures', *Oxford Economic Papers*, vol. 23 (1971), p. 342.

3. B. Balassa (ed.), *European Economic Integration* (Amsterdam and Oxford: North-Holland. New York: American Elsevier, 1975), Ch. 3.

4. See EFTA Secretariat, *The Trade Effects of EFTA and the EEC 1957–1967* (Geneva: EFTA, 1972).

5. Balassa, *op.cit.* pp. 108–12: In this study, manufactured goods were divided into 91 categories which were then ranked according to the value of intra-EEC trade.

6. Grubel and Lloyd, *op.cit.*, p. 136.

7. Meyer, *op.cit.*, p. 180.

8. See the review of national attitudes in G. Moorhouse, 'Recent trends in industrial protectionism in the EEC', in Stevens (ed.), *Survey 2, op.cit.* It is suggested that Italy has had a strong commitment to free trade but that this is giving way to an increasingly protectionist stand.

9. European Commission, *The Competitiveness of the Community Industry* (Luxembourg: EC, 1982), p. 38.

Chapter 5

1. H. Glejser, 'Empirical evidence on comparative cost theory from the European Common Market experience', *European Economic Review*, vol. 3 (1972), pp. 247–58.

2. Cited in *The Economist*, 19 September 1981, p. 68.

3. *Ibid.* See also Commission of the EC, *Twelfth Report on Competition Policy* (Luxembourg: EC, 1982), pp. 176–82.

4. Meyer, *op.cit.*, pp. 47–51.

5. Commission of the EC, *Assessment of the Function [sic] of the Internal Market*, COM(33), 80 final, Brussels, 24 February 1983, p. 8.

6. European Parliament, *Report on Barriers to Internal Community Trade in Agricultural Products*, Working Document 1–672/82, 15 October 1982.

7. Commission of the EC, *The Customs Union*, European Documentation Series, (EDS) 4/1980, Luxembourg 1980, p. 23.

8. Commission of the EC, *Removal of Technical Barriers to Trade*, COM(80), 30 final, Brussels, 24 January 1980, p. 7.

9. Commission, COM(83)80, *op.cit.*, pp. 24–8.
10. *Bulletin of the EC*, vol. 16/3, 1983.
11. Commission of the EC, *GR 1980*, pp. 85–6.
12. *Ibid.*, p. 313.
13. Commission of the EC, *GR 1981*, p. 80.
14. Commission, COM(83)80, *op.cit.*, p. 16.
15. Commission, EDS 4/1980, *op. cit.*, p. 13.
16. *Official Journal of the EC*, vol. 23, C59 of 10 March 1980, p. 67.
17. Commission, COM(83)80, *op.cit.*, p. 22.
18. The VAT system was not applied in all of the six original EEC countries until January 1973.
19. For a discussion of the trade implications of tax harmonisation, see H.G. Johnson and M.B. Krauss, 'Border taxes, border tax adjustment, comparative advantage, and the balance of payments', *Canadian Journal of Economics*, vol. 3 (1970), pp. 595–602.
20. Commission, COM(83)80, *op.cit.*, p. 19.
21. A most valuable review of the state of the EEC internal market is given in House of Lords, Select Committee on the EC, *The Internal Market of the EEC*, Session 1981–82 17th Report (London: HMSO, 1982).

Chapter 6

1. See, for example, F. Forte 'Principles for the assignment of public economic functions in a setting of multi–layer government' in Commission of the EC, Report of the [MacDougall] study group on the role of public finance in European integration, vol. II Collection Studies Economic and Financial Series No. B13, Brussels, April 1977.
2. *Ibid.* pp. 357–97, 'Perspectives for the place of the EC in the sectoral economic functions of government'.
3. The study group does not elaborate this argument in relation to trade policy but it might be suggested that democratic control could be strengthened if, for example, it proved easier to resist narrowly–based but well–organised protectionist pressure groups at the EEC, compared with the national, level. It should be added, however, that in practice protectionist pressure groups tend to be well–orchestrated at the EEC level, and that the powers of the European Parliament are very limited.

4. The EEC's use of trade sanctions against Argentina during the Falklands conflict in 1982 may be interpreted as a modest step in this direction.
5. These products were set out in List G of Annex I to the Treaty of Rome, and the duties and certain tariff quotas were agreed in March 1960. The duties on manufactured tobacco and certain petroleum products were fixed in 1962 and 1964, respectively.
6. M. Constantopoulos, 'Labour protection in western Europe', *European Economic Review*, vol. 5 (1974), pp. 313–29.
7. *Ibid.*
8. 'The effective rate [of protection] expresses the nominal tariff on the final good minus the weighted average of the tariffs on its inputs as a proportion of value–added per unit at free trade prices, where value–added includes the non–traded content.' (Corden (1974) *op.cit.*, pp. 382–3.)
9. M.A.G. van Meerhaeghe, *International Economic Institutions* (London: Longman, 1971, 2nd edn), pp. 276–7.
10. *Ibid.*, p. 277.
11. N. Vaulont, *The Customs Union of the European Economic Community* (Luxembourg: EC, 1981) p. 27.
12. See W.M. Corden, 'The structure of a tariff system and the effective protective rate', *Journal of Political Economy*, vol. 74 (1966), pp. 221–37.
13. E. Grilli and M. La Noce, 'The political economy of protection in Italy: some empirical evidence', *Banca Nazionale del Lavoro Quarterly Review*, no. 145 (1963), pp. 143–61.
14. A.V. Deardorff and R.M. Stern, *The Effects of the Tokyo Round on the Structure of Protection* (Institute of Public Policy Studies, the University of Michigan, Discussion Paper no. 182, January 1983).
15. The 1983 version is given in *Official Journal of the EC*, vol. 25, L366 of 27 December 1982.
16. The rules are set out in *Official Journal of the EC*, vol. 23, L134 of 28 May 1980.
17. See Vaulont, *op.cit.*, pp. 67–8.
18. *Ibid*, p. 57.
19. See House of Lords (1982), *op.cit.*, pp. 165–6.
20. *Official Journal of the EC*, vol. 22, L339 of 31 December 1979.
21. *Bulletin of the EC*, 1979, no. 5, p. 26.
22. *Official Journal of the EC*, vol. 25, L35 of 9 February 1982.
23. See L.M. Gard and J. Reidel, 'Safeguard protection of

industry in developed countries: an assessment of the implications for developing countries', *Weltwirtschäftesliches Archiv*, vol. CXVI, pp. 471–92.

24. *Official Journal of the EC*, vol. 25, L186 of 30 June 1982.
25. *Official Journal of the EC*, vol. 24, L83 of 30 March 1981.
26. J. Pearce, 'Export credit: the implications of the 1982 revision for developing countries', in C. Stevens (ed.), *The EC and the Third World: a Survey 3* (London: Hodder & Stoughton, in association with ODI and IDS, 1983).
27. E. Wellenstein, *25 Years of European Community External Relations* (Luxembourg: EC, 1979), p. 18.
28. These committees are part of an extensive network of bilateral contacts which the Community maintains with the aim of identifying problems at an early stage and finding agreed solutions. Since 1973/4, for example, the Community has had twice yearly consultations at a high level with the governments of the US, Japan, Canada, Australia and New Zealand.
29. R. Dahrendorf, 'External relations in the European Community', in H. Corbet and R. Jackson (eds), *In Search of a New World Economic Order* (London: Croom Helm, 1974)

Chapter 7

1. T.K. Warley (ed.), *Agricultural Producers and Their Markets* (Oxford: Basil Blackwell, 1967), Ch. 7.
2. For a critical review of the CAP see B.E. Hill, *The Common Agricultural Policy: Past, Present and Future* (London: Methuen, 1984).
3. The problems facing the EEC steel industry are examined in R.W. Crandall, 'The economics of the current steel crisis in OECD member countries', in *Steel in the 80s: Paris Symposium February 1980* (Paris: OECD, 1980).
4. In 1980, textile operatives' wages per hour were £2.95 in the UK and 8p in Sri Lanka *(Financial Times*, 17 February 1982).
5. Details are given in *Official Journal of the EC*, vol. 25, L83 of 29 March 1982.
6. Negotiations with Argentina were unsuccessful; the EEC imposed unilateral restrictions on imports from Argentina and Taiwan.
7. I. Frank, *Trade Policy Issues of Interest to the Third World* (London: Trade Policy Research Centre, Thames Essay 29, 1981), pp. 15–18; see also B. Hindley, 'Voluntary export

restraints and the GATT's main escape clause', *The World Economy*, vol. 3 (November 1980), pp. 313–41.

8. *Official Journal of the EC,* vol. 25, L374 of 31 December 1982, Article 7.

9. For Taiwan the reduction was 10 per cent.

10. C. Farrands, *op.cit.*, p. 37.

11. Based on C. Hamilton, *Voluntary Export Restraints and Trade Diversion* working paper (Stockholm: Institute for International Economic Studies, 1983).

12. A.Neu estimated that the quota restrictions on clothing imports to Germany had equivalent effects to a tariff of 45 per cent, in W.M. Corden and G. Fels, *Public Assistance to Industry* (London: Macmillan for TPRC, 1976), p. 181.

13. The German industry is more competitive than that in other EEC countries partly because of its modern equipment and specialisation at the top end of the market, and partly because goods can be shipped across the border to the GDR for cheap processing.

14. See, for example, G. Curzon *et al.*, *MFA Forever?* (London: TPRC, 1981).

Chapter 8

1. M. Judge, 'Co-operation between the EFTA countries and the EC', *EFTA Bulletin*, vol. XXIV, 1 (January–March 1983), p.6.

2. For a discussion of the EFTA experience, see H. Corbet and D. Robertson (eds), *Europe's Free Trade Area Experiment* (Oxford: Pergamon Press, 1970); and V. Curzon *The Essentials of Economic Integration, Lessons of EFTA Experience* (London: Macmillan for the Trade Policy Research Centre, 1974).

3. Finland has been an associate member since 1961.

4. V. Curzon, *op.cit.*, p. 85.

5. H. Shibata, 'The theory of economic unions: a comparative analysis of customs unions, free trade areas and tax unions', in C. Shoup (ed.), *Fiscal Harmonisation in Common Markets, Vol. 1* (New York: Columbia University Press, 1967).

6. EFTA Secretariat, *op.cit.*

7. Williamson and Bottrill, *op.cit.*

8. Mayes, *op.cit.*

9. EFTA Secretariat, *op.cit.*

10. Mayes, *op.cit.*, p.12.

11. Quoted in Palmer *et al., op.cit.*, p. 365.
12. V. Curzon, *op.cit.*, p. 230.
13. For a more detailed account, see *ibid.*, Ch. 9.
14. *EFTA Reporter* (March 1983), pp. 1–2, 6–10.
15. See the European Court's ruling on the Polydor case, G. Aschenbrenner, 'The interpretation of the free trade agreements', *EFTA Bulletin* vol. XXIV/2 (April–June 1983), pp. 14–18.
16. See e.g. EFTA, *Fifteenth Annual Report of the European Free Trade Association* (Geneva: EFTA, 1975), p. 19.
17. EFTA, *Nineteenth Annual Report of the European Free Trade Association* (Geneva: EFTA, 1979), p. 18.
18. *Bulletin of the EC*, 1975, no. 11, p. 54, and 1977, no. 3, p. 68.
19. Except for Finland, the Free Trade Agreements envisaged that relations might be extended to other fields.
20. *Bulletin of the EC*, 1976, no. 9, pp. 15–18.
21. Commission of the EC, *GR 1980* (Luxembourg: EC, 1981), pp. 232–3.
22. Commission of the EC, *GR 1982* (Luxembourg: EC, 1983), p. 231.
23. See also M. Judge, 'Ten years of free trade, changing trends in the trade of EFTA countries', *EFTA Bulletin*, vol. XXIII/4 (October–December 1982), pp. 8–12.
24. See *EFTA Bulletin*, vol. XX/6 (August–September 1979), pp. 2–5.

Chapter 9

1. The EEC currently has trade agreements with all the countries of the Mediterranean littoral except Libya and Albania.
2. A. Tovias, *Tariff Preferences in Mediterranean Diplomacy* (London: Macmillan, 1977), p. 67.
3. Algeria did not become independent until 1962; in 1958/9 87 per cent of Algerian exports went to the EEC (6); the corresponding shares for Tunisia and Morocco were 73 and 64 per cent, respectively.
4. S. Henig, *External Relations of the European Community* (London: Chatham House and PEP, 1971), pp. 48–51.
5. Council of the EC, *20th Review of the Council's Work 1972* (Luxembourg: EC, n.d.), p. 152.
6. R. Pomfret, 'Protectionism and preferences in the European Community's Mediterranean policy', *The World Today*, vol.

38 (February 1982), p. 63.

7. See Tovias, *op.cit.*, Ch. 5.

8. P.F.R. Artisien and S. Holt, 'Yugoslavia and the EEC in the 1970's', *Journal of Common Market Studies*, vol. 18 (June 1980), pp. 355–69.

9. S. Musto, 'The Mediterranean and the Middle East', in Stevens (ed.), *Survey 3, op.cit.,* pp. 127–8.

10. G. Yannopoulos, 'The effects of the full membership on the manufacturing industries', in L. Tsoukalis (ed.), *Greece and the European Economic Community* (Oxford: Oxford University Press, 1978), p. 58.

11. Commission of the EC, *Greece in the Community—Assessment and Proposals*, COM(83), 134 final, Brussels, 29 March 1983, p. 24.

12. *Bulletin of the EC*, 1982, no. 3, p. 90.

13. Commission, COM(83), 134, *op.cit.*, p. 3.

14. Commission of the EC, *The Commission's Proposals for the Integrated Mediterranean Programmes*, COM(83), 24 final, Brussels, 23 March 1983.

15. Commission, COM(83), 134 *op.cit.*

16. A. Da Silva Ferreira, 'The economics of enlargement: trade effects on the applicant countries', *Journal of Common Market Studies*, vol. 17, (December 1978), pp. 120–41.

17. C. Vaitsos, 'Transnational corporate behaviour and the enlargement', in D. Seers and C. Vaitsos, *The Second Enlargement of the EEC* (London: Macmillan, 1982), p. 158.

18. C. Ritson, 'Impact on agriculture', in Seers and Vaitsos (eds), *op.cit.*

19. Commission of the EC, *Olive Oil in an Enlarged Community*, COM(83) final, Brussels, 1 March 1983, p. 2.

20. L. Tsoukalis, *The European Community and its Mediterranean Enlargement* (London: Allen & Unwin, 1981) p. 100.

21. *Ibid.*, pp. 186–7.

22. *Ibid.*

23. The effects on developing countries of EEC enlargement are discussed in Seers and Vaitsos (eds), *op.cit.*: P. Mishalani, 'The Mahgreb and Mashreq countries'; B. Bayliss, 'The ACP countries', and K.W. Kim, 'The Asian NICs'.

24. European Parliament, *Report on Mediterranean Agriculture and the Problems of the Enlargement of the EEC towards the South*, Working Documents 1–785/82, 3 November 1982.

25. See also R. Pomfret, 'The impact of EEC enlargement on non–member Mediterranean countries' exports to the EEC',

Economic Journal, vol. 91 (September 1981), pp. 726–9.
26. Seers and Vaitsos, *op.cit.*, p. 16.
27. S. Musto, in *ibid.*, p. 76.

Chapter 10

1. Commission of EC, *Memorandum on the Community's Development Policy*, COM(82), 640 final, Brussels, 5 October 1982, p. 1.
2. For an introduction to the role of trade in economic development, see K. Morton and P. Tulloch, *Trade and Developing Countries* (London: Croom Helm, 1977), Ch. 1.
3. See A.I. MacBean, *Export Instability and Economic Development* (London: Allen & Unwin, 1966).
4. Trade problems of developing countries are examined in Morton and Tulloch, *op.cit.*, Ch. 3, 4 and 5.
5. For a critical review of Prebisch's terms of trade argument, see B. Södersten, *International Economics* (London: Macmillan, 1970), pp. 190–203.
6. Commission, *op.cit.*, p. 8.
7. A concise account of the call for a NIEO is given in J.R. Behrman, *Development, the International Economic Order, and Commodity Agreements* (Reading, Mass.: Addison-Wesley, 1978) Ch. 2.
8. An informative and up-to-date review of developments in EEC relations with the Third World is given in the annual volumes, C. Stevens (ed.), *EEC and the Third World: a Survey* (London: Hodder and Stoughton in association with ODI and IDS, 1981, 1982, 1983).
9. See e.g. H.G. Johnson, *Economic Policies Towards Less Developed Countries* (London: Allen & Unwin, 1967), Ch. VI.
10. See R. Lawrence, 'Primary products, preferences, and economic welfare: the EEC and Africa', in P. Kenen and R. Lawrence (eds), *The Open Economy* (New York: Columbia University Press, 1968), pp. 240–60; reprinted as 'Reading no. 19', in P. Robson (ed.), *International Economic Integration* (Harmondsworth: Penguin, 1971).
11. Inherited from the member countries.
12. Unless the African countries could agree to restrict supplies to the EEC market by a system of export quotas.
13. If the assumption of a completely elastic world supply is

relaxed, then increased consumption in the EEC could lead to higher world prices from which the African countries could benefit.

14. R.E. Baldwin and T. Murray, 'MFN tariff reductions and developing country trade benefits under the GSP', *Economic Journal,* vol. 87, (1977) pp. 30–46.

Chapter 11

1. For a summary of the origin and development of the association agreements, see Diddy R.M. Hitchins, 'The European Community and Africa, the Caribbean and the Pacific', in Juliet Lodge, *The European Community: Bibliographical Excursions* (London: Frances Pinter, 1983). A more detailed account is given in J. Moss, *The Lomé Conventions and Their Implications For the United States* (Boulder, Colorado: Westview Press, 1982), Ch. 1.
2. Moss, *op.cit.*, p. 1.
3. 'In international relations, association arrangements provided a formal link between full members of an international organisation and other political units that participate in some of the activities of the organisation but lack the full rights of membership.' (Hitchins, *op.cit.*, p. 16.) The eighteen associated African areas were: Burundi, Cameroon, Central African Republic, Chad, Congo (Brazzaville), Dahomey, Gabon, Ivory Coast, Madagascar, Mali, Mauritania, Niger, Rwanda, Senegal, Somalia, Togo, Upper Volta and Zaire.
4. The 20 Commonwealth countries were: Barbados, Botswana, Fiji, Gambia, Ghana, Guyana, Jamaica, Kenya, Lesotho, Malawi, Nigeria, Sierra Leone, Swaziland, Tanzania, Tonga, Trinidad and Tobago, Uganda, Western Samoa and Zambia.
5. Ethiopia, Liberia, Equatorial Guinea and Sudan.
6. Moss, *op.cit.* p. 52.
7. C. Cosgrove Twitchett, *A Framework For Development: the EEC and the ACP* (London: Allen & Unwin, 1981) p.25.
8. For a detailed discussion of the agricultural aspects of the Lomé Convention, including an analysis of the markets for vegetable oilseeds, fruit and vegetables, beef and cereals, see Simon Harris *et al.*, *The Re-negotiation of the ACP–EEC Convention of Lomé, with Special Reference to Agricultural Products* (London: Commonwealth Secretariat), Commonwealth Economic Papers, no. 12, 1978.

9. Moss, *op.cit.*, p. 57.
10. Cosgrove Twitchett, *op.cit.*, p. 43.
11. European Parliament, *Europe Today 1980–1981* (Luxembourg: EC, 1981), point 6.34143.
12. For a critical view, see D. Wall, *The European Community's Lomé Convention: Stabex and the Third World's Aspirations* (London: Trade Policy Research Centre, Guest Paper no. 4, 1976).
13. For sisal the rule is 5 per cent.
14. Moss, *op.cit.*, p. 94.
15. A. Hewitt, 'Stabex: analysing the effectiveness of an innovation', Stevens (ed.), *Survey 3*, *op.cit.*
16. Wall, *op.cit.*, p. 13.
17. 'Dossier: STABEX', *The Courier*, no. 79 (May–June 1983), pp. 68–82.
18. In May 1983, the EEC rejected demands from ACP countries for an extra $450 millions under STABEX to help offset the effects of the 1980–81 shortfall on the grounds that the latter was caused by freak conditions. *(Financial Times*, 20 May 1983.)
19. Iron ore was covered by STABEX in the first Lomé Convention but was to be phased out in the second Convention.
20. European Parliament, [*The operation of STABEX*] Working Document, 1–698/80 (1981) pp. 14–16.
21. Moss, *op.cit.*, p. 92.
22. *Ibid.*, p. 115.
23. In 1982, Zaire and Zambia were loaned 40 million ECU and 55 million ECU, respectively for copper and cobalt operations, and applications from Rwanda in respect of tin and Guyana for bauxite were under consideration. Commission of EC, *GR 1983*, p. 280.
24. For details of the EDF programme and other aspects of the Lomé Convention, see *Annual Report of the ACP–EEC Council of Ministers* (Brussels: ACP–EEC Convention of Lomé Secretariat, annual).
25. See Cosgrove Twitchett, *op.cit.*, Ch. 2.
26. Moss, *op.cit.*, Table 2.1, p. 35.
27. *Ibid.*
28. *Ibid.* A version also appears in Stevens (ed.) *Survey 3*, *op.cit.*, Ch. 10.
29. The statistical test used was the non-parametric, Wilcoxon–Mann–Whitney (w) test; this is discussed in Appendix B of

Moss (1982), *op.cit.*
30. L. Mytelka and M. Dolan, 'The EEC and the ACP countries', in Seers and Vaitsos, *op.cit.*

Chapter 12

1. Indonesia, Malaysia, Philippines, Singapore and Thailand.
2. Most of the larger non-associated countries have negotiated non-preferential commercial and economic cooperation agreements with the Community, which provide for mutual MFN treatment and for consultations over trade problems, together with joint programmes in such areas as research. In particular, agreements have been negotiated with Bangladesh (1976), China (1978), India (1974 and 1981), Pakistan (1976), Sri Lanka (1975), Argentina (1972, but discontinued in 1980), Brazil (1974 and 1982), Mexico (1975) and Uruguay (1974). In 1980, the EEC signed a cooperation agreement with the ASEAN group and has been negotiating a similar arrangement with the Andean Group in South America.
3. In addition, tariff-free quotas have been agreed for handmade goods from Bangladesh, India, Indonesia, Iran, Laos, Malaysia, Pakistan, the Philippines, Singapore, Sri Lanka and Thailand: for jute from Bangladesh, India and Thailand and for coir from Sri Lanka. India has a small sugar quota subject to similar treatment to ACP sugar (see section 11.2, *Special treatment for CAP products.*)
4. Under the Food Aid Convention of the International Wheat Agreement the Community and the member states have a joint commitment of 1.65 million tonnes a year, of which about two-thirds is contributed by the Community.
5. Commission of EC, *GR 1982*, pp. 266–8.
6. T. Murray, *Trade Preferences for Developing Countries* (London: Macmillan, 1977), p. 15.
7. Under the new rules agreed in the Tokyo Round, a waiver is no longer required for generalised preferences in favour of developing countries.
8. The Commission has published a very useful explanatory guide to the GSP; *Practical Guide to the Use of the European Communties' Scheme of Generalised Preferences* (Luxembourg: EC, 1 April 1982).
9. *Official Journal of the EC*, vol. 26, L362 of 24 December 1983.
10. House of Lords, Select Committee on the EC, *Generalised*

System of Preferences, Session 1979–80, 61st Report (London: HMSO, 1980), p. 10.

11. *Official Journal of the EC*, vol. 25, C274 of 18 October 1982.
12. Murray, *op.cit.*, p. 54.
13. House of Lords, *op.cit.*, p. viii.
14. Murray, *op.cit.*, p. 55.
15. Commission of the EC, *Guidelines for the EC's Scheme of GSP for the Post-1980 Period* (Brussels: EC, 7 March 1980), COM(80) 104, p. 6.
16. Under the 1981 revision, the previous system of fixing global limits to tariff exemption for all sources of supply was changed to one which fixes limits for individual countries.
17. Note that only about 3–4 per cent of total EEC imports of sensitive goods entered under the GSP in 1976 and 1977 (Commission, *op.cit.*, Annex p. 4).
18. *Official Journal of the EC*, vol. 25, L363 of 23 December 1982, pp. 8–53.
19. The Commission had suggested 40 per cent, which would have made the scheme much more flexible, if more difficult administratively. See *Commission Proposals to the Council fixing the Community's Five-year Scheme of Generalised Tariff Preferences for the Period 1981–1985 and the opening of the scheme applicable in 1981*, COM(80), 395 final, Brussels, 10 September 1980.
20. Commission of the EC, *Guidelines ....*, *op.cit.*, Annex p. 3.
21. Index to the *Official Journal of the EC, 1982*.
22. See Murray, *op.cit.*, pp. 74–7.
23. Some 35 countries are recognised by the EEC as least developed, including Bangladesh and many of the African countries.
24. e.g. Murray, *op.cit.*, pp. 111–13.
25. e.g. an UNCTAD study suggested that the introduction of the GSP may have boosted US imports of GSP products from the developing countries by rather less than 20 per cent between 1974 and 1977 (UNCTAD Secretariat DOC TD: B:C 5/66 of 20 February 1980).
26. A. Weston *et al.*, *The EEC's Generalised Scheme of Preferences—Evaluation and Recommendations for Change* (London: ODI, 1980).
27. House of Lords, *op.cit.*, p. 22.
28. R.J. Langhammer, *Asean Manufactured Exports in the EEC Market*, Kiel Working Papers no. 122, May 1981.
29. *Ibid.*, p. 21.

30. *Ibid.*, Table 15*, p.62.
31. House of Lords, *op.cit.*, pp. 5–7.
32. Langhammer, *op.cit.*, Table 9*, p. 56.
33. *Ibid.*, p. 35.
34. *Ibid.*, Table 9*, p. 56.
35. *Ibid.*
36. *Ibid.*, Table 20*, p. 67.
37. The amount of EEC tariff revenue forgone under the GSP is estimated at about £200 millions a year (House of Lords, *op.cit.*, p. 16).
38. R.E. Baldwin and T. Murray, *op.cit.*, estimated that trade creation would be ten times greater than trade diversion, but see Z. Iqbal, 'The GSP examined' *Finance and Development* (September 1975) pp. 34–9.
39. Baldwin and Murray, *op.cit.*
40. UNCTAD Secretariat, *Multilateral Trade Negotiations: Evaluation and Further Recommendations Arising Therefrom* (Geneva: UNCTAD, 1979); see also J. Ahmad, 'Tokyo Rounds of trade negotiations and the GSP', *Economic Journal*, vol. 88 (1978), pp. 285–95.
41. *Official Journal of the EC*, L363, 23 December 1982; for agricultural products 'an appreciable' is substituted for 'a large'.
42. House of Lords, *op.cit.*, p. 8.
43. *Ibid.*, p. xi.
44. A. Weston, 'Who is more preferred? An analysis of the new GSP', Ch. 5 in Stevens *(ed.)*, *Survey 2, op.cit.*, p. 85.
45. These agreements are surveyed in C. Nappi, *Commodity Market Controls* (Lexington, Mass.: Lexington Books, 1979).
46. See Behrman, *op.cit.*, Ch. 3.
47. Cocoa, coffee, olive oil, sugar and tin, for which agreements already existed, plus bananas, cotton, hard fibres, jute, meat, rubber, tea, tropical timber, bauxite, copper, iron ore, manganese and phosphates.
48. Behrman, *op.cit.*, pp.93–5. The argument is that when commodity prices rise high above their trend they cause inflation that is not reversed when the commodity prices subsequently decline.
49. But see *ibid.*, pp. 66–7.
50. T. Josling, 'The CAP and International Commodity Agreements' in M. Tracy and I. Hodac, *Prospects for Agriculture in the EEC* (Bruges: De Tempel, 1979), pp. 275–87.
51. Commission of EC *Memorandum on the Community's De-*

velopment Policy, COM(82), 640 final, Brussels, 5 October 1982.

Chapter 13

1. In the 1947 negotiations tariffs on dutiable US imports were reduced by a weighted average of 18.9 per cent; the US was willing to make tariff cuts on its imports against 'sham' tariff cuts by the European countries which did not become effective until later on when quota restrictions were abandoned. MacBean and Snowden, *op.cit.*, p. 70.
2. Trade Policy Research Centre, *British, European and American Interests in the Forthcoming International Negotiations on Industrial Trade* (London: Trade Policy Research Centre, Staff Paper no. 1, 1973), p. 2.
3. G.P. Casadio, *Transatlantic Trade, USA–EEC Confrontations in the GATT Negotiations* (Farnborough: Saxon House, 1973), pp. 229–30.
4. *Financial Times*, 21 July 1977.
5. S.A.B. Page, 'The revival of protectionism and its consequences for Europe', *Journal of Common Market Studies*, vol. 20 (September 1981), pp. 17–40. Note that the percentages cited for both years are based on the structure of trade in 1974 and hence are not influenced by changes in the pattern of trade.
6. *Ibid.*, p. 23.
7. *Ibid.*, p. 30.
8. *Ibid.*, p. 29.
9. See e.g. V. Roningen and A.J. Yeats, 'Non-tariff distortions of international trade: some preliminary empirical evidence', *Weltwirtschaftesliches Archiv*, vol. 112 (1976), pp. 613–25.
10. The texts of these codes are reproduced in *Official Journal of the EC*, vol. 23, L71 of 17 March 1980.
11. For critical views of selective safeguards, see V. Curzon Price, 'Surplus capacity and what the Tokyo Round failed to settle', *World Economy* vol. 2 (1979), pp. 305–19.
12. See F. Hubert 'Résultats des négociations commerciales multilatérales au GATT' in Tracy and Hodac (eds), *op.cit.*, pp. 250–62.
13. *Financial Times,* 30 November 1982.
14. T. Josling, *op.cit.*
15. Frank, *op.cit.*, pp. 15–18.
16. Curzon Price, *op.cit.*, p. 306.

17. A.V. Deardorff and R.M. Stern, 'A disaggregated model of world production and trade, applied to the Tokyo Round', *Journal of Policy Modeling*, vol. 3 (1981), pp. 127–52. For an earlier review of quantitative studies of the effects of the Tokyo Round, see M.E. Kreinin and L.H. Officer, 'Tariff reductions under the Tokyo Round: a review of their effects on trade flows, employment, and welfare', *Weltwirtschaftes-liches Archiv,* vol. 115 (1979), pp. 543–72.

18. It is assumed, perhaps very optimistically, that for the non–defence public procurement that governments had tentatively agreed to open up to foreign bidding, the propensity to import would become the same as in the private sector.

19. Cline *et al., op.cit.*

20. Trade Policy Research Centre, *op.cit.*, p. 10.

21. See G.K. Bertsch, *East–West Strategic Trade, COCOM and the Atlantic Alliance* (Paris: Atlantic Institute for International Affairs, 1983); S. Woolcock 'East–West trade: US policy and European interests', *The World Today*, vol. 38 (February 1982), pp. 51–9: S. Woolcock, 'The Versailles Summit and East–West trade', *The World Today*, vol. 38 (July–August 1982), pp. 251–3.

22. For a stimulating review of economic relations between the EEC and Japan, see L. Tsoukalis and M. White, *Japan and Western Europe* (London: Frances Pinter, 1982).

23. J. Abegglen, in Tsoukalis and White, *op.cit.*, p. 55.

24. C. Sautter, *ibid.*, p. 197.

25. B. Meynell, *ibid.*, p. 109.

26. M. Hanabusa, *Trade Problems Between Japan and Western Europe* (Farnborough: Saxon House for the Royal Institute for International Affairs, 1979), pp. 2–5.

27. B. Meynell, in Tsoukalis and White, *op.cit.*, p. 114.

28. G. Shepherd, *ibid.*, p. 151.

29. Y. Satoh, *ibid.*, p. 193.

30. *Bulletin of the EC*, 1983, no. 2, p. 9.

31. *Ibid.*

32. Y. Sazanami, 'Possibilities of expanding intra-industry trade in Japan', *Keio Economic Studies*, vol. XVIII/2 (1981), pp. 27–43.

33. L. Tsoukalis, in Tsoukalis and White, *op.cit.*, p. 214.

34. *Financial Times*, 30 November 1982.

35. *Ibid.*

36. The GATT Declaration and the EEC's qualifying statement are given in *Bulletin of the EC*, 1982, no. 11, pp. 87–94.

Chapter 14

1. This section draws particularly on European Parliament, *Report on Relations between the EC and the East European State-trading Countries and the CMEA (COMECON)*, Working Document 1–531/82, 28 July 1982.
2. Commission of the EC, *GR 1982*, p. 263.
3. European Parliament, *op.cit.*, pp. 18–31.
4. Trade between the FRG and GDR amounted to $5.2 billions in 1981, equivalent to about 3 per cent of the FRG's trade with non-EEC countries.
5. F. Rösch and F. Homann, 'Intra-German trade', *Zeitschrift für die gesamte Staatwissenschaft*, vol. 137/3 (1981), pp. 549–55.
6. Bertsch, *op.cit.*
7. See S. Woolcock, (February 1982), *op.cit.*
8. Commission of the EC, *Towards a European Energy Policy*, European File 8/79 (Luxembourg: EC, 1979), p.3.
9. Commission of the EC, *GR 1975*, p. 260.

Chapter 15

1. *Financial Times*, 17 March 1983.
2. See especially, Cable, *op.cit.*
3. A. Dunkel, 'The new protectionism—who pays?', *EFTA Bulletin*, vol. XXIII/2 (April–June 1982), p. 1.
4. See General Agreement on Tariffs and Trade, *International Trade 1981/82* (Geneva: GATT, 1982), p. 11.
5. Dunkel, *op.cit.*, p. 1.
6. A.P. Thirlwall, 'Foreign trade elasticities in centre–periphery models of growth and development', *Banca Nazionale del Lavoro Quarterly Review*, no. 146 (September 1983), pp. 249–61.
7. W.R. Cline, 'Reciprocity and comparative advantage', *Economic Impact* no. 43 (1983), p. 31.
8. W. Hager, 'Protectionism and autonomy: how to preserve free trade in Europe', *International Affairs*, vol. 58 (Summer 1982), pp. 413–28.
9. B. Hindley, 'Protectionism and autonomy: a comment on Hager', *International Affairs*, vol. 59 (Winter 1982/83), pp. 77–86.
10. M. Wolf, 'The European Community's trade policy', in R. Jenkins (ed.), *Britain and the EEC* (London: Macmillan, 1983).

Index

inward processing 83
intra-EEC trade 49–54, 59–73
intra-industry trade 15, 27, 53,
    62, 185, 231, 234, 258
invisibles: trade in 50, 245–6

Jobert 245
Johnson 25–6

Kennedy Round 6, 79–80, 221,
    259
Kreinin 28
Lancaster 14
Langhammer 207
level of government assignment
    analysis 74–5
liberalisation list 86–7 (see also
    quotas)
linear tariff cuts 41, 221–2
Lloyd 29, 36, 53
Lomé Convention 7, 8; aid 183–
    5; conclusions on 192–4;
    future of 218; origins of 170–
    2; trade provisions 97, 99,
    173–83; trade effects 185–92
London Communiqué 119
Long Term Arrangement on
    Cotton Textile Trade 108

MacDougall study group 74–5
management of trade 54–5,
    112, 264
Marshall Aid 42
Massell 22–4
measuring trade effects of EEC
    50–4
Mediterranean trade policies 5,
    7; conclusions on 153–5;
    global approach 136–42;
    'mosaic' 135–6; and second
    enlargement of EEC 146–53;
    trade developments with
    EEC 49, 142–6; trade
    restrictions 89, 108–9
Messina conference 1
Meynell 239
MINEX 181–3

monetary compensatory
    amounts 66–7, 103
Moss 188–92
most-favoured-nation
    treatment 39–40, 79, 83, 141,
    202, 257
movement certificate 85
Multi-Fibre Arrangement 8, 87,
    107–12, 139, 245
multilateralism 39–40 (see also
    GATT)
Murray 169, 209

New International Economic
    Order 95, 160–2, 177, 192–3,
    211–12, 215
New Protectionism: and new
    industries 262–5; and old
    industries 259–62 (see also
    non-tariff restrictions)
'new trade policy instrument'
    93
Nomenclature for External
    Trading Statistics
    (NIMEXE) 82
'non-application of Community
    treatment' (Art 115) 88–9,
    208
NICs: competition from 8, 9,
    90, 220, 234, 264; and EEC
    enlargement 152; and GSP
    206, 210; and selective
    safeguards 92, 97, 227; trade
    growth 46–7, 49, 106, 160,
    202–3; and trade restrictions
    217, 222
non-reciprocal (one-way) tariff
    preferences 98, 113; and
    GSP 196–211; and Lomé
    Convention 173–7; and
    Mediterranean countries
    141–2; trade effects of 161–9
non-tariff barriers: and EFTA
    133; and GATT 41–2; and
    intra-EEC trade 62–73; and
    sectoral policies 101–13; and
    Tokyo Round 223–7 (see

Index of countries and regional groups